Psychoanalytic Explorations of What Women Want Today

In this book, international psychoanalytic writers address the question "What do Women Want Today?" from a variety of lenses, bringing into focus the creative, resilient forces shown by women in their multiple social and psychological tasks.

The book reviews classic psychoanalytic theories about the feminine within a new cultural context. It challenges hegemonic gender prejudices and discusses new conceptions that do not pathologize "different" lifestyles and family configurations. With chapters by leading, international thinkers in the field, this book explores how to think about new feminine scenarios, gender identities, gender dynamics, motherhood, and desire, in light of modern psychoanalytic theories. In presenting how these changing contemporary notions of the feminine challenge classic psychoanalytic theory and practice, this book will compel both training and experienced analysts to think about new psychoanalytic theories and engage with their own prejudices regarding changing notions of the feminine.

Offering ideas relevant to psychoanalysis, sociology, gender studies, psychology, and activism, this book will be of great interest to professionals, teachers, and students in addition to any with an interest in psychoanalytic theory and women's studies.

Margarita Cereijido, Ph.D., is a Training and Supervising Analyst and Faculty Member of the Washington Baltimore Center for Psychoanalysis. She has written and taught on the areas of gender, culture, and prejudice. She organizes the Culture and Psychoanalysis annual conference at the Washington Baltimore Center for Psychoanalysis and is a member of the Committee of Women and Psychoanalysis (COWAP) at the International Psychoanalytic Association.

Paula L. Ellman, Ph.D., ABPP., is a Training and Supervising Analyst in the Contemporary Freudian Society, Washington DC, and the Washington Baltimore Center for Psychoanalysis. She is Overall Chair of the IPA Committee on Women and Psychoanalysis and Chair of the IPA Inter-committee Work Group on Prejudice and Race. She is on the Editorial Board of the *International Journal of Psychoanalysis* and is a Board Member of the North America Psychoanalytic Confederation (NAPsaC).

Nancy R. Goodman, Ph.D., is a Training and Supervising Analyst with the CFS and the IPA and a faculty member for the Wuhan Training Program, China. She writes about trauma, symbolizing processes, female development, and unconscious fantasy. She is a member of the Asia-Pacific Planning Committee of the International Psychoanalytic Association and Founder and Director of the online Virtual Psychoanalytic Museum with IP Books, and she maintains a psychoanalytic practice in Bethesda, Maryland.

Psychoanalysis and Women Series

Series Editor: Frances Thomson–Salo

Titles in the series:

Changing Notions of the Feminine: Confronting Psychoanalysts' Prejudices
Edited by Margarita Cereijido

When a Child has been Abused: Towards psychoanalytic understanding and therapy
By Frances Thomson-Salo and Laura Tognoli Pasquali

The Courage to Fight Violence Against Women: Psychoanalytic and Multidisciplinary Perspectives
By Paula L. Ellman

Changing Sexualities and Parental Functions in the Twenty-First Century: Changing Sexualities, Changing Parental Functions
By Candida Se Holovko

Psychoanalytic Explorations of What Women Want Today: Femininity, Desire and Agency
By Margarita Cereijido, Paula L. Ellman and Nancy R. Goodman

For further information about this series please visit www.routledge.com/ Psychoanalysis-and-Women-Series/book-series/KARNACPWS

Psychoanalytic Explorations of What Women Want Today

Femininity, Desire and Agency

Edited by
**Margarita Cereijido, Paula L. Ellman,
and Nancy R. Goodman**

Routledge
Taylor & Francis Group

LONDON AND NEW YORK

Cover image: © Getty Images

First published 2022
by Routledge
4 Park Square, Milton Park, Abingdon, Oxon OX14 4RN

and by Routledge
605 Third Avenue, New York, NY 10158

Routledge is an imprint of the Taylor & Francis Group, an informa business

© 2022 selection and editorial matter, Margarita Cereijido, Paula L. Ellman, Nancy R. Goodman; individual chapters, the contributors

British Library Cataloguing-in-Publication Data
A catalogue record for this book is available from the British Library

Library of Congress Cataloging-in-Publication Data
Names: Cereijido, Margarita, editor. | Ellman, Paula Lisette, editor. | Goodman, Nancy (Nancy R.), editor.
Title: Psychoanalytic explorations of what women want today : femininity, desire and agency / edited by Margarita Cereijido, Paula L. Ellman and Nancy R. Goodman.
Description: Abingdon, Oxon ; New York, NY : Routledge, 2022. | Series: Psychoanalysis and women series | Includes bibliographical references and index.
Identifiers: LCCN 2021056868 (print) | LCCN 2021056869 (ebook) | ISBN 9781032017808 (hardback) | ISBN 9781032017815 (paperback) | ISBN 9781003180036 (ebook)
Subjects: LCSH: Women–Psychology. | Women and psychoanalysis. | Women–Social conditions.
Classification: LCC HQ1206 .P767 2022 (print) | LCC HQ1206 (ebook) | DDC 155.3/33–dc23/eng/20220121
LC record available at https://lccn.loc.gov/2021056868
LC ebook record available at https://lccn.loc.gov/2021056869

ISBN: 978-1-032-01780-8 (hbk)
ISBN: 978-1-032-01781-5 (pbk)
ISBN: 978-1-003-18003-6 (ebk)

DOI: 10.4324/9781003180036

Typeset in Bembo
by Newgen Publishing UK

Contents

Acknowledgments

Earlier versions of Chapter 9 were presented at a conference on "What Do Women Want Today?" sponsored by the Committee on Women and Psychoanalysis of the International Psychoanalytical Association in Washington, D.C., on 9 November 2019; and at the Seattle Psychoanalytic Society and Institute on 19 January 2021.

I thank Margarita Cereijido and Paula Ellman for their creativity and motivation to develop this volume. I love working with them. I thank all of the psychoanalytic writers in the book for their passion about bringing psychoanalytic understanding to "what women want today". My husband Louis Goodman and my children and grandchildren are loving and supportive about the time I devote to thinking, writing, and editing. Thank you.

Nancy R. Goodman, Ph.D

I thank my husband Thomas Palley for his support at every step of the project. I am grateful to everyone who collaborated in this book: my co-editors Paula Ellman and Nancy Goodman, and the colleagues who contributed chapters, Virginia Ungar, Patricia Alkolombre, Leticia Glocer Fiorini, Adriana Prengler Graciela Abelin Sas-Rose, Rosemary Balsam, Adrienne Harris, Cecile Bassen, Janice Lieberman, and Arlene Kramer Richards. It was a pleasure working with all.

Margarita Cereijido

I extend my loving appreciation to my husband, Douglas Chavis and my children, Anna Chavis, Sam Chavis and Jennie Chavis, and Karl Rodger and Richard Mullin for their ongoing support of my work. I appreciate my co-editors and collaborators, Margarita Cereijido and Nancy Goodman for our learning and working together, and all of our contributing colleagues whose creative thinking deepens our understanding of "what woman want today". Thank you.

Paula Ellman

Part I

1 What do women want today?

Margarita Cereijido

Notions of woman and the feminine have changed dramatically over the last century. Today, we are undergoing a further round of change that is introducing new feminine scenarios. Women increasingly see themselves as subjects with their own desires and projects, and who stand as peers vis-à-vis men. As part of this, they are exploring new gender identities, new gender dynamics, and new family configurations.

This book aims to explore and support these new notions of the feminine. A natural starting point for such an enterprise is to revisit and seek contemporary answers to Freud's classic question, addressed to Marie Bonaparte in 1925, "What do women want?"

Freud's response to his own question, which became the classic response, was that women want to be loved. Psychoanalysts widely agree that women (and men) want to be loved. However, living in a different cultural context today, we also conceive of women as being subjects and agents with desires and projects of their own.

The book reviews classic psychoanalytic theories about the feminine within this new cultural context. It challenges hegemonic gender prejudices, and discusses new conceptions that do not pathologize "different" lifestyles and family configurations. Today, psychoanalysts tend to be less focused on what a "normal" woman should look like, and more interested in being attuned to each woman's personal and social realities, subjectivities, and desires.

The book also discusses new theories, such as replacing Freud's notion of penis envy with "power envy." Additionally, it explores how the characteristics earlier attributed to women – such as masochism, passivity, and narcissism – are no longer viewed as innate. Instead, they relate to the place women occupy in society. The new psychoanalytic theories conceive of the feminine – and gender notions in general – as something that transforms itself. Gender ideals change within the cultural context, and each woman has her singular notion of the feminine.

This introduction to the book consists of four parts. The first part deconstructs the question by identifying the historical context in which the question is asked, who is asking the question, who is a woman, and what it means "to want." The second part provides some answers to the question "what do women want

DOI: 10.4324/9781003180036-2

today?" The third part discusses how to explore and support new notions of the feminine within psychoanalysis. The fourth part briefly describes the structure of the book.

The question "what do women want today?" is rhetorical. It is meant to be thought-provoking and deconstructed

Who is asking the question?

The question was originally asked by Freud to Marie Bonaparte, whom he was analyzing. Traditionally, all important enterprises were conducted by men. They were the observers who defined the world. That is meaningful, because in general, we have lived in a phallocentric culture where everything has been constructed from a male's point of view. Most "great thinkers" who conceived of and defined the world have been males.

Consequently, as Glocer Fiorini (2022) points out, the subject studying an object has traditionally been male, and the object being studied has been female. That renders the male as the active subject who desires, and the female as the passive object being desired. The female and her perspective have traditionally been thought of as "unknown," "different," "mysterious," or "other." If the observer is a male, it follows that he would think of females in this way, and think of his own perspective as the known established model.

As a result of a hegemonic culture where everything has traditionally been conceptualized from a male's point of view, women have also tended to share a phallocentric ideology and have perceived themselves as passive objects of desire. This book demonstrates that there is a powerful change occurring now. Women are adopting more active roles, perceiving themselves as human beings with desires and agency. They are re-conceptualizing culture through their own experiences and asking their own questions. From their perspective, they are no longer "the other" nor "a mystery." And while "women (and men), want to be loved," they also want to love and to sublimate and have their own ideals.

Today, many criticize Freud for his apparently misogynistic theories. However, everything should be understood in its cultural context. Freud was *avant garde* when he articulated his theories almost a hundred years ago.

What is a woman?

Today, psychoanalysis is reexamining its conceptions of "women." Freud proposed the contradictory ideas that anatomy is destiny and that gender identity is something culturally attained through the resolution of the Oedipus complex (Glocer Fiorini, 2017). On one hand, Freud's oedipal theory accentuates a binary theory by taking the subject to a masculine or feminine position via a heterosexual outcome. On the other hand, he goes beyond this masculine–feminine binary. In "The Psychogenesis of Homosexuality in a Woman" (Freud, 1920), he maintains that the subjective gender construction involves three variables: somatic sexual characters, psychic sexual characters (masculine or feminine attitude), and type of object choice (homosexual or heterosexual). He maintained that these three variables mix in different combinations.

Today, most new theories are in line with Freud's (1920) notion. Anatomy is always culturally signified and is seen as only one variable in the subjective construction of gender. Culture has a strong binary reference, but people are increasingly conceptualizing their gender identity as non-binary and having characteristics traditionally associated with the opposite gender.

The feminine: Many theorists consider that while being female refers to being born with a particular anatomy, being a woman or being feminine are subjective social constructions. Each individual develops her own singular notion. In her opening remarks at the last International Psychoanalytic Association meeting, Julia Kristeva paraphrased Simon de Beauvoir as follows: "We are (biologically) born female, but 'I' (psychosexual conscious unconscious) become (or not) feminine" (Kristeva, 2019).

There is a difference between "woman" and "feminine." The latter concept is based on the masculine–feminine dichotomy. It is a cultural and psychoanalytic notion which can apply to women, to men, and non-binary gender identities. We can talk about "feminine" aspects of men. In this way, the concept of the feminine is not universal, and it is necessary to deconstruct it through a non-binary model.

While adhering to the notion that being feminine is a subjective construction, theorists vary in the role that they attribute to anatomy in the development of gender identity. Kristeva stresses the notion that "the body – far from being a solely biological fact – is a psychosomatic construction that takes form as the speaking subject emerges in its relationships with the paternal and maternal instances" (Kristeva, 2017, p. 68; Balsam, 2022). The body does not exist in a vacuum. It can only be conceived as the person emerges within the subjective relationship with its maternal and paternal objects.

Balsam (2022) stresses the importance of the female body's capacity to engender life. She thinks there is a cultural fascination with it, and she maintains that those subjects who possess a female anatomy will have to take this into account as they deal with themselves, interact with others, and develop their subjective gender identification.

Butler, on the other hand, challenges conventional notions of gender identity and maintains that being a woman is unrelated to anatomy. According to the author, gender identity is performative. It is continuously redefined by performing certain behaviors, which are in turn related to the place occupied in society (Butler 1990).

Today, most authors understand gender conceptions as related to social constructions. Those social constructions are informed by conscious and unconscious identifications. They are also the product of the history of the places women and men have occupied within their families and societies. Once the infant is born, it is assigned a masculine or feminine gender. Even before conception, it is the object of the projections and expectations of all the ideals and values that its parents and culture have about gender stereotypes. Laplanche (1997) refers to these projections and expectations as "messages of gender assignment." The child gradually understands who she is and what others expect from her.

A study done 30 years ago with a newborn baby in a nursery illustrates the extent to which gender characteristics are assigned. The baby was first dressed in light blue, and both men and women observers said it looked "powerful and wise." The same baby was then dressed in pink and the same observers said it looked "pretty and delicate."

Parents contribute to the child's gender identity through the way they relate to the child in reference to its gender and through the identificatory object they provide.

Subjects born with a male anatomy can be feminine, be women, and have maternal feelings and attitudes. That is especially relevant for gay men and transgender women. Subjects have the right to identify themselves with a particular binary or non-binary gender.

What is to want?

We can talk about two types of desires. The first concerns sexuality and drive. The second concerns "want/wills" which refers to sublimated desires related to creative work and the ideal of how to be in the world. That latter meaning is particularly relevant today as women are developing new self-ideals.

As for sexuality and drive, women want passively to be loved. They also want to actively love. As for want/wills, just like men, they sublimate their desires and pursue their own ideals and projects.

Kristeva maintains that Freud's classic question does not refer to "desire," but to "want/will." "It's the pillar of the choice of an ethical life. It refers to the relationship of the feminine to the ideals of life, and to life itself, inseparable from cultural ideals" (Kristeva, 2019).

The notion of "will" has an immediate connection to "agency." To have agency is to own your will. Ellman (2022) discusses how women have been historically identified with a passive role, and are now struggling with their ambivalence about having agency.

Each woman is a unique human being and wants something different

The new psychoanalytic theories conceive of the feminine – and gender notions in general – as something that transforms itself. Gender ideals change within the cultural context.

A woman's sexual desires will include her psychic sexual character and her choice of object. Traditionally there was no freedom of choice regarding desire – not from the sexuality dimension nor from the "will" dimension. From the sexuality dimension, it was inconceivable not to follow the anatomical mandate and have a heterosexual object choice. From the "will" dimension, it was unimaginable to have ideals outside of being a wife and mother. Today, women can explore those two dimensions. They can aspire to different gender identities and to new professional ideals.

The specific desires of a woman are shaped by the interaction of her drive, family, and social culture. The social cultural context is a convergence of her race, social class, and religious beliefs, among other things. Today, as we challenge traditional hegemonic concepts and attempt to be more appreciative of each person's unique values and backgrounds, we are paying closer attention to those social variables.

Although each woman is different, we can still conceptualize "women" as a heterogeneous collective group.

What do women want today?

Now that we have deconstructed the question "what do women want today?" and identified its many implicit components, we can attempt an answer. As we will see, that answer is complex and manifold. What women want today is different from what they wanted when Freud asked his question in 1925.

From a social perspective, we can argue that the most fundamental of what women want is not to be the object of violence

For privileged women, there are many rights – such as absence of domestic violence, egalitarian treatment at work, and controlling one's own body – that seem obvious. However, most women in the world continue to fight for those rights. What those women want is not to be the object of violence.

Historically, a culture that has implicitly seen women occupying a denigrated place in society has tolerated violence against them. Immersed in that culture, women found it difficult to challenge such violence and some even identified with the aggressor.

As Patricia Alkolombre points out, that is changing. Today, there is less tolerance for misogyny. Popular women's movements like "Ni una menos" in Argentina are taking on femicide. And movements like "Me too" in the United States are confronting sexual harassment. These new movements are having a powerful effect on culture and women's conceptions about themselves. They are creating new ideals and identificatory models. Instead of being submissive, some women identify with these movements and feel supported and empowered to challenge violence against them. Argentina just legalized abortion after many persistently demanded to be in charge of their reproductive rights.

Cultural changes interact with the desire and the possibilities of sublimation of each woman, creating new ideals and identificatory models

Many factors are contributing to these cultural changes. The feminist movement has had many important effects. It has helped change women's conception of themselves, helped change cultural attitudes toward women, helped change women's standing regarding the law and society, and helped women see that they are deserving of equal status in the workplace. The changes in culture include the decline of the patriarchal paradigm and a questioning of the central place of the long-accepted classical family. Those efforts have been assisted by a shift toward an economy powered by technology rather than physical strength, which has diminished the significance of a historical male attribute and created openings for women in the workplace.

Those developments mean that getting married and having children is no longer the only way of becoming fulfilled and having financial support. Work provides women with an alternative source of fulfillment and financial independence.

Traditional and new feminine ideals now co-exist

We live in a transitional time – the construction of new subjectivities is influenced by the values of both traditional and contemporary cultural models.

Some women feel pressure to live up to both our traditional and new ideals. They feel the need to be perfect professionals, partners, and mothers. They have developed idealized and impossible to reach demands. The mere existence of new models is a potential source of anxiety. Having multiple reference can lead to ambivalence, conflict, and additional anxieties. Moreover, choosing models other than their mothers can lead some women to feel that they are devaluing their mothers. This can lead to feelings of guilt and fantasies that their mothers will not love them. Some working mothers feel guilty for being less involved with their children than their mothers were.

While there have always been conflicts between ideals and realities, this is much more exacerbated today. There is more freedom and possibility to explore and access new ideals, including new gender identities and family configurations.

Taking on these multiple roles, inside and outside the home, requires that women have partners who also take on multiple roles. That said, many couples are negotiating their roles. They face the challenge of having both stereotypical and contemporary gender ideals. For younger generations the gender dynamics are more fluid, which facilitates women having multiple roles and living up to their ideals. Among the young there is little stereotyped binarism, and both sexes have roles that were previously characteristic of the other.

Motherhood

Motherhood is being affected by all the current developments. The access to birth control on one hand and to assisted fertility technology on the other, further contributes to separating motherhood from "nature" and making it something cultural. Contemporary authors, such as Schwartz (1994), also challenge the notion that motherhood is instinctive. They maintain that being a mother requires the cultural desire to be one.

Society has become more open to different gender roles and family configurations. Women increasingly see motherhood as a choice and not a necessity, and it is easier for them to conceive of having a child without a partner. Single motherhood by choice has become more common. As a result, women can now make choices that are not experiences as defying an established social structure. They are less likely to feel they are "transgressing" and also less likely to feel ambivalent and guilty.

As fertility technology has become more common, it is more incorporated into fantasies and, therefore, more possible to elaborate and symbolize. Today's fertility techniques also offer a continuum of options that further help elaborate this previously alien process. An example is the chance to freeze eggs allowing for the option of future artificial insemination.

Most psychoanalysts conceive motherhood as a wonderful, gratifying, and very special aspect of the feminine. However, some are also concerned that the sanctification of motherhood can inhibit women who want to pursue other avenues of fulfillment.

Leadership

Women's efforts to attain equal status as whole human beings are a central theme in this book. Equal status relates to how they conceive of themselves and their place in society.

After struggling throughout history to be recognized, many women are establishing themselves as leaders. Whereas many pioneers felt they had to adopt a traditionally masculine style to lead and be respected, today's women leaders are cultivating their own feminine leadership styles. As Adriana Prengler (IPA's vice-president) maintains, women have found their own feminine voice. Virginia Ungar, the first woman president of IPA in 102 years, associates leadership by women with Kristeva's notion of "the transformative capabilities of the feminine" (Kristeva, 2019), and with the analytic attitude: the capacity to receive, to contain, to think before acting, and to tolerate ambiguity and the unknown (Ungar, 2022). She also quotes Harriet Wolfe, who is IPA's second woman president, "the transformative aspect is fundamental to institutional leadership…It is what I mean about receptivity and its relation to the feminine…A leader needs to 'hold' the organization with a benign, attentive, active receptivity" (Wolfe, 2021). Paula Ellman, COWAP's overall chair, maintains that women have to overcome misogynistic cultural mandates to feel comfortable with their self- agency and able to own their will to pursue the ideals of their choice.

In conclusion, today, women want to be free to develop and inhabit their own binary or non-binary, singular version of woman and the feminine. From a sublimated perspective, they "want" to be respected as whole human beings, to have equal power and authority (a "voice"), and to have choices. With that comes the demand that they not be the object of violence and that they have control over their bodies and choices related to their bodies.

How do we explore and support new feminine notions as psychoanalysts?

In my view, psychoanalysts can explore and support new feminine notions in three important ways. The first way is thinking about our own gender prejudices, which is something I want to invite readers of this book to do.

The second way is to develop new psychoanalytic theories that embrace, rather than pathologize, alternative choices. This book discusses how we can replace Freud's notion of penis envy with "power envy," and how the characteristics earlier attributed to women – such as masochism, passivity, and narcissism – are no longer viewed as innate, but instead relate to the place women have occupied in society.

The third way is to adopt an open curious attitude. Patients are coming in with new gender scenarios. They are developing new ideals and new interpersonal dynamics. Psychoanalysts must attempt to bring understanding to the meaning of each issue a woman brings to her sessions – to think of each woman as a singular woman, inhabiting her own set of circumstances.

The way in which we listen and give meaning to our patients' material about these new feminine scenarios is affected by our own subjective views of the world, and that includes our listening to new feminine scenarios.

From a psychoanalytic perspective, it is normal for everyone to have prejudices and to perceive the other (the new, the different) as "bad." This experience of "otherness" is part of developing a cohesive sense of identity. The infant needs to define itself in terms of another being who it is not. People with "different" notions of gender may challenge our own notions. We may unconsciously denigrate them in order to reassure ourselves that our constructs are the right ones.

So, we have to explore and understand our own gender prejudices and the effects they have in the counter-transference. And, we need to monitor them.

The psychoanalytic theories that we use to understand our patients can operate like prejudices. Theory poses epistemological obstacles. It limits our ability to hear what is foreign to us and to make room for the other's differences, with its unexpected or unknown elements. It can prevent us from listening to what is new and different when patients' discourse contains conceptions that denote an ideology that is inimical to ours. We may lose our suspended attention and focus excessively on certain problems. Nevertheless, while rigidly adhering to some concepts hinders the development of our discipline, we still need theories as they are mainstays of our work.

Because psychoanalytic theories are immersed in cultural context, the theories of the 1900s appear phallocentric today. In his 1905 "Three essays," Freud discusses the sexual development of girls and presents his thesis of infantile sexual monism. The thesis assumes that children of both sexes perceive the penis and the clitoris as the only sexual organs. Therefore, the sexuality of children of both sexes is of a masculine nature, and the girl is "castrated."

Authors who subscribed to these Freudian theories emphasized different aspects. Lampl de Groot (1928) focused on the identification of femininity with passivity. Deutsch (1932) viewed narcissism, masochism, and passivity as three essentially feminine traits. Despite being a time of phallocentric theory, there were analysts who disagreed, such as Klein (1975) and Jones (1927). They maintained that, from a very early age, girls had unconscious knowledge and sensations of their internal organs and vagina. In 1976, Stoller articulated his theory of primary femininity, which maintains that women have their own psychic constellations.

Many of us were taught theories in our psychoanalytic training that now appear phallocentric and misogynistic. An example is Freud's (1937) conclusion in "Analysis terminable and interminable," about the extent to which a woman can be understood and analyzed: "...with the wish for a penis and the masculine protest we have penetrated through all the psychological strata and have reached bedrock" (Freud, 1937).

Both the current revisiting of Freud and the new theories advocate an approach that depathologizes the "different" lifestyles and family configurations of transgender people, homosexuals, women who do not want to have children, and women who want to have children without a partner. As analysts, we need to help each woman explore and develop her own feminine notion of what she wants. We also have to be open and inquisitive in order to allow ourselves to hear new thoughts in our patients that challenge our own long-held beliefs.

At the time, Freud asked the question in 1925, the only acceptable ideal for women was to become mothers. A desire for a child within an adult heterosexual relationship was, according to classic psychoanalytic theories, the epitome of the development of female sexuality. There were no other choices. That has profoundly changed.

Brief description of the book's structure

The book explores and discusses the question of "What Women Want Today" in five sections: Introduction, Current Theories about the Feminine, Gender Relations Today, Psychoanalysis in the Community, and Contemporary Gender Scenarios.

The tone of the discussion is set by Virginia Ungar's paper about women wanting to have equal power, sustaining a feminine style of leadership, and overcoming historical difficulties exerting their power.

Next, a section on "Current Theories about the Feminine" features prominent authors in the field: Balsam Glocer Fiorini and Kramer Richards. The authors discuss new concepts of development and gender identification. They argue that gender stereotypes are reductionistic and that each woman has a singular conception of her own femininity. They all conceive the feminine – and gender notions in general – as transformative. Gender ideals change within the cultural context.

This is followed by a section on "Gender Relations Today," where Abelin-Sas Rose, Lieberman, Bassen, and Harris discuss the effect that changing notions of the feminine have on current gender dynamics. They also discuss the conflicts and anxieties that arise from dealing with conventional stereotypes and new gender roles.

In the next section, "Psychoanalysis in the Community" Prengler and Goodman discuss different aspects of women's struggle for equality in a misogynistic culture. Prengler discusses women's successful struggle to have "a voice," a power that has been suppressed through history. Goodman writes about the importance of active witnesses of the trauma caused by misogyny in both the analytic situation and out in the community.

The last section considers "New Female Scenarios" that arise today as women explore new gender identities and dynamics. Ellman discusses women's ambivalence about having agency and how they have historically inhibited their self-determination. Alkolombre examines contemporary motherhood considering the multiplicity of new scenarios (hetero-, homo-, single parent, assisted reproduction) which all bring an expansion of possibilities.

References

Balsam, R. (2022). *What Do Women Want Today? Femininity, Desire and Agency in Psychoanalysis.* London: Routledge.

Butler, J. (1990) *Gender Trouble.* New York: Routledge.

Deutsch, H. (1932). On female homosexuality. *Psychoanalytic. Q.* 1:484–510.

Ellman, P. (2022). *What Do Women Want Today? Femininity, Desire and Agency in Psychoanalysis.* London: Routledge.

Freud, S. (1905). Three essays on the theory of sexuality, *S. E.* 7:135–149.

Freud, S. (1920). The psychogenesis of a case of homosexuality in a woman. *S. E.* 18: 145–177.

Freud, S. (1937). Analysis terminable *and Interminable. S. E.* 23:216–253.

Glocer Fiorini, L. (2017). *Sexual Difference in Debate: Bodies, Desires and Fictions.* London: Karnac.

Glocer Fiorini, L. (2022). *What Do Women Want Today? Femininity, Desire and Agency in Psychoanalysis.* London: Routledge.

Jones, E. (1927). The early development of female sexuality. *Int. J. Psychoanalysis.* 8:459–472.

Jones, E. (1955). *The Life and Work of Sigmund Freud.* Volume II. London: Hogart.

Klein, M. (1975). *The Psychoanalysis of Children.* London: Hogarth.

Kristeva, J. (2017). Transformations of parentality, Ch. 7. Tsolas, V. Anzieu-Premmereur, C. (eds.) *A Psychoanalytic Exploration of the Body in Today's World: On the Body,* p. 68. London: Routledge.

Kristeva, J. (2019). Prelude to an ethics of the feminine. Opening Lecture Given at the 51st IPA Congress, July 24, London, United Kingdom.

Lampl de Groot, J. (1928). The evolution of the Oedipus complex in women. *Int. J. Psychoanalysis.* 9:332–345.

Laplanche, J. (1997). The theory of seduction and the problem of the other. *Int. J. Psychoanalyst.* 78:653–666.

Schwartz, A. (1994). Taking the nature out of mother. Bassin, D., Honey, M., Kaplan, M.M. (eds.), *Representations of Motherhood* (pp. 240–255). New Haven, CT: Yale University Press.

Stoller, R. (1976). Primary femininity. *J. Am. Psychoanalytic Assoc.* 24 (Supplement): 59–78.

Ungar, V. (2022) Actitud analítica (Psychoanalytic attitude). Ungar, V. (ed.). *What Do Women Want Today? Femininity, Desire and Agency in Psychoanalysis.* London: Routledge.

Ungar, V. (2021). *What Do Women Want Today? Femininity, Desire and Agency in Psychoanalysis.* London: Routledge.

Wolfe, H. (2021). Female leadership: difficulties and gifts, Plenary APsaA Meeting, 2022. Ungar, V. (ed.). *What Do Women Want Today? Femininity, Desire and Agency in Psychoanalysis.* London: Routledge.

2 Authority, power and gender in institutional life

Virginia Ungar

Firstly, I would like to thank the Committee on Women and Psychoanalysis for inviting me once again to address issues that have been discussed for some time now. And I would also like to tell you that my appreciation is in no way a mere formality.

From a personal point of view, ever since I was elected to the position of President of The International Psychoanalytical Association (IPA)in 2015 – becoming the first woman President of the Association – I have started to think about subjects which previously I had not been used to addressing.

Because of this, then, I would like to thank The Committee on Women and Psychoanalysis (COWAP) sincerely as, in inviting me on a number of occasions to work on issues that are of great relevance in themselves and which are also major points of discussion in the world today, you have made me read, study, listen, think and write about women in contemporary society.

In 2018, I participated in the COWAP Congress held in Los Angeles, which was wonderful for its organization, format and content and also for the warmth that was in the air during the event.

In July 2019 and between the two meetings of COWAP, we had the London Congress under the title "The Feminine" with 2500 participants, 500 of them candidates. We also had the honour of Julia Kristeva giving the opening address, which was entitled "Prelude to an Ethics of The Feminine".

Also, in 2019, the Sexual and Gender Diversity Studies Committee, with the help of COWAP, organized two meetings, one in Brussels and the other in Buenos Aires. That is to say, that we are very much involved in the issues that are the focus of debates all around the world in the present day.

At the London Congress, I took part in a panel – sponsored by COWAP – together with the ex-President of the IPA, Claudio Eizirik, and the president elect, Harriet Wolfe – three "Presidents" together. The panel was chaired by Patricia Alkolombre and the title was, as it happens, "Women in Leadership: A Psychoanalytic Perspective".

Now, let us turn to the subject of this book. The title *Femininity, Desire and Agency in Psychoanalysis: What Do Women Want Today?* leads me to mention a similar question that Kristeva asked during her presentation at the last IPA Congress when she took up again what she herself calls the *enigmatic* question

DOI: 10.4324/9781003180036-3

Freud outlined to Marie Bonaparte: "What does woman want?" or "*Was will das Weib?*" But Kristeva immediately explains that the question does not refer to *desire* (*Wunsch*), but to *want/will* (*Wollen*). For Kristeva, this is in fact the pillar of the choice of an ethical life. Then, she goes on to explain further that "The elusive ('what…want') refers to the relationship of the feminine to the ideals of life, and to life itself, inseparable from cultural ideals" (Kristeva, 2019).

The question here **is not** what woman wants. We are not talking here about *desire*, but about *want/will* (*Wollen*), the axis of an ethical position according to Kristeva. She also asks if Freud might not have pursued an ethical refounding through the Feminine, and says that the biopolitics of modernity force the enigmatic question on us now more than ever.

Today, it is possible to ask this question as set out by Kristeva. In the past, this was simply not possible. Nowadays, a woman can ask many things, and first if she wants to be a woman. And also, if she wants to be a wife, if she wants to be a mother. In Freud's times, there was absolutely no space available for these questions.

This historic question for psychoanalysis seems to have originated in a session of analysis with Marie Bonaparte, who took notes when her analyst, none other than Sigmund Freud himself, said to her: "The great question that has never been answered and which I have not yet been able to answer, despite my thirty years of research into the feminine soul, is 'What does woman want?'"

This question remains relevant up to the present and leads Freud to give, at different times in his career, different tentative answers to the idea which refers in some way to a dark territory.

We could say that Freud positions the question at an abstract level: what does woman want? Today, after some time has passed and with the enormous cultural and social changes that have taken place in recent times, we can finally talk about exactly that: what women want. And, indeed, women want different and particular things; not all want the same thing.

I can also imagine what a teenager in my home country, Argentina, might answer if I asked her that question: "What kind of question is that?" she would say, continuing "I would never think of asking the question in that way. Women are, above all, human beings".

But going beyond the question of the times and the way young people are setting aside binarism, I believe that a first reply would be that women want equality, parity.

Even if we can see that Feminism has been doing great work and women's movements have established a new way of doing politics, we cannot deny that equality of access and opportunities do not exist today for women, not to mention even the lack of recognition for the non-remunerated work that women do in the home. And, what's more, we must also admit that violence against women in its most aberrant forms, such as femicide, is continuing to rise.

These are the voices of the women suffering these situations that can still be heard and which, necessarily, must continue speaking as well as they can, and today even more so considering what is being facilitated on the internet.

Returning to the question: what do women want today? Even if I am in favour of the ceding of more space to the plural, I must pause for a second to underline the fact that, although it has been the women's collective which has made our voices heard, the area of psychoanalytic work deals with singularities.

This is the nature of our essentially singular task. But this singularity always maintains a relationship to the context in which that person lives. This "externality" is always plural.

Freud posed the question in a context in which the collective was essentially the family. There was no other collective such as the women's collective movements that exist today.

Having made this clarification, I would now like to take up once more the question of what women want today, and what comes to mind is a game where I try out some of the possible answers to the question in Freud's work which remains unanswered. I said that women want equality, parity, but at the same time they want differences to be respected. Continuing the game, I'll add another possible response which perhaps should precede the previous one: women want to be heard. It is only in this way that we can understand massive movements like *Ni Una Menos* that was born in Argentina, marches around the world, and the mass movement in my country in favour of legal and safe abortion. These huge gatherings and vigils were born of a collective cry first of women, but now of women, men, adolescents and children.

We must remember that we are preceded by a history full of silence, of forced silence and stifled voices.

There is a book by Mary Beard which helped me to understand this point, published in 2017 and entitled *Women & Power: A Manifesto* (Beard, 2018). In it, the author traces the mechanisms of the silencing of women which have been so ingrained in Western civilization. I would like to convey here all that I learnt from Beard, but for reasons of space I will mention just a few central points. In her book, Beard traces this regime of the silencing of women to the very start of the Western literary tradition near the end of the 8th century BC according to some scholars: *The Odyssey* by Homer. As we know, this work tells of the difficulties and challenges faced by Odysseus at the end of the Trojan War in his efforts to return home where his wife Penelope awaits him. It is also the story of Telemachus, their son. In a scene in the first book of the tale, Penelope comes down from her quarters to the hall of the palace and finds there a minstrel singing to a group of suitors about the difficulties the men were having returning home from the war. She does not like the song and so asks the minstrel to sing a happier one. Right there, her son Telemachus says to her: "Mother, go back to your quarters and attend to your own works, the loom and the spindle, […] Talking must be the concern of men, and mine in particular. I am the master of the house". Penelope retires to her bedchamber.

Beard takes this fragment of *The Odyssey* as the first written proof in Western culture that women's voices should be silenced in public and further, she writes that what appears here is the concept that a man must learn to control public discourse and silence women as part of his development as a man.

There is also historic evidence from the 2nd century AD of other cases of loathing of those women who tried to speak in public. One example was where women were allowed to speak as martyrs just before their deaths, as in the Roman circus. Another was to let women speak to defend their own interests, but never to speak on behalf of men. In other words, oratory was a practice which defined masculinity as a gender.

According to Mary Beard then, we inherited the tradition of gendered speaking. One of the consequences of this is that it is still possible, right up to the present, to see how women who demand to be heard in public are seen as androgynous.

These same questions arise when we look at the harassment of women online, from insults to death threats. If we examine the difficulties faced by women in the exercising of power, we will find some very interesting situations. Without needing to go too far back in history, we will rapidly come to the conclusion that the cultural and mental model that we have of the powerful person continues to be invariably male. And simply observing the way leaders such as Angela Merkel and, on the campaign trail, Hilary Clinton dress shows us how this image persists: a suit of jacket and trousers, all in neutral tones. This leads me to think that we should pay close attention to the degree to which this male dimension is ingrained in our own mindsets, to the extent of having been absorbed by women also.

We are now working towards a possible answer in the game of trying to find a response to Freud's enigmatic question, and indeed there is one which is based on and includes the previous two: women want to have equality of access to positions of power. This is an issue which deserves to be studied deeply because, in my opinion, it does not refer to the struggle of an individual, of one or two women, to access those positions and keep them in spite of all the adverse reactions that they may attract. To do so, it is enough to monitor the varying strengths of misogynistic reactions on the internet during election campaigns. When it comes to the construction of the exercising of power, a male mark can still be seen. The current model is one of domination and the deconstruction of this model of the application of power is made necessary as it originates in times when women were not even considered for the exercising of power.

From this perspective, it is interesting to think that, at a time when his female patients did not have a voice to be heard and arrived with hysterical symptoms of conversion, Freud offered them the possibility "to freely associate and relate what is going through her minds". He gave them a voice and the symptoms receded. Today, the fact of being in a position of power implies for a woman a great responsibility and an enormous commitment. We would all agree that gender is a social construction and, as already proposed by Judith Butler, this construction is born of a performative process. Judith Butler recently stated that the occupying of public spaces by women's movements is also performative in the sense that it is a construction of power and she presents this as an inevitable task of our times if we truly want to achieve change in this world (Butler, 2019).

The exclusion of women from the spaces of power has a long history in which the darkest and most terrible experiences serve as a background which we should never ignore. It is part of a series of practices noted not only by History, but also by Literature. Yet another major instance is the question of the hunting down and burning of the witches that was immortalized in *The Crucible* by Arthur Miller. A highly recommendable book on the subject is *Caliban, the Witch: Women, the Body and Primitive Accumulation* by Silvia Frederici which analyses in masterful depth the history of women in the transition from feudalism to capitalism. According to the author, "It also provided a genealogy of the modern concepts of femininity and masculinity that challenged the post-modern assumption of an almost ontological predisposition in Western Culture to capture gender through binary oppositions" (Frederici, 2004). Frederici also makes a critique of the theory of the body by Michel Foucault who, in his analysis of the techniques of power and the disciplines to which the body has been subjected, ignores fundamental issues such as reproduction, and bases the histories of men and women in an undifferentiated whole. In this way, he manages to leave aside the "disciplining" of women to such an extent that he does not even mention the most horrifying attack against the body in the Modern era: the burning of witches. The author believes that the history of sexuality could not be written today from the point of view of an abstract, asexual and universal subject.

We cannot ignore this milestone in history given the context that we find ourselves in today, so I propose coming back to the theme of authority and power in relation to gender. Power is an attribute and not an object. In fact, it has to do with relations and has no material corporality. Even if in the popular imagination power is something that is acquired and used, power is actually constructed in a process which can have a number of nuances. It is said that if you study the biography of a leader it is easy to find precedents which reveal a personality that was constructed in order to exercise power.

I must now return once more to authority and its relationship to power and I would like to tie it in with the question of having a voice because perhaps, as Beard suggests, we need to recognize the necessity of an awareness of a *voice of authority* for women and how we have come to create it. This voice of command is still operating as masculine in the binary code of the collective imagination. What's more, the issue of authority and its relation to other concepts such as power and obedience have been studied for a long time now in the field of the social sciences.

It is a subject that needs a multidisciplinary approach, but which we must also think of both in relation to our practice as psychoanalysts as well as in the insti-tutional field. I only want to introduce the issue and to do so I will go back to the inescapable reference to the notion of authority that was set out by Hanna Arendt in the article "What Is Authority?" (Arendt, 1961). Here, she describes her position early on saying that not only has authority been dissipated in the Modern era, but also that the word has been emptied of meaning, this applying not solely in the political sphere but also in those where it had its origin in the pre-political era: education and the raising of children.

Our times have been characterized by the so-called "crisis of authority" and its expression in the greater social and cultural process is the *questioning of authority*, including that linked to knowledge. Teachers and lecturers, and also those who work in the field of law, come up against these variations all the time and the analyst is also questioned because of both the devices and the tools that we use. In fact, when we talk about *authority* and power we do so in the arena of relations, something that always implies a certain amount of asymmetry. If this component does not exist, there is no room for resistance, so that the exercising of authority includes resistance to it, something that is also part of power relations.

Authoritarianism is a type of authority which is not based on consensus, but on submission. In this sense, it is not an *excess* of authority, something that "got out of hand"; it is not quantitative, a "too much". They are completely different experiences. Authority, or the commanding voice, is arrived at through mechanisms such as recognition and legitimization and it is not possible to impose these – they are achieved only when consensus is obtained.

To give it a simple definition, authority is connected to the attribution of knowledge, while power is connected to the possibility of the regulation of a series of forces in a legitimate manner which then allows for a series of actions to be carried out. It is a permanent collective construct.

Authority, power, suggestion and transference

Before addressing the issue of authority and power in personal analysis and in psychoanalytic institutions, it is necessary, even briefly, to look at this topic and its relation to the very core of the psychoanalytic process: transference. There is something that takes place in analysis that we cannot overlook, and this is the fact that analysts' words have an effect of authority that is not based solely on the rationality of their statements. It is tied instead to the nature of a device that is typical of psychoanalysis and that we call the transference. One of its components, suggestion, supports patients' attribution of authority to the analyst, which occurs after the development of transference neurosis.

We know that Freud adopted hypnotic suggestion early on to abandon it later as a practical method. In other words, he gave up the use of direct suggestion. Yet we can also assert that he never abandoned the idea that suggestion was part of the cure. When Freud stops using hypnosis to order that the symptom cease, he incorporates the invitation to associate freely. This operation constitutes an attempt to recruit patients' will so that they may let their unconscious manifest itself. Along with the analyst's evenly suspended attention, such manifestation will set the course to be travelled by the analytic couple until the end of its journey.

We cannot overlook the fact that this invitation to associate is but an aspiration. There is nothing less free than patients' discourse at the beginning of a treatment, when they are trapped between their anxiety and their symptoms. If they are able to engage in free association, we are approaching the end of analysis. Now, if patients have accepted being part of the analytic device – lying on the couch, losing their ability to use their gaze to control the subject who is willing to listen to them – something has taken place that has to do with trust, with the attribution of knowledge. In this sense, while suggestion is part of every human relationship and, to a greater extent, of curing phenomena, what concerns us today is its role in the transference in the context of the analytic cure.

Suggestion is present across Freud's writings – from "Papers on Hypnotism and Suggestion" (1888–1892) to "An Outline of Psychoanalysis" (1940). Examining the evolution of this concept, however, would exceed the scope of this paper. In the manner of an overview, let us say that in 1912, past the pre-analytic stage, Freud states that to a certain extent, "the results of psycho-analysis rest upon suggestion" (Freud, 1912, p. 106). In his 28th introductory lecture, in turn, he establishes the essential difference between suggestion and the transference. Hypnotism "makes use of suggestion in order to forbid the symptoms (…) but (…) leaves all the processes that have led to the formation of symptoms unaltered". Analytic treatment, by contrast, "makes its impact further back towards the roots, where the conflicts are which gave rise to the symptoms, and uses suggestion in order to alter the outcome of those conflicts" (Freud, 1916, p. 450–451). In this sense, suggestion *helps* analysts to work with their patients towards overcoming resistance. Further, in a very enlightening paragraph Freud talks about what analysts do with suggestion, that is, with the attribution of authority. "In psycho-analysis", he states,

> we act upon the transference itself, resolve what opposes it, adjust the instrument with which we wish to make our impact. Thus, it becomes possible for us to derive an entirely fresh advantage from the power of suggestion; *we get it into our hands.*
>
> (ibid., pp. 451–452; emphasis added)

For the purpose of this discussion, the key to the relationship between authority and the transference lies here, in the tight line analysts must walk in order to use the position of knowledge where they have been placed (in Freud's words, that they "get into their hands") to promote the cure by paying constant attention to the transference-countertransference dynamics. Such is the only possible route for analytic treatment. In this sense, suggestion helps therapists to recruit patients' will, but not so that patients will follow, we might say, the "pleasure principle" or take on a submissive position. Instead, the goal is that they let their unconscious express itself and produce. As to analysts, they cannot use what patients place on their hands, their trust, to seduce or to teach; they must keep it within the realm of the transference-countertransference interplay.

We thus get into the sphere of the potential misuse of suggestion in analysis. Here we must take into account several factors that play a role in the analytic situation, namely, the attribution of knowledge to the analyst, the analytic frame and neutrality. The attribution of knowledge takes us back to the notion of authority, which is favoured by the device of *the frame*. It is worth asking to what extent such device – the use of the couch, which means that the analyst is out of sight and patients' contact with him or her is limited to the voice, and the indefinite duration of the treatment – contributes to creating an environment that promotes suggestion. At the same time, there is no doubt that the ways in which therapists operate the frame will determine, to a great extent, the fate of suggestion in the analysis. In this context, we should not merely maintain the oft-cited analytic regression but create an environment that can be traced back to a kind of infantile, projective dependence discussed by Meltzer (1998), with his conception of adolescence as a state of mind. For this author, adolescence starts with puberty, that is, with the break of the configuration developed during latency (characterized by the presence of obsessive dams), a configuration whereby children are willing to perform the work of leaving the realm of the family in order to socialize and learn. Psychoanalytic practice with children teaches us that they are able to do so because they *rely* on the belief that parents know everything about them. When this certainty collapses and, at the same time, children come into contact with their sexual impulses, their newly foreign body and the idea that their parents *do not know* bring about unusual emotional turmoil.

There is a coincidence between this prepubertal state and the beginning of analysis. Patients rely on their confidence that analysts know about them. Otherwise, it would be hard to accept becoming part of the analytic device. The suggestive aspect of the transference is hence essential, especially in the early stages of an analysis, but it must necessarily evolve; it must transform. Donald Meltzer delves lucidly into this process when he discusses patients' attitude towards mental pain. He notes that the self must progress, at the unconscious level, in its relations with its internal objects. These relations will go from *projective* dependence, to *obedience*, to *introjective* dependence on the internal parents, which constitutes the basis for an inspired independence (Meltzer, 2008). In addition, subjects' confidence in the object's kindness, in its ability to be fair, and in its availability to listen and to respond to requests for help will determine their attitude towards mental pain. Meltzer finds that trusting that the parent or the analyst will introject and preserve them and that both parent and analyst will sacrifice their own pleasure to satisfy their needs is pivotal to children's and patients' development as well as to the evolution of the transference.

The third of the factors mentioned above, *neutrality*, is a key psychoanalytic concept that was never used by Freud but has been widely debated in psychoanalytic literature. We could say that it is closely linked to the rule of abstinence. This rule lies at the core of the analytic attitude, but I do not believe it should be prescriptive. When analysts respond from inside the analytic frame instead of meeting patients' demands, they are not doing so only because they should not satisfy these demands. Rather, they just *cannot* satisfy them. Neutrality, then, remains an aspired ideal that is supported by the rule of abstinence.

To summarize, in analysis, the word of the analyst has an authoritative effect which is not only based upon the rationality of the affirmations made by the analyst, but also on the nature of a device native to our task which is called transference. One of the components of the transference – the suggestive – is that which upholds the attribution of authority which the patient carries out once the transference neurosis has settled in. From the references stated before, we may understand that the key to the relationship between authority and transference is to be found there, in the balance that the analyst must strike in the handling of the attribution of the knowledge which he/she has (as we see in Freud: "We get it into our hands") and how it is used towards a cure, working on the transference-countertransference relationship as the sole pathway in analytic treatment. And, regarding the attribution of knowledge, this mechanism leads us to the concept of authority mentioned at the start and fits nicely in the frame device. It is worth asking ourselves to what extent the frame that we suggest – the use of the couch, the suppression of sight of the analyst, contact only with the voice, suggesting a duration for treatment without a definite time limit – contributes to the creation of an atmosphere favourable to suggestion. The destination of that suggestion will obviously determine to a great extent how the therapist sets it out.

Authority, power and personal analysis

Given the current "crisis of authority" and general sociocultural transformations, our discipline cannot avoid being called into question. From my point of view, authority seems to be more closely linked to the analytic process and power to institutions. The problem is when the logic of power, which is the logic of institutions, invades the consulting room, or vice versa. We should recall here that while the transference refers to the analytic device, there are also institutional transferences, especially in spaces associated with the medical cure.

Not only is the psychoanalytic institution implicated in the process of the cure, it is also traversed by a variety of transferences insofar as analytic training is the basis of its existence. Much has been said about power and the use and abuse of authority in these cases. I believe that it is very important not to lose sight of the magnitude of power at play in training analysis. At the same time, this analysis is essential for psychoanalytic training. In this sense, Bion (1962) developed a very fruitful conception of learning as the product of an emotional experience that can be thought. Thinking, in turn, will lead to personality change. The author also claims that any type of learning that does not involve experience will result in a mere accumulation of information.

From this perspective, people can only become analysts if they have gone through the experience of an analysis with all the vicissitudes of the analytic process. This will be the sole way of introjecting such an experience, which will sustain therapists' analytic attitude. For this reason, candidates' motivation to undergo a training analysis must be addressed from the start, when the power of suggestion is at its peak. Meltzer says it in a very poetic way in *The*

Psychoanalytical Process: "We were beggars when we thought we were patrons, patients when we thought we were students" (Meltzer, 1967, p. 11).

Yet for this learning experience to be profitable, analysts of "analysts in training", as colleagues who are training are called in Argentina, must strike a delicate balance between acknowledging the attribution of knowledge they have been granted and viewing training analysis almost as any other individual analysis. Training analysts' position in the institutional structure lends them an additional authority, a place of knowledge that can favour the slippage of the transference relationship, essential for the analytic process, to an asymmetrical power relationship.

Both training analysts and the institution, therefore, are faced with a difficult task. Training analysts must constantly remember the specificities of the analysis of an analyst in training and, while taking into consideration the presence of institutional politics in the consulting room, prevent it from affecting their bond with their patients. The institution, for its part, must carefully analyse the training function, how it is granted, and the possibility of creating a revalidation system precisely because we are dealing with a function, and a very sensitive one.

The transference involves patients' trust in the object, a trust that places them in a situation of demand and vulnerability regarding the therapist. In the case of training analysis, such vulnerability is compounded by the positions occupied by analyst and analysand in the psychoanalytic institution. In this sense, how we use this power of suggestion that, according to Freud, we have in our hands becomes an ethical issue.

Authority, power and gender in psychoanalytic institutions

Entering into the political-institutional dimension of an analyst's training, it is important to mention the extraordinary lecture given my Max Weber entitled "Politics as a Vocation" (Weber, 1946). There, the German sociologist asks himself about the virtues of a politician and points to three: passion, a sense of responsibility and prudence. The passion, as a positive factor, is the commitment to a cause. It is the passion to a cause which makes us man, Weber says, and we should add "women" if we are to include the gender perspective. In fact, today, this should read "complex human beings". However, passion is not enough. The sense of responsibility to the cause is what orientates political action. And prudence rounds off the configuration of political subjectivity. In times such as these, in times when it is necessary to reconsider the conditions of the very exercising of our profession and the sense of its institutions, nothing seems more accurate. Or might it be the case that we could imagine and construct new territories for psychoanalysis, for example, without passion, responsibility and prudence?

It now seems that the moment has arrived to consider the task of institutional management. There is much to consider about leadership and I am going to use that term with the qualification that it could lead us onto the slippery slope to the exaltation of individuality.

It is necessary to underscore something that I have previously referenced on a number of occasions: when we access the management of institutions, we quickly realize that the analytic training which we received was not oriented to preparing us for these types of positions. We learn as we go along and by trial and error.

We are forced to confront crises and, at some times, we come into contact with very chaotic levels of group functioning in which the most primitive layers of the personality come into play together with the most archaic defences. And here, it is important to mention the great contribution made by Bion when he states that the possible emergence of the basic assumption configuration always lies beneath work groups (Bion, 1962).

It would seem to me that these moments of extreme conflict are in fact necessary as they test whether we are true to our own convictions. It is a time when we start to think again about the deepest personal reasonings which bring us to take up the position that we are in and to which we dedicate our energy and ability. It is also during times of crisis that we find and are forced to recognize our personal limitations, something that can persuade us to make the changes and adjustments that are necessary.

Being true to oneself does not necessarily imply either dogmatism or being chained to a position that cannot be modified. On the contrary, it is the time when we most need to listen to others and at the same time be ready to change our stance. Susana Malcorra, an Argentine woman who has held positions high up in business and was even appointed the Chef de Cabinet to the Executive Office at the United Nations by Ban Ki-moon – after which she became the Argentine Minister of Foreign Affairs holding the post until last year – put it in a very poetic way when referring to the *plasticity of the self*. "In a crisis, the best strategy is always to be true to oneself in a flexible way that helps you to adapt to the new circumstances" (Malcorra, 2018).

Being true to your own principles implies not imposing them on others, and much less attacking others but rather thinking and acting to the benefit of the community that you are working for, often involving the setting aside of personal interests. Being in leadership positions means that we often get to see ourselves with intractable narcissisms, but it is simply part of a task which has similarly other features that are also part of our clinical work.

Some years ago, I wrote a paper on Analytical Attitude and I still think today that it is this attitude that we internalize gradually over the years, first in training and later in the day-to-day practice of psychoanalysis. The analytic attitude has a number of components: receptivity (the willingness to receive whatever the patient needs to place in us), the capacity to contain, the possibility to think before acting and the ability to tolerate ambiguity and the unknown, that is, receive, contain and avoid saturating the space with explanatory interpretations which could actually be there to calm the anxieties of the analyst himself/herself. (Ungar, 2000). These abilities are put to the test in the most rigorous way in institutional conflicts. Each and every situation challenges them and it is important that we retain the ability not only to reflect, but also to listen to those whose position is different from our own.

Now, let us turn to the question of gender. Harriet Wolfe, in an excellent presentation that she gave at APsaA in February 2019, talked about the question of leadership by women and said:

> Leadership means attending to the "dark continent" aspect of an organization, the unarticulated and often unrepresented within it. We must be sensitive to what voices are not being heard within the organization and how our ideologies that make us feel certain might also blind us to important truths.

She continues "It is the transformative aspect that is fundamental to my understanding of leadership. It is what I mean about receptivity and its relation to the feminine". Later she says "A leader needs to 'hold' the organization with a benign, attentive, active receptivity to hear what is loud as well as what is so soft as to be almost inaudible" (Wolfe, 2019). It has a strong impact on me to go back and read her words once more after hearing Julia Kristeva, at our last Congress in London, talk about the transformative capabilities not of woman, but of *the feminine*. According to Kristeva, this is not innate, and neither is it acquired. Rather, it is tirelessly conquered through the two stages of the incomplete Oedipus complex.

I can find no better way to conclude than through her words in the hope that future generations of analysts, no matter their gender, may be inspired by them.

> Madam President, women do not own the transformative and always becoming FEMININE, which participates, with the masculine, in the psychosexuality of speaking and imagining beings. Since Freud and continuing in today's socio-historical mutations, the feminine appears to us at the heart of the psychoanalytic experience. Might Psychoanalysis be one of the feminine's possible (or even ultimate) sublimations?
>
> For the clinician that you are, "psychoanalytic listening" is alert to the "presence of change in certain dimensions of psychic functioning" – from the sensorial to the linguistic (from the "semiotic" to the "symbolic") and capable of inducing the patient "to collaborate with the task of transforming [these] elements". And you warn: only "an improvement on the attachment to the analyst and her/his capacity to receive and contain his/her anxieties make this transformation possible".
>
> As President of the IPA, your plasticity is and will surely continue to be greatly solicited, always discreet, and effective! "Rebirth has never been beyond my powers", wrote Colette (1873–1954), one of those "transformative" feminine geniuses whose works revitalize us. May that phrase stay with you.
>
> (Kristeva, 2019)

References

Arendt, H. (1961). What is authority In *Between Past and Future: Eight Exercises in Political Thought*. New York, NY: The Viking Press, pp. 91–141.

Beard, M. (2017). *Women & Power: A Manifesto*. New York; London: Liveright.

Bion, W.R. (1962). *Learning from Experience*. London: Heinemann.

Butler, J., Cano, V., Fernández Cordero, L. (2019). *Vidas en lucha. Conversaciones.*, Buenos Aires: Katz editores.

Frederici, S. (2004) *Caliban and the Witch, Women, the Body and Primitive Accumulation*. New York, NY: Autonomedia.

Freud, S. (1898). Papers on hypnotism and suggestion. *S. E. 1*: 61–72.

Freud, S. (1912). The dynamics of transference. *S. E. 12*: 106.

Freud, S. (1916). Introductory lectures on psychoanalysis (Part III). *S. E. 16*: 241–463.

Freud, S. (1940). An outline of psychoanalysis. *S. E. 23*: 141–208.

Kristeva, J. (2019) Prelude to an ethics of the feminine. Opening lecture given at the 51st IPA Congress, July 24, London, United Kingdom.

Malcorra, S. (2018). *Pasión por el resultado*. El liderazgo femenino ante las grandes decisiones, Buenos Aires: Paidós.

Meltzer, D. (1967). *The Psychoanalytical Process.*, Perthshire, Scotland Great Britain: Clunie Press, p. 11.

Meltzer, D., Harris M. (1998). *Adolescentes*, editado por L. Jaschevasky y C. Tabbia, Buenos Aires: Spatia.

Meltzer, D. (2008). *Sexual States of Mind*. London: Karnac Books.

Ungar, V. (2000). "Actitud analítica" [Psychoanalytic Attitude]. XXII APdeBA Symposium, Buenos Aires, Argentina.

Weber, M. (1946). "Politics as a Vocation," originally a speech given at Munich University, 1918, *Essays in Sociology*. New York, NY: Oxford University Press.

Wolfe, H. (2019). Female leadership: difficulties and gifts, Plenary APsaA Meeting, February 8.

Part II

Current theories about the feminine

Introduction by Margarita Cereijido

This section introduces the reader to the main current theoretical understandings of women and feminine gender identification. Rosemary Balsam, Leticia Glocer Fiorini, and Arlene Kramer Richards challenge hegemonic gender prejudices. They discuss new conceptions that make room for new gender identifications which do not pathologize the new feminine scenarios.

All of the authors approach women as "human beings" and whole persons who desire, sublimate, and create. They also all agree that gender stereotypes are reductionist and that each woman has a singular conception of her own femininity.

In her chapter "Liberating 'Female' from 'Femininity': Helene Deutsch and the Past to Dianne Elise and the Present," Rosemary Balsam discusses the use of the concept "feminine," and warns about the dangers of its indiscriminate use. She argues that it is preferable to refer to just the anatomy as "female," without other expectations. This allows each person to have her own subjective "sense of femaleness," a concept proposed by Dianne Elise.

Balsam maintains that instead of making an external assessment of "femininity," we have to carefully listen to our patients' own subjective experiences of it. She also discusses the impact of the female body's capacity to engender life. She argues that gender stereotypes are reductionist, and she illustrates her theories with a rich clinical vignette.

In "The Feminine: Plurality of Desires," Leticia Glocer Fiorini deconstructs Freud's question – "what do women want?" She explores many aspects of it, including the concept of the feminine. She also deconstructs the concept of otherness linked to the feminine, and she rethinks the concept of sexual difference. Understanding gender identification requires using a non-binary paradigm.

Glocer Fiorini points out that sexual and gender differences reflect relations of domination and violence. By deconstructing and analyzing these differences, we can see the values promoted by the current social discourse. She posits that each woman is different and thinking of women's desire as a universal category hinders understanding of the plurality of desires of each singular woman.

In her chapter "What Women Want and What is Wanted of Women," Arlene Kramer Richards maintains that women want to be heard, valued, and seen

DOI: 10.4324/9781003180036-4

as equals to men. Kramer Richards argues that patriarchy is very entrenched. Women want to pursue their own projects, but they also want to be desired by men, while men want women to look after them.

Like Glocer Fiorini, Richards maintains women have a plurality of desires. In this regard, she discusses the gender dynamic complications that arise from women having both traditional and contemporary gender ideals.

Kramer Richards also discusses the paradox that while Freud put forth the idea that penis envy was bedrock, he granted women important places in the psychoanalytic world. She writes about Freud's transformative psychoanalysis of the poet, Hilda Doolittle, whose writing block he helped resolve.

Balsam, Glocer Fiorini, and Kramer Richards maintain that today women have multiple desires, inside and outside the home. That is a big departure from classic psychoanalytic theory, according to which the desire for a child within an adult heterosexual relationship was the epitome of the development of female gender identity.

The three authors conceive of the feminine as changing with the cultural context. They pose open-ended questions and want to promote an ongoing discussion about these new theories.

3 Liberating "female" from "femininity"

Helene Deutsch and the past to Dianne Elise and the present

Rosemary H. Balsam

The linguistic differentiation (in English) among "the feminine," feminine, femininity, and female is an important topic that affects the anglophone terminology of psychoanalytic theory affecting female development. It has great importance for the way analysts communicate with each other and pass on information about gender portraiture. The confusion among these words operates in the present, as well as representing a continuity of many burning and still smoldering societal conflicts about gender and sex from past eras in many cultures, that can become automatic and inbuilt and taught as actual theoretical concepts in psychoanalysis. If I were Joan Baez, I'd sing her sad refrain about us never seeming to learn from our past pain. Her song, "Where have all the flowers gone?" was about the sacrifice to the death of young men going to war, never to return. Our song, on the other hand, is about life, but no less about war. It is about the subjectivity and experience of living in a female body – about the social and legal battle over the heartbeat of new life, and the virtual war that women seem to need to fight in every era for autonomy over their own bodies and their social and professional destinies (Balsam, 2015; Lament, 2015; Toronto, et al 2017; Brody and Arnold 2019); and the related ongoing battles of those who were not born female, but have the spirit and civil right to participate in affective or embodied ways, should they so wish. There is inevitable fall-out from these virtual wars, and the repetitive social resistance of daily life, the inner and outer contributions. How are these tensions created, manifested, and unwittingly or even wittingly sustained? The language used bears the history of these tensions. Unfortunately for our field, in spite of having greater access to the trust of female psyches than most, we too can contribute unthinkingly to sustaining gender and sex confused value systems that are dubious for the welfare of females. Our focus in psychoanalysis is the subjective experience of women's participation in her mental growth, bodily development, internalizations of family environs and culture, thus we have opportunities to study how these words are used both by patients and analysts.

DOI: 10.4324/9781003180036-5

"The eternal feminine"

"The feminine" (with a definite article), can a slither over into theorizing about "women" as if they were a monolithic genre (Chodorow, 1994; Balsam, 2012). I found it unfortunate, for example, that for a welcome conference that addressed "women's" issues, such as the International Psychoanalytic Association Congress of 2019 in London, the organizers would title it "The Feminine To-day." In this usage, because of the polysemy of the subjectivities involved, "feminine" – if it is not instantly problematized – can be normalized. The term is frequently toxic in our theories, and thus clinically, for our patients. What are the subjectivities embedded in those concepts that make them ambiguous and slippery? I appreciate the thoughtful examination of "femininity" in the work of others like Wolfe (2019), A.K. Richards (2019), Scarfone (2019), Glocer Fiorini (2019), and, for example, Kulish (2000), Elise (1997), and Chodorow (1994).

The feminine

What do we actually mean by "'the' feminine" when used with a definite article? This links to both the concepts of "the eternal feminine" and "femininity." With all due respect to those who still freely use these notions, I believe that these terms are so problematic that they have become useless for theory-building at this point in our evolution (Balsam, 2012; Balsam 2015). I would like readers actively to question for themselves, how they are using these terms, and ask what they mean exactly wherever they encounter them in a psychoanalytic context. Some may disagree with me, but that is a good discussion about choices rather than an acceptance as received wisdom.

Some of the pre-judged and co-opted subjectivity of "feminine" emerges within the generic concept of "The Eternal Feminine" as an ideal. This notion emerged eons ago, especially in religions of both the West and East, as if all women contain a mysterious essence of womanhood. Should we yearn for an over-arching commonality between our ancients and more modern ancestors – but without needing to evoke the supernatural – we can note a fascination in common with them all about "the spark of life." This recalls Freud's original question that he cited as common to all children, "Where do babies come from?" In turn, this links to the knowledge of how sexually mature men's and women's bodies combine to kindle this spark of generation and renewal. Women's bodies utterly do transform in fruitful pregnancy, and offspring amazingly are produced from within themselves. This, I believe, is the deepest source of apparent female magic and mystery. To this day the biological forces that produce "quickening" and the first flutters of life from within the maternal body, or the moment of the water breaking are indeed unclear. Biological features such as these surrounding birthing, all females for ever have had in common. These seem to me as outstanding – forgive the pun – as awesome and fearsome as earth's manifestations of sun, darkness, or storms – and of course – the storied phallus! (see Balsam 2019 for a fuller view of this argument).

Conception and our power to create life is deeply significant for our own hopes and fears of both life and death and of eternal significance. The body thus becomes the peoples' Rorschach (Dimen, 2000). Qualities of magical animation become embedded in the anatomy and geography of this female materiality and the attendant imagination. Values are "agglutinated," to use Hartmann's s apt term, to create mystery and awe (Kristeva, 2014; Balsam, 2019). They freight the female body and transform her materiality by sublimation, worshipfully and fearfully into such exaltation as "The Eternal Feminine." This is a species of "Homo Fictus," after E.M. Forster, who pointed out its major difference from "Homo Sapiens"! (Smith, 2019).

In reactive response to the fundamentally female anatomical gift of biological transformation in fecundity, definitions of "female" existence can quasi-defensively skid into abstractions, or, in psychological terms become more sublimated. To quote from Wikipedia, "Although the definitions of the Eternal Feminine are myriad and complex, and …there is no one clear definition, … a careful inspection of these definitions allows one to ascribe …[to]…the Eternal Feminine… Beauty, Truth, Good, Love." The founders of psychoanalysis would have looked to Nietzsche or to Goethe's Faust. Goethe's "Eternal Feminine" (das Ewig-Weibliche) is a transcending figure promising salvation from evil, and analogized by scholars, for example, with the ancient Grecian perfect world of Platonic ideals (Eros), or in Hinduism, Shakti, the Indian Feminine Goddess, or the Pagan bountiful "Mother Nature," etc. Goethe's "Eternal Feminine" also recalls the Christian Virgin Mother. Böhme, the 16th c. German mystic, considers the Eternal Feminine as "the inexhaustible source of all life, of all creativity. God, or the Divine is the Eternal Feminine symbolized by the Divine Sophia," thus marked as the territory for mystics and theologians (Eric, 2014). "The Eternal Feminine" is a symbol of life's triumph over death and life, and thus the idealized image carries far too much on her shoulders for the fundamental building blocks of any basic theory about an individual inhabiting a female body. This form of "She" is an embellishment. It is compelling to see these connecting threads within imaginative culture to Freud's belief in women's psychology as a "dark continent," and one of abiding mystery. Not only Freud. I was shocked to read the other day that even the great contemporary theoretical physicist, Stephen Hawking, a man of great learning and a vocal supporter of women's rights, when asked about what he thought about most during the day, said: "Women, they are a complete mystery!"

I would like to offer the painting as a late 19th c. struggle for emergence from such a worshipful status. Many have seen it instead as the political interpretation of "poor Paris" weeping in the Franco-Prussian war of 1871 and the Paris Commune. Note the avidity of the scrutinizing fully clothed men encased and defended in the full regalia of their own professions – bishop, painter.

My reading of Cezanne's 1877 painting is that he seems to be struggling here with a path away from such a worshipful status of women. He seems to appreciate the role of male pressure to create this fictive image, and the difficulty for both men and women in trying to emergence from such a worshipful stance.[1]

Figure 3.1 The Eternal Feminine by Paul Cezanne, 1877.
Digital image courtesy of the Getty's Open Content Program.

We can note the avid postures of the scrutinizing fully clothed men focused on the central woman, some seemingly surprised in their concentration by the presence of the painter, and all encased and defended in the full regalia of their own professions – bishop, painter, banker, etc. In contrast, she lies naked, in vague outline, looking unfinished and uncomfortable, on her obligatory long blond unkempt locks, with red, blotched out eye-sockets. She is the object of their imaginative fervor and curious gaze – some would say gawking? admiration and celebration.

The use of "Feminine" to describe qualities as belonging to women, just because they are female, as in "The Eternal Feminine."

Much unintentional "biological essentialism" (*see* Chodorow, 1994 for a good account) is brought to bear on the conflation of what is female with supposedly "feminine" qualities. I make a marked distinction between therapists' and theoreticians' external assessments of "femininity," as contrasted with descriptions of a patient's own meticulously registered individual subjective experience of owning a quality that she identifies as "feminine." For example, one patient said, "I am very touchy and easily hurt, and it's part of being feminine and sensitive, because my mother was just like that": Or another, "I rarely take offence and have a stiff upper lip, because my mother and aunt were like that. That's what I grew up with – being their girl, and I think that's characteristic of my femininity." These statements are from women describing a contrasting quality as "feminine," because it belongs to her internal experience in assessing her own womanhood.

For comparison, here is a random example of "feminine" being used generically and therefore obscurely, followed by one of greater acuity. These examples are taken from comments on the back cover of Arlene Richard's and Lucille's Spira's 2019 edited book, "Myths of Mighty Women: Their Application in Psychoanalytic Psychotherapy." The following blurb writer is of course very well meaning and well-disposed toward women. But she seamlessly refers to "the feminine universe" and also "the feminine psyche" implying "Don't we all know about that?" That touches on my complaint about obscurity. We actually do not know what each other mean, whether favorable or unfavorable.

Another comment, in contrast provides greater clarity. It alludes to "psychosocial and therapeutic models of female ambition, power, identity and independence" that are seen as "depictions of the many facets of femininity." This expression "many facets," then, does not blur in theory into a generic oblivion. Grounded in more lucidity, we can then see further layers of questions arise. We can, say, investigate issues like claims to innate femininity, or innate "maternal instinct" that turn out to reveal embedded biological essentialism and stultified polarities of gender. (Kulish, 2000, on the topic of questioning "primary femininity"; and Hilferding, 1974, very early in psychoanalysis, in 1911, on the topic of questioning "the maternal instinct").

Liberation from "femininity" and ideas of a "feminine universe"

We can liberate our analytic sensibilities, then, by scrutinizing our terms closely. We can also ask ourselves, what ideas from the past have been useful? We can range back over our repertoires of teachers and readings. Within this whole swirling psychological arena of shifting individualities and manifest and latent biases, I have found a solid ground with Freud's earliest fascination with the body itself, and in the greater consensual reliability of the body – the materiality of the sexed female body's biological development, with a sense of gender as simultaneously being constructed in psychological growth. It is important to say that there is no place for linear certainties in psychological growth as in, because this and then that happens, then such and such inevitably follows. Because a female body has a vagina, it does not follow that the owner necessarily will have a proclivity for domestic duties. Because a male body has a penis, the owner will not necessarily enjoy climbing mountains. However, if the subject possesses female anatomy, she, zee, or they will need to take their natal body housing into account, and right into the mental complexities of dealings with themselves, others, the world, their past, and their future. This principle of theory building does not dictate anything of what they as individuals may feel about their bodies, or how they may handle them in relation to others. They may survive by dissociating from their bodies – but our analytic theories of average expectable mental life and growth do not need to echo suit.

Shifting the grounds of thinking about theory brings out of the shadows former pseudo-theoretic models of the human mind where heterosexual social ideals or condemnations are conflated with standards of "normality vs. deviance." One man married to one woman to create a family is easy in our Western society, but once that is declared by a metatheory of mind as "normal," then one woman married to one woman in a family with two mothers becomes "deviant," and thus a deviation from the norm. A "variant" is thus a liberating accuracy for our theory of object choice or sexual practice, as opposed to a "deviant." Physical females who possess wombs when sexually mature frequently bear children. That is straightforward. No choice need be made what circumstance uniting an ovum and a sperm is in any way is normal or deviant, or what form of marriage is or isn't acceptable to society as that changes with the times. Language matters profoundly in psychoanalytic theory-making.

Femininity's social style affecting psychoanalytic theorizing

Being "unfeminine" within an old-fashioned but lingering social code of nicety that may actually deny the female body of the owner, may well reflect unconscious bias and a deep anxiety associated with the female in the act of childbirth – the female situation where the subject is principally at the mercy of her specifically female body. This is an idea that is undeveloped in psychoanalysis. Julia Kristeva may be the sole other analyst who has specified difficulties with the state of corporeal femaleness as a hugely problematic influence showing through all of psychoanalytic body/mind theory. She has said sarcastically to make the point in her drawing attention to the absence of consideration of maternal eroticism, for instance,

> To live and to think the maternal as erotic, wouldn't that be as provocative as to speak of infantile sexuality?
>
> (Kristeva, 2014, p. 2)

As an example of social feminine niceties amounting to an inadvertent unconscious attack on inhabiting the body, here is an excerpt from "Etiquette for Every Day" by Mrs. Humphry, 1902–1904 published in London at the same time Freud was writing "Dora." Here is her advice about mounting a carriage:

> There is an art in getting in and out of a carriage, and anyone who has noticed how some people flounder in and out must acknowledge that to acquire the art is worth some trouble. It consists partly in folding oneself together almost telescopically, then gradually emerging, with caution, but not too slowly. A well-shod foot and ankle first appear, and the head comes next, with a little hand ready to lean on the footman's arm (not to take

his arm), or in the absence of a footman, to grasp the side of the door. It is much more difficult to descend gracefully from a covered carriage than from an open one.

(p. 325)

One can hear that as a "feminine" person, a female is expected to be physically dainty, delicate, and – only in a controlled and muted fashion – lean on a man, without holding on to him; show just a little foot and ankle but no more, presumably, lest she would be exhibitionistic; perform gymnastics hidden from view, in order to take up less than no physical space, yet show her full face at the same time to the public – no doubt with a charming smile. An analyst might unconsciously compare the act of emerging from a covered carriage as a delicate and visually pleasing childbirth. The "ungraceful" and unfeminine woman says Mrs. Humphry, has a "heavy flump... making the horses start" she "flops into a corner," "scrambles," or "trips over the front" of her gown. (p. 325). What is loud-voiced, impatient, flopping, flumping, scowling etc. is "not good breeding" (p. 336). Self-control is seen as the essence of good breeding. (Even this word "breeding." Isn't that about childbirth too?) But all this is, is a catechism for being "feminine." The women closer to nature, as it were, the servants, are screaming, rough-housing, harridans where bad breeding is more acceptable, and at one point the envy is written the text by saying they are allowed to have a "good howl."

Tears

Tears, too, may be imagined in the pain of delivering a child, or in the devastation and loss should the child die or prove to be damaged.

Mrs. Humphry says:

> Tears are often very bad manners... [W]hen a woman loses her purse and begins to cry in the street... or on an omnibus, she is behaving like a baby. If she loses her train – tears; if her husband is home half an hour late – tears. This copious lacrimation is extremely irritating, not only to men but to women... Servants are the worst sinners. A cut finger is the cause of floods of tears.

Men crying evokes different sentiments from Mrs. Humphry: "Men's own stern code forbids them the relief of tears" (p. 232). There is much admiration for men's lack of tears. But then, from the unconscious socio-psychological point of view, the male body does not have to enact this dreaded act of childbirth, making it seem more easily admirable in its role that demands less physical stress. The admiration of seeming male body non-birthing ease of "control" could be easy to follow in terms of comparison to the previous attitudes of female birthing body out-of-control self-denigration.

Helene Deutsch

Born in 1884 in Poland, the youngest of four children, to a Jewish lawyer father whom she worshipped, and a housewife mother whom she denigrated, Helene Deutsch was involved in socialist movements when young, and was proudly nationalistic Polish. In a patriarchal family, against the will of both parents, she fought with them as a female for permission to go to medical school. She did so in Vienna, and subsequently became involved with Freud and psychoanalysis.

After an early affair with the socialist leader Herman Lieberman, Helene married Felix Deutsch in 1912, and gave birth to a son, Martin. In 1935 she fled Germany, and the family immigrated to Boston. She (and Felix) became well-known analysts and she worked there till her death in 1982.

Helene Deutsch, in 1944 and 1945, famously wrote two volumes that spanned early girlhood to old womanhood. She is one of only a handful of analysts worldwide, who have written about female development over the life cycle. It is said that she saw 60,000 female cases in her long career. The vivid accounts of her clinical work these days are best valued if they can be separated from her theory. Deutsch, powerful, and lauded in her day, has fallen into ill repute with contemporary feminist theorists.

Femininity in Deutsch's Terms: She wrote three relevant chapters to this examination of "femininity." The first is Chapter 5 in Volume 1 of The *Psychology of Women: A Psychoanalytic Interpretation*, called: "Eroticism: The Feminine Woman" (p. 185).[2] (Immediately preceding chapters were on "Puberty and Adolescence," and "Menstruation," leading to young adulthood). The second is Chapter 6, "Feminine Passivity," and the third is Chapter 7, "Feminine Masochism." Her overall theory links these concepts.

Deutsch writes concerning eroticism: "Many adolescent features are carried over to the years of maturity…" momentarily appearing modern in her view of oscillating growth. But this is quickly spoiled by her erroneous pronouncement: "and this is especially true of women" (p. 185). She thinks that numerous women are psychologically healthy but that means very "adolescent." What on earth does that mean? This is just the old saw that women are less mature emotionally then men. Deutsch frequently compares women and men in this fashion, for example, A young girl's fearful (but to her "masochistic") dreams of rape and burglars are compared unfavorably to the lucky boy who, she implies, experiences only pleasure in his nocturnal emissions! (p. 255). An irksome feature of her writing is its certainty, with insistent recurring choruses of comparisons and contrasts between women and men that are sometimes positive, sometimes negative, but always value-laden. Thinking such as Deutsch's is unfortunately labeled "classical," and then agglutinated negatively to "American ego psychology." As Kulish (2010) writes:

> many gender theorists, such as Foucault (1978) and Butler (1990), question the basic premises and terminology of gender. For such theorists, the

terms masculinity and femininity, or male and female, have no real or fixed meanings, but are always defined by context and culture.

(p. 232)

The postmodern relational social constructivist thinkers and postmodern scholars like Foucault (1978) and Butler (1990) use this association as paradigmatic of traditional psychoanalysis. They claim rightly, though, that masculinity and femininity "have no real or fixed meanings but are always defined by context and culture." Theirs are valuable opinions about the valueless role of comparisons such as fill Deustch's thinking, but it is also too bad to put this slippery, personally derived masculinity/femininity comparison that leads to binaries, and that has masqueraded as psychoanalytic "theory" at the very heart of a psychoanalytic gender theory as also symptomatic of all contemporary thinking. We need to try to separate and individualize these categories of "male and female, masculine and feminine," in order to create a cohesive theory that is able to capture the infinite varieties of gender within female development and yet leave room for the obvious biologic housing of individuals. The nefarious comparison of women to men is culture bound, but admittedly lingers in our own era in terms of compulsive comparisons between male and female. The point is that psychoanalytic theory should beware of compounding or echoing this social problem.

Deutsch's other irksome trait is in generating a constant stream of generalizing assertions offered as "knowledge": such and such women do this or that. Her so-called "feminine" women, offered in the corsets of these categorizations are recognizable, but hopefully would be problematized by a contemporary analyst.

Deutsch writes about female romance like a novelist of bodice-rippers! "Every woman has a masochistic need to experience the torments of longing and the sufferings that deep love can bring. In the same recess there is a narcissistic wish for great proofs of the partner's love and readiness for self-sacrifice" (p. 199); or, "The woman who is harmoniously erotic who is most "feminine" and represents the best achievement of her Creator, often declares in the evening of her rich and happy love life, "I have not always been faithful, but actually I have been in love only once" (p. 200). What on earth does that mean? She idealizes a woman's "longing to be loved." Women choose to marry the ideal father – a very active and masculine type who needs her support to fulfill himself, she says. Deutsch sees this as the motherly component of "feminine eroticism." Two types of love choices are often made she says – a daughter to a father, or a mother-relation to a man. (Note that siblings are left out of her calculus.)

1   There are further misleading major theories offered with confidence. Deutsch claims the "feminine woman" "has a passive-masochistic character" as a fundament of psychic structure. Feminine masochism, she says (no reason given), "lacks the cruelty, destructive drive, suffering and pain by which masochism manifests itself in perversions and neuroses" (p. 191). Instead, she talks of it

as "activity directed inward" that is "parallel to a man's intensified activity directed outward, and her masochism is parallel to the masculine aggression that accompanies his activity, particularly at the end of adolescence" (p. 191). What on earth does that mean? The notions here seem driven by a need to imagine women and men as opposite and complementary as one whole. Yin and Yang. Activity directed outward: activity directed inward. This is her 'biological essentialism' that is manifest as Deutsch sees it, in a female's natural "masochism" necessary to tolerate childbirth. Later, both Breen (1993) and Hoffman (1999) noted how long it took for straightforward aggression in females to be acknowledged as part of their human psychic composition. Deutsch's version of eroticism in feminine women is cloying to modern ears – a "facility in identifying with man in a manner that is most conducive to the happiness of both partners…[making] ideal life companions for men" (p. 192): "The woman …leaves the initiative to the man and out of her own need renounces originality" (shades of Freud's denigration) "…[M]aking the man happy can be expressed in the formula, "He is wonderful and I am a part of him" (p. 192). Enough said!

Deutsch divides feminine types into three as they relate to men.

a   When erotically desired the first type of feminine erotic woman "finds it very difficult to refuse… [T]he guardian… has not established his post at the entrance door… . The gates of the front yard often remain open" (p. 193). Deutsch sees the "conquering" of this woman by a man as a dialectic between "passive-masochism" and "feminine narcissism" where the latter protects against the former.
b   The second type has a "narcissistic guardian… posted at the very entrance door to her erotic and emotional life" (p. 193). Deutsch approvingly thinks that "the guardian" preserves this woman's personality till she wants to open her "inner gates" (p. 194).
c   The third type is in love with herself as a narcissistic barrier – that can "come down" or "barricade" her from her own downfall of being masochistic.

Deutsch is fond of numbering bullets. Each number defines a woman's behavior toward a man or a child. None is described as if she were an independent entity capable of generating her own wishes or fantasies, or as if she were in relation to another woman. Narcissism seems like a chastity belt or a male guardian to the woman's so-called masochistic surrender. "[M]an's sexual desire is intensified if he has to overcome obstacles before achieving sexual union with woman," she avers and says the woman awaits her "defeat" in "joyful excitation" (p. 195). This may remind a reader of watching mating iguanas on the rocks by the sea in the Galapagos, where the females flee up the beach aggressively pursued by ardent males, who are apparently endowed with double penises!

Any of these attitudes, (one hopes) psychoanalysts would now find relationally problematic.

All of this is bound up with Deutsch's thoughts about reproduction. If a woman is adjusted to reality she must cope with physical pain – "even where it most serves pleasure. The dangers inherent in women's service to the species impel her to assimilate her feminine masochism and her human anxiety…" (p. 277). Deutsch's accounts are indeed a hymn to biological essentialism – fantasy rationales associated with pregnancy and childbirth. However, at least she really does consider procreative uses of the female body far more seriously than most psychoanalysts since her time. Her greatest problem is the phallocratic certainty, which her theory expresses and assumes.

There are some positive points that Deutsch also noticed and described. Deutsch's clinical stories and empirical theory make far more contemporary sense than her metatheory. For example: laudably, but quietly, she challenges a shibboleth of Freud in that it is "erroneous that the girl gives up her first mother relation in favor of the father" (p. 205). She challenges Freud also in seeing the birth of a sibling is the great first stimulus to envy – not penis envy alone. Also, presaging a modern view: "…in relation to her own child, woman repeats her own mother-child history, and seeks to continue the … new triangle." Deutsch also observes that "the real personality of the mother has a strong effect" (p. 214). This was an unpopular point of view with early analysts who downplayed the environment, and she knows too that a "domineering mother … provokes hatred of the daughter and nourishes self-exactions in her" (p. 214).

In a modern vein she states: "The woman's choice of love objects is to a great extent determined by her past emotional ties and her psychological readiness for motherhood" (p. 191). This apt developmental thread is not even mentioned in most contemporary case studies (Balsam, 2012, 2019). Deutsch can occasionally write with a fresh elegant vision: "Every love relation of the feminine woman psychically contains the germ of a child" (p. 208). Might that be so – if we just say "woman" instead of insisting "feminine woman"?

Dianne Elise's idea about representing subjective femaleness

Dianne Elise (1997) has given us a contemporary way out of all the confused cacophony of differing ways people challenge or repeat elements of our past dealings with these words. Her suggestion is to use "a sense of femaleness" instead of the murky, slippery adjectival noun "femininity." The clinical beauty of application, and accuracy of her idea for thinking about gender construction, is that a person can thus only report a "sense of femaleness" from her inside emotional story. And this safety of checks and balances in values can allow "my femininity" to be designated by me, secondarily to be the subject of genuine analytic enquiry by you as an analyst, no matter the morphology of my natal body is. It can be a matter of life and death to shift the thinking of blind categorization behind misapplied gendered nomenclature. Especially gay males and trans women have been tortured and murdered by society for value-ridden external perceptions of "femininity" hurled as violent insults.

Clinical instance of gender individuality and use of "a sense of femaleness" or "a sense of maleness"

This patient was a highly intellectual young single woman of 29, who wanted help with sustaining long-term relationships. She wanted to be able to find a life partner. She was doing a Ph.D. thesis on black holes in the universe. Let's call her Vi. She had always wanted to fly since she was little. She grew up on a farm in Vermont, loving in the late summer to lie on a grassy hill in a meadow in the pitch dark, feeling the soft soil and blades of grass beneath her, surrounded by the crickets clicking, lost in the cosmos of the black velvet sky filled with its winking diamonds and passing dark clouds: and sometimes there was a large shiny moon. She loved the sky. She was an only child, but never lonely. Her mother owned show horses, was an equestrian of Viennese extraction, and an expert in dressage. This style of riding is very precise and demanding of exquisite and delicate the mutual attunement between horse and rider.

The mother was utterly absorbed in her horses according to her daughter. (This was persuasive in the transference, because every scrape that the analyst made behind the couch was alarming as a sign of total self-absorption, and the patient subjected it to scrutiny for wandering thoughts.) The female analyst was found guilty often, but eventually Vi trusted her enough to allow anger at that. However, paradoxically, for a while this self-absorption of the analyst with her own interests set her up in the patient's mind as an ideally absorbed professional good at her work, also like mother. Vi's father was a rough and tumble sort of burly guy who had wanted to be a veterinary surgeon, he so enjoyed animals. But he had ended up instead running the family farm, caring tenderly for the birthing cows, mares, and foals, and the nurturance of endangered piglets. He apparently would weep when his wife was disappointed in the show ring, though she rarely showed her emotions – to humans, at least.

These characteristics are emphasized as this man and woman, this father and mother couple could be classical reversals of what is considered stereotypically as "masculine" and "feminine." However, it is he who melts over baby animals, and she who is all reason, control, and precision. The little daughter I think escaped to the sky, but she lay on her father's fields, in his arms as it were. And she thought of stars giving birth to other stars and dying. And she used her precision instruments in her lab as she grew, with all the rationality and love of her internalized mother expressed through the accuracy of her calculations and measurements.

Physically she was tall and slim, her brown shiny-clean hair in a practical cut, neatly dressed in unisex jeans and a sweater. She was socially pleasant, mannerly, and considerate.

How could one have judged here what is "feminine" and what is "masculine"? An analyst could have seen her as primarily gendered masculine with her outdoors interests, her love of physics, her loner style, and her lack of flirtatiousness. Romantically she told a story of one yearned-for boyfriend, the object of her heterosexual fantasy life, who was like dad, but who turned out to be gay.

The only way to have a sense of Vi's gender composition or ability to formulate it, would be to wait for stories, memories, dreams, and spontaneous moments in the analytic interactions, remembrances of her own body in relation to the maleness of her father's body, and the femaleness of her mother's body, and listen to the attached emotional agglutinations. Only then she and the analyst might, by her own reporting, find her own "sense of femaleness" or her "sense of maleness." Or alternatively discover a profound sense of inner gender identity confusion in relation to her body, that became a focus of interest in this particular analysis, with her puzzling feelings, sensations, and the conundrum of personal construction of inner meaning.

Our labs are our offices. There are two bodies and two complicated psyches in those rooms, but until the patient's gendered imagery used is shared and understood together, there is little way for us to know, and little way for the individual to own up to and take charge of and own an autonomous sense of her, his, or their own gender narrative.

Clinical resonances of "femininity" and its conundrums

This patient's mother had had four close pregnancies (the patient being the oldest), plus three bloody and domestically disruptive miscarriages. For many years on a daily basis this patient, who was a middle aged heterosexually married woman, railed against this "useless" mother, for example, burning the grandchildren's rice on the stove while talking on her cell phone to her stockbroker. The analyst would think privately, for example – "But your kids like her rough-housing – and she's got a talent in making money." This was a painful point of countertransference, of course. The poor daughter felt so alone because the outside world, like her analyst, liked this mother. The symbolism of "burning the rice in the pot" was important as the "inside story" of the mother/daughter entwined stories of procreation.

A bitter complaint of this patient was that her mother was "unfeminine and manly." The mother would tell the daughter how beautiful she was – "so much more beautiful than me." But mother was "horsey, tweedy, big-boned, coarse, abrupt, abrasive, tough, strong, sharp, hard-muscled, and obsessed with her own physical prowess." She had a heavy, firm "flat-footed" tread when she walked the stairs. The patient described herself in contrast as soft and smooth, a lover of fine pastel cashmere sweaters that she said showed off her curves. She told the analyst unabashedly that she had "an exquisite profile." Her mother had told her so. Again – there was little objectivity about any of these complimentary statements. The analyst, for example, reported her as long-faced, thin, and yes, in beautiful pale pink cashmeres and loose blue silks, but bent over and "caved-in" in appearance. The analyst imagined that she was hiding her breasts, height, and nice legs, but she described pride in them. The analyst's separate reaction was therefore definitely not related to the patient's owned self-image, and clearly an unreliable guide to the patient's assessments. The patient saw herself as a startling beauty, and she worried that others were envious of her willowy beauty. She styled herself as very "feminine."

This meant to her that she was the total opposite of mother. The analyst was to understand her to be the exact opposite of this hateful mother but to admire her through her mother's eyes. The patient had a heavy gait much as she described a hated feature of her mother.

This phenomenon, tactfully broached – not easy – became the route to understanding the burned pot. The mother, it turned out, pregnant before marriage in a puritanical household, had tried to fall downstairs to induce an abortion. The mother's sexuality had suffered from her rigid background. The patient's soft pastel appearance had been much more influenced by her nanny. Pregnancy for my patient was where the conflicts really became heightened, and much influenced by her mother's and her own past. She teetered between losing the child and keeping the child, facing the future as a childless motherly nanny, or birthing a child and fearing turning into her abrasive, "masculine" mother. Understanding the intermingled tonalities of the mother's and daughter's physical bond would have been erased by a pronouncement the analyst's own external assessment that this or that between this mother and this daughter was either "feminine" or "masculine," after the style of Deutsch and many others subsequently. A reader might appreciate how this would have been dramatically at odds with this patient's own inner complexity.

Alas I cannot say that Dianne Elise's 1997 idea about using "the sense of femaleness" instead of "femininity" has caught fire. It does astonish me that people did not take it up as a solution to the confusions and obscurity that is so common in texts about sexuality.

If we claim her primary "sense of femaleness" we acknowledge the co-existence of the material biological body with the mind in interaction. Kristeva (2016), too, says "the body – far from being a solely biological fact – is a psychosomatic construction that takes form as the speaking subject emerges in its relationships with the paternal and maternal instances." I think that what makes "feminine and femininity" so obscure and enigmatic is an attempted divorce from the body's impact and import on those sensibilities. If the natal body is allowed to be central, then all observations fall into place as perceptions, the stuff of individuality – the stuff of subjective reactions – the stuff of dreams and in that sense, we well know that:

We are such stuff
As dreams are made on.
          (Prospero) (Shakespeare, The Tempest Act 4, scene 1, 148–158)

Notes

1 There is also a political interpretation of this work which is of "poor Paris" weeping in the Franco-Prussian war of 1871 and the Paris Commune.
2 The most interesting part of the chapter is its beginning, where she sees young women as essentially full of romantic fantasy. (Mostly Deutsch writes with a heterosexual assumptions). She thinks that young women should not have sex too

early, otherwise the girl doesn't have a chance to allow these ideals to be contained, indulged, and run their course, and gradually become blended into sensual love with an ordinary man. Deutsch thinks that if these idealizations are bypassed and curtailed, it leaves some women with a lifelong hunger for a "grand passion." One thinks associatively of the avid female audiences for Danielle Steel's pink- and blue-silver covered paperback bodice-rippers sold in airports, or "50 Shades of Gray" or the female audience for chickflicks and soap operas … and one wonders if perhaps she is onto something about female erotic fantasy lives.

References

Balsam, R.H. (2012). *Women's Bodies in Psychoanalysis*. London: Routledge.

Balsam, R.H. (2015). The War on Women in Psychoanalytic Theory Building: Past to Present. *Psychoanal. Study Child*, 69:83–107.

Balsam, R.H. (2018). Response to John Steiner's "Overcoming Obstacles in Analysis: Is It Possible to Relinquish Omnipotence and Accept Receptive Femininity?" *Psychoanal. Q.*, 87:21–31.

Balsam, R.H. (2019). The Natal Body and its Confusing Place in Mental Life. *J. Amer. Psyoanal. Assn.*, 67(1):15–36.

Breen, D. (1993). Introduction. In D. Breen (ed.), *The Gender Conundrum: Contemporary Psychoanalytic Perspectives on Femininity and Masculinity*. London: Routledge, pp. 1–39.

Brody S., and Arnold, F. (eds.) (2019). *Psychoanalytic Perspectives on Women and Their Experience of Desire, Ambition and Leadership*. London: Routledge.

Chodorow, N. (1994). *Femininities, Masculinities, Sexualities: Freud and Beyond*. Kentucky: University of Kentucky Press.

Chodorow, N. (2017). *Individualizing Gender and Sexuality: Theory and Practice* (Relational Perspectives Book Series). London: Routledge.

Deutsch, H. (1944). *The Psychology of Women: A Psychoanalytic Interpretation Vol 1. Girlhood*. New York: Bantam Books; 2nd edition (1973).

Dimen, M. (2000). The Body as Rorschach. *Studies in Gender and Sexuality*, 1(1):9–39.

Elise, D. (1997). Primary Femininity, Bisexuality, and The Female Ego Ideal: A Re-Examination of Female Developmental Theory. *Psychoanal. Q.*, 66:489–517. Eric (2014). Goethe and the Concept of The Eternal Feminine. Available at www.ilovephilosophy.com/viewtopic.php?f=1&t=186899.

Glocer Fiorini, L. (2019). Deconstructing the Feminine: Discourses, Logics and Power. Theoretico-Clinical Implications. *Int. J. Psychoanal.*, 100:593–603.

Hilferding, M. (1974). On the Basis of Mother Love. Scientific Meeting Jan 11 1911 Presentation. In H. Nunberg and E. Federn (eds.), *Minutes of the Vienna Psychoanalytic Society Vol III: 1910-1911.* . New York: I U.P. p. 112–126.

Hoffman, L. (1999). Passions in Girls and Women: Toward a Bridge between Critical Relational Theory of Gender and Modern Conflict Theory. *J. Amer. Psychoanal. Assn.*, 47(4):1145–1168.

Humphry, Mrs. (1902). *Etiquette for Every Day*. London: Alexander Moring Ltd., The De la More Press.

Kristeva, J. (2014). Reliance, or Maternal Eroticism. *J. Amer. Psychoanal. Assn.*, 62(1):69–85.

Kristeva, J. (2017). Transformations of Parentality, Ch. 7. In V. Tsolas and C. Anzieu-Premmereur (eds.), *A Psychoanalytic Exploration of the Body in Today's World: On the Body.* . New York, NY: Routledge.

Kulish, N. (2000). Primary Femininity: Clinical Advances and Theoretical Ambiguities. *J. Amer. Psychoanal. Assn.*, 48:1355–1379.

Kulish, N. (2010). Clinical Implications of Contemporary Gender Theory. *J. Amer. Psychoanal. Assn.*, 58(2):231–258.

Lament, C. (2015). The War against Women in Psychoanalytic Culture. *Psychoanal. Study Child*, 69(1):35–40.

Richards, A.K. (2003). Rage and Creativity: Second Wave Feminists and the Rejection of "Freudian" Thinking. *Mind Human Interact.*, 13:145–155.

Richards, A.K., and Spira L. (eds.) (2019) *Myths of Mighty Women: Their Application in Psychoanalytic Psychotherapy (Psychoanalysis and Women)*. London: Routledge.

Scarfone, D. (2019). The Feminine, the Analyst and the Child Theorist. *Int. J. Psychoanal.*, 100:567–575.

Smith, E. (2019). Homo Fictus: Two Approaches to Reading Characters in Novels. *TLS Sept.* 20: 26.

Toronto E., Ponder, J., Davisson K., and Kelly K. (2017). *A Womb of Her Own*. London: Routledge.

Wolfe, H. (2019). The Feminine in Leadership Address given at the 51st Congress of the International Psychoanalytic Association, London.

4   The feminine: Plurality of desires

Leticia Glocer Fiorini

The androcentric viewpoint

In the first part of this text, I would like to emphasize that the question – what do women want today? – *is an inquiry originally constructed from a masculine point of view*. This question was formulated by Freud but also by scholars in philosophy and other disciplines that came before him (all of whom were men). This question refers to a mystery they were not able to access. The question in itself reveals its origin as well as its distortion with regard to the feminine position. The viewpoint of the investigator and its neutrality is at stake. In fact, we should say that desire is always an enigma for every human being.

The question also opens up the need to investigate how power relations between the sexes and genders act. It refers to a male researcher, a subject investigating an object of knowledge, which is female. It is well known that the researcher interprets "difference" in terms of the feminine enigma because it does not coincide with the accepted male "model" from a narcissistic point of view.

Moreover, it is not a mere coincidence that the researcher is so frequently considered the subject of desire and that the object to investigate is equated to the object of desire. Indeed, many women consider themselves only as objects of desire and identify with the position they have been traditionally assigned.

Following this line of thought, the question about what do women want reveals a trap since women have been thought of as objects of desire throughout the course of history. We should recall that modernity did not recognize the position of desiring subjects for women.

This viewpoint has been replicated in psychoanalysis. The denial of the position of subject is a point of particular importance regarding women. An analytical Superego, from a theoretical and clinical point of view, denies the place of subject for women. We should remember that, in the case of the young homosexual woman (Freud, 1979c), the position of subject of desire, active, in search of the object of desire, was interpreted by Freud as corresponding to a masculine position. In the same way, Freud (1979d) equated the active position with the masculine and the passive with the feminine, although he also posited that the drive was always active for both sexes.

DOI: 10.4324/9781003180036-6

On the other hand, the question equates all women from the point of view of desire and this implies considering them as a class, as a universal category, denying a singular position for each woman.

From this assertion another question arises: why should we focus on women if, as we pointed out, desire in itself has a certain enigmatic character in both men and women, as well as in other subjectivities.

These ideas lead to a notion, *the feminine conundrum that* I have discussed in other publications (Glocer Fiorini, 1998; Glocer Fiorini, 2007; Glocer Fiorini, 2017). This notion is still maintained and intimately linked to the question: what do women want? At the same time, this inquiry is connected to the position of otherness that is assigned to women and the feminine. *We can say that women, the feminine, enigma, and otherness form a set of equivalences that need to be deconstructed.*

In his lecture "Femininity," Freud (1979f) addressed his audience affirming that there was a conundrum related to women and the feminine. He posited that this was an enigma for men, but he acknowledged to the female audience that indeed they were not an enigma for themselves.

It is necessary to rethink the notion of feminine enigma in psychoanalysis since there is a displacement by which the conundrum of sexual and gender difference is relocated onto women and the feminine. Deconstructing that displacement is a fundamental task in the psychoanalytic field and impact on our conceptualizations of desire in the field of the feminine. My proposal is that the riddle is the category of "sexual difference" itself and not women as a universal category (Glocer Fiorini, 2007).

Moreover, as we will posit in this text, it is necessary to distinguish the category of "difference" as a symbolic operation from sexual and gender difference.

The notion of feminine enigma arises from an androcentric perspective that has always infiltrated the relationship between men and women from the trans-subjective, intersubjective, and intrasubjective point of view. Gender mandates have strongly shaped subjectivities and have naturalized the modality of inter-subjective relationships. When Bourdieu (1999) studied the populations of Cabilia, he analyzed how male domination was naturalized over the course of time so as to become ahistorical. In this tribal society, women walked hunched over, and this culture interpreted this position as being part of a woman's nature. Bourdieu pointed out that this was the result of power relations typical of patri-archal societies. In this context, one of the main goals is to *historicize what has been dehistoricized*. So, the question proposed is part of the androcentric circuit organized as a systemic structure. I also include psychoanalysis and specifically psychoanalytic theory about the feminine, women, and sexual difference within this assertion.

There are differences between the concept of the feminine and women, but there are also connections. *We consider the category of "the feminine" as a principle of culture, with various attributes, different from the masculine, and whose meanings should be deconstructed.*

It is also crucial to distinguish the concept of femininity (including its stereotypes), female sexuality (which is not unitary), motherhood, and women. All these notions coexist; they are different but also related. In this frame, we will assume the polysemy of these notions as well as its ambiguities.

Psychoanalysis at the borders

Many things have changed, principally in contemporary western cultures. In this context it is necessary to address how the relationships between social and cultural norms impact the construction of subjectivity. This issue was already raised at the beginning of psychoanalysis. Let us recall Karen Horney (1977) and many other psychoanalysts who emphasized the role of cultural determinations on the position of women in society as well as in psychoanalysis. Later on, these ideas adopted more complex developments. However, they were not included in the core of the psychoanalytic theory. It is important to recall that the central core of a theory, its hard center, is always difficult to be rethought. Thus, relevant discussions took place at the frontiers of psychoanalysis that became a place of important debates and proposals on these increasingly sophisticated topics.

In my view, working on the interface, on the frontiers, is fundamental to deconstructing concepts and categories with strong psychic inscription and its consequence in the construction of sexed subjectivity. The expectation is to expand and, moreover, decenter the core of the psychoanalytic theory regarding the feminine position and the question about desire. This aim includes the need to analyze the relationships between, on one side, desire(s) and the drive; and on the other side, cultures and subcultures in force over time. In these intersections, sexed subjectivity is constructed and this inevitably includes the role of the Other.

The concept of performativity (Austin, 2007), is an important proposal concerning this area of study. Austin proposed that "words are acts" and, in this way, a symbolic effect is produced. Butler (1990) took to this concept with regard to gender and its performative construction. This author also clarified that the power of performativity is not absolute. In this sense, performativity allows intertwining of bodies, the drive, and gender identifications; all of them crossed by the effect of Otherness. These variables cannot be separated; their connections respond to a systemic net.

If we follow this line of thought, we need to further investigate *the specific mechanisms by which the social contract rules on gender norms and its psychic inscription.* In this context, we should remember that gender theories obviously did not exist in Freud's time, although the Freudian theory about women is a gender theory, with many blind spots.

There have been in recent decades many changes in social, discursive, and cultural domains. Major movements claimed for changes in the place of women in society, although not all social classes, cultures, and subcultures were part of these changes. We find, however, that even in the most privileged classes and in the most developed countries, the glass ceiling still remains.

At the time I am writing this chapter, the coronavirus pandemic is going on. The effects of confinement put on stage the traditional sexual division of labor. This fact is frequently verified, even in the most progressive families of Western societies. At the same time, femicides and gender violence are strongly increasing, at least in Argentina (my country). Social theories on women and the feminine are at the core of these hierarchical relations and, even more, psychoanalytic theory is not excluded from this plot. So, there is a strong relationship between gender violence and theories that support them.

The concept of feminine enigma as well as establishing women as objects of desire, as the Other of the subject of desire, greatly contributes to gender violence. Power relations are at stake. Those conceptions remain through time although coexisting with the important changes already mentioned.

Therefore, it should be reaffirmed that there are strong psychic inscriptions on sexual and gender differences that are maintained despite legal and cultural changes at work in daily life. Gender stereotypes are permanently acting in men and women's subjectivities. This fact strongly marks the paths of desire – of what is allowed and what is forbidden.

On the other hand, an important point must be highlighted: undoubtedly, social, discursive, legal, and cultural changes influence the self-perception, desires, longings, and projects of each woman. This means that desire(s) do not only depend on the inner world. They are not an essence that would be impossible to analyze and deconstruct, especially with regard to the strong influence of gender norms.

Here I would like to recall two particularly important contributions to specific mechanisms of transmission that impact the psyche: (a) Castoriadis-Aulagnier (1977) and the identification project with its transmission of maternal enunciations. These enunciations also bring implicit knowledge, desires, and longings regarding the gender of a child although the author did not include this specific proposal. (b) The enigmatic signifier proposed by Laplanche (1989) which is a notion that allows a better comprehension of what is conveyed from the external world not only in terms of desire, but of gender expectations including its stereotypes.

In this frame, I want to make it clear that desire and gender are not autonomous one from the other. Messages circulate and are in permanent movement: gender mandates and stereotypes impact on the itineraries of desire. On the other hand, itineraries of desire always restrict the domain of gender. So, both categories are not independent.

These proposals allow us to understand more precisely that it is not just a question of focusing on the influence of cultural norms and legalities, but of investigating the precise mechanisms by which they are internalized and interact with the drive and the field of desire.

Before moving forward, I would like to emphasize that there is an inherent imprecision in the terms in use. That is to say, we need to support the distinction between women as a collective group with regard to their rights and each woman in particular in terms of the construction of sexed subjectivity. In other words, it is a heterogeneous collective group. It is a kind of coexistence between the categories of the general and the particular in which, on the one hand, women as a collective group share problems because of their secondary position in different societies but, on the other hand, there is an absolute singularity and diversity with regard to their subjectivity and desires.

As I have tried to emphasize, the search for equal rights and freedom is inducing important changes in existing cultures. Recursively, these changes reverberate in the itineraries of desire and the possibilities of sublimation of each woman. But there are also resistances that appear as a consequence of the threat to the male collective group or, better yet, to those who are placed in a rigid male position. These resistances express what we can call *neopatriarchy*. This is why I underline the coexistence between nowadays social/cultural changes and traditional mandates concerning women in contemporary societies. Even more, this is the point at which equivalences between women, object of desire, enigma, and otherness are still sustained.

"What do women want" according to Freud's infantile sexual theories

Infantile sexual theories (Freud, 1979a, 1980a) are in the origin of psychoanalytic thoughts on the feminine position.

Freudian infantile sexual theories assume the belief that there is only one genital organ for both sexes – the penis. This would define sexed positions for the girl and the boy. Freud develops his theory by taking the male child as a model. In the phallic phase, the vision of the female genitalia binds to the castration anxiety. In other words, the threat of castration takes on value through the vision of female genitalia interpreted as a lack. This is linked to the child's incestuous desire for the mother, which in turn is connected to childhood masturbation and fear of the imminence of a punishment. This imaginary plot is linked with the boy's construction, on a narcissistic level, of the theory of castration by which the organ has been amputated in the girl. Therefore, sexual difference is interpreted by the boy as "castration," – representing punishment for his incestuous desire, as Freud posited. But, we know that the girl doesn't lack anything anatomically; she is just different from the male. Only from one point of view, that of the male, can it be interpreted that something is missing – but only because (a) it is not what the male has; and (b) the point of view is androcentric. The point is that this infantile sexual theory, created by Freud (1979a) from his interpretation of the experience of the male child – Little Hans case (Freud, 1980a) – is later established as an adult theory and loses the interpretative character of infantile sexual theories and, in this way, becomes a "proven" truth.

I am focusing on infantile sexual theories as they were described and interpreted by Freud. These theories sustain the Oedipal plot with different resolutions for boys and girls, according to ideals and norms in force. Indeed, Freud's proposal leads to blind spots that have strong consequences on clinical work. The main obstacle is to duplicate social norms for the masculine and the feminine positions, ignoring the multiple paths of desire in both sexes/gender.

Moreover, it is also an impediment for its comprehension with regard to other subjectivities (Glocer Fiorini, 2019b).

The boy as a researcher is guided by his own narcissism concerning the interpretation of sexual difference and, accordingly, the girl is branded as "castrated," and imprisoned by penis envy as an effect of an internal drive/desire condition. If the imaginary basis of infantile sexual theories is forgotten, its origin in an intertextual, discursive, and cultural plot will be lost.

The interesting point is that the Freudian girl seems to share this theory: she feels castrated. Kristeva (1986) posited that the girl is identified with the masculine *semblant*.

In this research, the topic of castration arises: the researcher subject discovers the sexual difference and attributes a lack to the girl. In this way, sequences of "knowledge" are established in which the presence-absence, phallic-castrated and male-female polarities are equated. However, it is still necessary to emphasize that this "lack" can be only thought as a consequence of a previous framework of "knowledge" in which difference is interpreted as a lack with regard to women.

And here we should talk about the phallic value of the penis in different cultures; it is a phallic value linked to power which is inscribed in the psyche of men and women. Hence, it is of great importance to emphasize that the penis or the phallus (either symbol or signifier) respond to a phallic, hierarchical value. For ancient Greeks, the phallus was a symbolic value of power. In psychoanalysis we can see how this concept was developed from different perspectives. It was established early on that the penis, the anatomical organ, was not the phallus. For Lacan (1971), the phallus is a signifier of desire, of lack, which he calls a master signifier. This author set up the phallus as a fundamental signifier, an organizer of the psyche and the construction of sexed subjectivity. For Lacan (1981), sexuation is defined around the phallic function.

Lacan posits that this signifier does not refer to a meaning, as De Saussure (1974) proposed; instead, meanings arise in the game of the signifier's slippages. In this way, the question of why a signifier of desire is named "phallus," since it is very difficult to disarticulate it from its meaning, is at play. Undoubtedly, the only explanation is its relationship to anatomy and its significance as a phallic value. Continuing with Lacan (1981), it should also be noted that in the "formulas of sexuation" the feminine position always corresponds to the place of the Other, the other sex, even though the concept of the barred Other is more encompassing. It is also striking that although it can be occupied by a man or a woman, this position is named as feminine.

In this context, it is essential to distinguish between the Freudian phallic phase, with its imaginary character, typical of the children's fantasy, and the concept of phallus as a master signifier, universal, with no sex, around which sexuation would be defined. We are reminded that Derrida (1998) posited that the phallus could not be a master signifier, since it contradicts the concept that one signifier slips to another and in that movement significance occurs. We can also consider, as some authors do, that by describing the phallic phase and the penis envy in the girl, Freud is describing the state of things in a given socio-cultural context (Mitchell and Rose, 1982). We can add that he referred mainly to the hysterical patients he treated and this is a limit for the comprehension of the diverse routes of desire.

In this frame, the question "what do women want today" is strongly linked to the theories described above, which in turn are supported in a cultural and discursive network.

It is important to notice that, according to Laplanche (1988), psychoanalytic theories can double infantile sexual theories. Certainly, this equivalence has strong consequences if the analyst cannot distinguish their imaginary and meta-phorical aspects. Thus, it is crucial to make a deconstructive analysis of psycho-analytic theories about sexual difference and their relationship with infantile sexual theories.

Even more, it is necessary to disarticulate the seemingly impregnable chains between the Oedipus complex, symbolic castration, sexual difference, paternal function, and the Law with a capital "L."

This line of thought also implies questioning if there is a universal feminine desire or if this assertion is based on a substantial and essentialist approach to the inquiry proposed. We should revise the question in terms of rethinking what is beyond the masculine/fem-inine polarity, as we are going to develop later in this chapter.

The Oedipus plot: the girl

Going back to the origin of psychoanalytic theory from a genealogical perspective, we can see how the question "what do women want" (desire and sublimation included) was outlined, starting from the Oedipus complex.

The Freudian proposal (1979e) poses extra difficulties for the girl such as the change of object and zone; the girl must look for an object of another sex than that of the mother. This leads her on a long libidinal journey commanded by the penis envy beginning when in front of the vision of the anatomical diffe-rence she interprets her own condition as a consummate castration. For the girl, Freud (1979f) posits three paths with regard to the finalization of the Oedipus complex which he considered a secondary formation to her long pre-oedipal period:

1   Inhibition or frigidity: sexual desire is inhibited facing the disappointment for not possessing the penis;
2   The masculinity complex which, by not solving penis envy, could lead to homosexuality; and
3   Motherhood, as the *princeps* resolution for the girl's libidinal development.

In these three paths there are two issues, among others, to rethink:

First, motherhood is for Freud the fundamental goal of the girl's libidinal development. Second, there is no place for an autonomous female sexuality that is different from motherhood. We see that the Oedipus complex in the girl, as it was proposed, does not accept another goal beyond the symbolic equation penis-child, that leads from penis envy to the desire for a child, first from the father and then from another man. And, as we have already pointed out, any development concerning female sexuality not connected to the desire for a child is almost excluded. This leads to interpret, through penis envy, the desire for a child as a substitute of a fundamental lack. In this way the penis-child symbolic equation would become essential to understand the psycho-libidinal development of the girl and there would be no other convincing explanation about motherhood and other itineraries of desire.

Certainly, the symbolic equation is not a universal proposition to understand motherhood and it can be observed in the realm of hysteria. Nevertheless, in this case − the child as a substitute of an original lack − it would be impossible for the mother to consider the child as an Other. Certainly, the symbolic function of the father can lead to the mother/child separation, but does not necessarily determine that the mother accepts the child's otherness. In addition, this leads some analysts to an over interpretation of phallic envy in women and to homologate hysteria with femininity.

Now, if we move forward on the subject-object issue, we can reaffirm that Freud (1980a) installs the question of sexual/gender difference in connection with infantile sexual theories, as described by two adults − little Hans's father and Freud himself (Freud, 1979a). The child's investigation is theorized and interpreted by adults.

This is linked with the myth described in *Totem and Taboo* (Freud, 1980b). This narrative recalls that in the origin culture, women were possessed by the father of the horde and, under these conditions, objects of exchange. This last position is linked to Freud's (1979b) assertion telling us that the taboo discloses a basic fear of women to the point of making them into objects of horror. The female is different from the male, seems eternally incomprehensible, mysterious, and alien; therefore, she is hostile. Further, the male fears being weakened by the woman and then being revealed as incompetent. None of these fears have expired, on the contrary, they pervade through time under different presentations. Consequently, Freud points out, one of the causes of the taboo is that women are, for men, strange beings, hostile, foreign and, as such, in possession of a threatening power.

These narratives establish the castrated other in the girl, subjected to penis envy and embodying little Hans' fear: castration (Freud, 1979a). At the same time, they also set up women as objects of desire and this poses an interesting paradox because what would be most desired for the masculine position would be what, on the other hand, causes "horror."

Winnicott (1982) raises another point of view. He detaches the feminine from the woman, which Freud had already done with his theory of bisexuality. Let us remember that Freud never abandons the theory of bisexuality, mainly in the field of fantasy. There are identification movements that allude to male and female positions coexisting in every subject, and the complete Oedipus complex would be an example. However, in this framework, there are no other options beyond male/female dualism.

Going back to Winnicott, he points out that there is a primary femininity that concerns "being" and we could interpret this proposal in relation to the maternal other. He adds that masculinity is connected to the drive and "to have" – that is – the first one is linked to existence, the second to the category of having. Winnicott's position is important for analyzing these factors in each singular subject, although it would be debatable to assign to these categories (being and having) a fixed relationship with the feminine and the masculine, respectively. This debate makes more complex the question of desire with regard to placing it exclusively in the feminine or masculine side of this dichotomy.

From this point, let us remember that in psychoanalysis the subject-object relationship is outlined in the field of sexuality. But, as we have already suggested, it occurs inevitably and concomitantly in the field of knowledge.

This path introduces us to the contributions, but also to the contradictions and aporias of the Oedipus-castration complex, concerning contemporary problems focused on the multiple itineraries of desire. Freud himself argued that feminine and masculine were categories of uncertain content so they should be derived to active and passive, and that even that movement was doubtful. He pointed out that the male-active and female-passive equations did not even have correspondence in the animal kingdom.

Beyond binary thought

The central hypothesis of this chapter is that binary thought (masculine-feminine, phallic-castrated) is a limit to approach the challenge of thinking about desire in the broad field of women and the feminine. This central hypothesis connects with other secondary hypotheses that we are developing in the course of this text. Among them: that the phallic order does not encompass the complexity of the notion of sexual difference and, moreover, of the category of "difference." In addition, it is necessary to deconstruct the male-female, phallic-castrated dichotomies, and, at the same time, disarticulate the homologation of the presence-absence, nature-culture, rational-emotional polarities with the masculine/feminine dualism.

At this point, it is crucial to think on how women are defined and, even more, to distinguish women from concepts such as "the feminine" and femininity. This can help us to approach the proposed question. Is it just the information of the anatomy or the genetics? Is it gender? Is it sexuality, or is it motherhood alone? Is there a specific characteristic of desire in women? There is a complex relationship between these variables that cannot be ignored. None is independent from the others. They are heterogeneous among them and generally do not reach a dialectical, harmonic solution. Even more, their concordances and discordances are different for every woman. This fact is fundamental to the psychoanalytic thought in order to avoid stereotyped interpretations in the clinical work. It is incomplete to speak of desire as a unit as well as to consider women as a unitary class, except with regard to their rights as it was suggested before, even though there are different cultural approaches regarding this point.

Undoubtedly, it is impossible to ignore the presence of bodies. Anatomy, however, does not define the itinerary of desire in women if we think psycho-analytically in terms of psychosexuality. Sexuality does not mean "having sex," nor is it only a biological practice of human beings. Social ties radically change these variables. First, because bodies are signified and interpreted by culture (Laqueur, 1994); second, because fantasies are plural and determine that desire cannot be locked inside a universal definition, masculine or feminine; and third, because erogenous zones are changeable – albeit some of them are privileged erogenous zones. *Therefore, at least three variables are at stake: bodies (always signi-fied); fantasies (plurality of identifications including gender); and desires, avoiding mono-causal determinism. These variables are crossed by the role of the significant other, at first by the maternal other, in the frame of body contacts and closeness. The primacy of the other (Laplanche, 2001) is at play. Each of these factors intersects with the others.*

We can say that there are recursive messages between drives and gender (Faure-Oppenheimer, 1986). The drive informs gender and gender informs the drive. In these crossings, desire is outlined. Desire has internal sources but is outlined by those "messages" coming from language, discourse, and culture, by way of the parental unconscious. This means thinking beyond the so-called paradigm of simplicity as pointed out by Morin (1995). So, while desire always tends to work exceeding rules, it is also limited by those same rules. These are insoluble contradictions, which need to be sustained.

In other words, I believe it is essential to think of these variables in terms of interfaces of intersections, without discarding any of them and without holding a single category as an exclusive one. It is necessary to approach *the interrela-tionship between bodies, drives, gender, identifications, and desire.* These are variables that are not independent or that work autonomously. There are no pure ana-tomical determinations; the same applies to gender, the drive, identifications, or desire. There are cross-relationships between these variables, which work in constant tension. All of them respond to meanings coming from culture and language and should be deconstructed. *This way of thinking – triadic or including more variables – goes beyond binary thought* and thus allows us to have another per-spective on the category of desire.

To turn back to the question "what do women want," it was stressed that it is problematic to agree with the Freudian proposal on motherhood as the *princeps* aim of female desire. What is at stake is the prospect of a non-maternal desire in women; in other words, to an independent desire from motherhood. It is very well known that there are women in whom the non-desire of a child prevails and this fact, that in other times was considered pathological, has been surfacing even if not all psychoanalysts agree with this assertion. Moreover, the symbolic equation that replaces the desire for a penis with the desire for a child is insufficient to explain the maternal desire in all its complexity and its sym-bolizing aspects.

On the other hand, women's sublimation requires a theoretical extension to be understood, in order to go beyond Freud's ideas (1979f) about women's limited capacity for sublimation. The aim is to find other alternatives within the psychoanalytic theory that could allow us to better understand the multiple variants of subjectivities and desires, not only with regard to women, but also with regard to people with other itineraries of desire and gender.

At this point, it is necessary to think about the Freudian conception of desire in the context of his hysteric patients, where "yes" meant "no" and vice versa. This became the paradigm of the feminine conundrum, of the inscrutable object of desire. But is this what we see in today's women in the frame of clinical consultation?

On the contrary, thinking of women as desiring subjects leads us to approach another horizon in the process of construction of subjectivity. We should remember that women are still equated to prostitutes in some cultures, as Aulagnier-Spairani (2016) stated; also, in the field of fantasies. This configures the so-called *alienation vel*. This category is a logical figure that refers to an impossibility which is neither one thing nor the other. She cannot develop her desire lest she be equated as a prostitute, nor can she take the place of the virgin mother because she risks denying her own desires. This impossibility requires deconstruction.

The issue, however, is even more complicated: it is difficult to assign a gender to desire. Only in a phallic order are there specific characteristics assigned to desire in men or women. They are considered as universal notions although Freud himself had already pointed out that it was a mistake to equate libido and masculinity – sustaining that the libido was always neutral.

As I pointed out, there is a plurality of desires that differ in every woman and, moreover, in every human being. This plurality of desires also requires an opening to rethink sublimation as well as other non-sexual, creative aspects, in women. In other words, what a woman wants is a broader question. It focuses on the point at which Freud admits his incompetency with regard to the area he failed to discern which he named the bedrock of femininity/castration. It is also a reference to desires beyond maternity, but that are unrelated to prostitution or to demeaning women.

Desire: from lack to *poiesis*

Raising the phallic function as the signifier of desire and lack in the context of sustaining a primacy of the phallus is a problematic position. Is it that the Oedipus complex embodies a narrative about the fantasies of desire in androcentric societies?

If we return to the question of what do women want today, we *have to differentiate between desire and want*. It is necessary to distinguish desire from the perspective of sexuality/drive from other desires (want?) with regard to sublimation and creative work. That is what we mean by plurality of desires, considered in a broad sense. There are sexual and non-sexual aspects which we could differentiate in terms of desire and want. We should also take into account the differences determined by diverse subcultures, religions, and ethnicities, among others.

In this context, my proposal is to think of desire or better yet, desires, in a poietic, productive sense as Deleuze, interviewed by Parnet, posited (Deleuze and Parnet, 1980). It involves conceptualizing desire not only as arising from an essential lack, which in women would be replaced – via penis envy – by the desire for a child through the symbolic equation penis/child. This allows us to frame the issue in an alternative way. It does not eliminate the notion of lack but challenges it as an original and absolute starting point for the emergence of desire. On the contrary, thinking about desire in terms of "desiring production" opens the possibility of addressing another perspective from a psychoanalytic point of view. It implies a non-substitutive approach of desire in general as well as involving another concept of motherhood, by way of considering other forms of production of desire, beyond the symbolic equation. Indeed, this proposition exceeds femininity and includes the masculine position and its avatars as well as sexual and gender diversities. Moreover, this approach generates the possibility of encompassing other desires within the context of creativity and sublimation.

In short, the conceptions of desire in a poietic sense would allow for the conceptualization of the desire for a child in a multicenter framework, and imply (Glocer Fiorini, 2001) the possibility of adding a plus to the system of substitutions typical of the symbolic equation penis-child, based on an original lack. This commands, in Freudian theory, the oedipal resolution of the girl toward a "normative" path. On the contrary, I posit another avenue of conceptualizing maternal desire – recognizing a productive character of the desire for a child that would exceed the symbolic substitutions of phallic logic. It provides other variables instead of the over-interpretation of phallic motherhood and specifies with greater precision the establishment of a symbolic third function of the mother.

The concept of phallogocentrism (Derrida, 1998) also alludes to this problem. The author's criticism underlines that the phallus appears as a transcendental element that reintroduces the metaphysics of presence. This happens even if it is argued that the phallus is a signifier of lack.

For Deleuze (Deleuze and Parnet, 1980), desire is not defined by any essential lack. He points out that lack refers to a positivity of desire and not desire to a negativity of lack. His thoughts are based on the work of Nietzche, who sustains the self-affirming character of the forces which, Deleuze *dixit*, are "desiring forces." The notion of desire as production comes from the field of philosophy and is therefore far from the current and everyday concept of positivity. The desiring forces and its creativity affirm the production of difference and novelty.

This proposal means to work with disjunctive conjunctions (Deleuze and Guattari, 1994). *It involves going through dualisms and reaching transitional synthesis as much as disjunctions, which sustain the heterogeneity of subjectivation processes* and allows focusing with a different perspective, such as to think on other non-maternal desires.

Undoubtedly, a non-substitutive conception of desire enables addressing the relationship between symbolic functions and women in another way. It is a reference to the symbolic functions that the mother can fulfill by promoting the separation of her children instead of retaining them. In other publications I named this function: *third party symbolic function* (Glocer Fiorini, 2013; Glocer Fiorini, 2017), in order to deconstruct the Paternal Function because of obvious patriarchal connotations. These connotations are, in turn, attached to the notion of *pater familias* of Roman law. Besides, fatherhood is more complex than this function. Benjamin (1997) stated that there are sufficient symbolic reserves in the mother to perform this function and this point deserves to be highlighted.

Finally, there is a question to be clarified: why the title of this text is about the feminine when the question is about women? My intention, as I said, is to differentiate the feminine as a broader category than as related to women. The feminine is a cultural and psychoanalytic concept which exceeds women and, in different ways, also encompasses men and unconventional sexualities and genders. On one side, the feminine goes beyond the masculine/feminine dichotomy. On the other, it is important to emphasize that its meanings are inevitably based on an androcentric viewpoint. Certainly, this proposal involves reviewing the concept of difference.

Desire and difference

In other publications (Glocer Fiorini, 2017; Glocer Fiorini, 2019a), I proposed that the category of "difference" exceeds that of sexual difference. Its polysemy: difference in the linguistic level, difference as distinction (Heiddeger, 1988), différance (Derrida, 1989), differendo (Lyotard, 1983), and difference within repetition as flows in becoming (Deleuze, 2002), as well as gender and psychosexual difference, all constitute a complex network indispensable to think on another conception of desire beyond the masculine-feminine dualism.

All these variables configure a plot in which there is always an "empty box." This means that "difference" always has an opacity which cannot be covered by a narrative. On the other side, it is inevitable to go through the category of "sexual difference" in culture, discourse, and clinical practice as long as we accept that it does not correspond to a biological fact or an immutable essence. This line of thought allows for the complexity as well as the polysemy and metaphorical aspects of the category of "difference." The point is whether the subject has psychically inscribed "difference" as a symbolic operation, including all the levels in which it is addressed in each singular person. This goes beyond how the object choice is resolved and points to the recognition of alterity.

Thinking about the category of difference in terms of the paradigm of complexity (Morin, 1995) allows us to go beyond the masculine-feminine polarity and its essentialist character. Although we cannot annul this dichotomy, it is possible to include it within a complex network. As we pointed out, this model of thought changes the way of thinking about desire in general and concerning women in particular.

In this context, should we think of a post-gender or beyond gender desire, perhaps a queer desire? In this way, the question – what woman wants – places tension on power/ knowledge relations involving women and the feminine in the complex framework of "differences."

This proposal takes us away from a comfortable position regarding knowledge. It implies an approach to another conception of desire, another conception of motherhood, and the possibility of rethinking symbolic and sublimation functions in women. This proposal encompasses the field of psychosexuality, gender, and creativity. In addition, this means reviewing the Freudian Oedipal resolution for the girl, with motherhood considered the privileged aim of femininity (Glocer Fiorini, 2001; Glocer Fiorini, 2007; Glocer Fiorini, 2019a).

Answering the question of what do women want is not only about detecting new and previously hidden desires of women, but also investigating how this impacts psychoanalytic theory, with the perspective of opening a review of postulates that are currently insufficient to think about women and the feminine. In sum, in light of the new positions and demands that are visible in today's society, Freud's question of what do women want is renewed and should be rethought. As it was pointed out, this is a question that traditionally starts from a male point of view: there is a subject of knowledge and desire which is male, investigating an object of knowledge, which is female, and is classically located as an object of desire. The concept of women's desires has created significant conflicts in different times. Moreover, thinking of women's "desire" as a universal category hinders the understanding of the plurality of symbolic and desiring movements of each woman, in the singular. It is necessary to adopt non-binary logic to deconstruct the concept of a feminine essence as a universal category to approach women and the feminine.

In sum, in light of the new positions and demands that are visible in today's society, Freud's question of what do women want is renewed and should be rethought. As it was pointed out, this is a question that traditionally starts from a male point of view: there is a subject of knowledge and desire which is male, investigating an object of knowledge, which is female, and is classically located as an object of desire. The concept of women's desires has created significant conflicts in different times. Moreover, thinking of women's "desire" as a universal category hinders the understanding of the plurality of symbolic and desiring movements of each woman, in the singular. It is necessary to adopt non-binary logic to deconstruct the concept of a feminine essence as a universal category to approach women and the feminine.

References

Aulagnier-Spairani, P. et al. (2016). *Le désir el la perversion*. Paris, France: Points.

Austin, J.L. (2007). "From the performative to the speech act." In: *Performativity*, Ed. Loxley, J., New York: Routledge, pp. 6–21.

Benjamin, J. (1997). *Sujetos iguales, objetos de amor*. Buenos Aires: Paidós.

Bourdieu, P. (1999). *La dominación masculina*. Barcelona: Anagrama.

Butler, J. (1990). *Gender Trouble*. New York: Routledge.

Castoriadis-Aulagnier, P. (1977). *La violencia de la interpretación. Del pictograma al enunciado*. Buenos Aires: Amorrortu.Deleuze, G. (2002). *Diferencia y repetición*. Buenos Aires: Amorrortu.

Deleuze, G. and Guattari, F. (1994). *Mil Mesetas*. Valencia: Pre-Textos.

Deleuze, G. and Parnet, C. (1980). *Diálogos*. Valencia: Pre-Textos.

Derrida, J. (1998). *Resistencias del psicoanálisis*. Buenos Aires: Paidós.

Derrida, J. (1989). *La deconstrucción en las fronteras de la filosofía*. Paidós: Barcelona: Paidós.

De Saussure, F. (1974). *Curso de lingüística general*. Buenos Aires: Losada.

Faure-Oppenheimer, A. (1986). *La elección de sexo*. Madrid: Akal.

Freud, S. (1979a). *Sobre las teorías sexuales infantiles*. Vol. IX. Buenos Aires: Amorrortu.

Freud, S. (1979b). *El tabú de la virginidad*. Vol. XI. Buenos Aires: Amorrortu.

Freud, S. (1979c). *Sobre la psicogénesis de un caso de homosexualidad femenina*. Vol. XVIII. Buenos Aires: Amorrortu.

Freud, S. (1979d). *La organización genital infantil*. Vol. XIX. Buenos Aires: Amorrortu.

Freud, S. (1979e). *El sepultamiento del complejo de Edipo*. Vol. XIX. Buenos Aires: Amorrortu.

Freud, S. (1979f). *La femineidad*. En *Nuevas Conferencias de Introducción al Psicoanálisis*. Vol. XXII. Buenos Aires: Amorrortu.

Freud, S. (1980a). *Análisis de la fobia de un niño de cinco años*. Vol. X. Buenos Aires: Amorrortu.

Freud, S. (1980b). *Tótem y Tabú*. Vol. XIII. Buenos Aires: Amorrortu.

Glocer Fiorini, L. (1998). "The feminine in Psychoanalysis: A complex construction." *Journal of Clinical Psychoanalysis*, 7:421–439. (In Spanish: "La posición femenina: una construcción heterogénea". *Revista de Psicoanálisis*, 51/3: 587–603, 1994). Buenos Aires: APA.

Glocer Fiorini, L. (2001). "El deseo de hijo: de la carencia a la producción deseante." *Revista de Psicoanálisis*, 58, 4:965–976. Buwinnicottenos Aires: APA.

Glocer Fiorini, L. (2007). *Deconstructing the Feminine. Psychoanalysis, Gender and Theories of Complexity*. London: Karnac. (In Spanish: Lo *Femenino y el Pensamiento Complejo*. Buenos Aires: Lugar Editorial, 2001).

Glocer Fiorini, L. (2013). *Deconstruyendo el concepto de función paterna. Un paradigma interpelado*. *Revista de Psicoanálisis*, LXX, 4, 671–681. Buenos Aires: APA.

Glocer Fiorini, L. (2017). *Sexual Difference in Debate. Bodies, Desires, and Fictions*. London: Karnac. (In Spanish: *La Diferencia Sexual en Debate, Cuerpos, Deseos y Ficciones*. Buenos Aires: Lugar Editorial, 2015).

Glocer Fiorini, L. (2019a). Deconstructing the feminine: Discourses, logics and power. Theoretico-clinical implications. *Int. J. Psychoanal.*, 100(3), 593–603.

Glocer Fiorini, L. (2019b). Polyphonies of sexuality: Debates about theories/ debates about paradigms. *Int. J. Psychoanal.* 100(6), 1256–1269. IJP Centenary Special Issue.

Heidegger, M. (1988). *Identidad y diferencia*. Barcelona: Anthropos.

Horney, K. (1977). *Psicología femenina*. Madrid: Alianza.

Kristeva, J. (1986). Revolution in poetic language. In: *The Kristeva Reader* Ed. Moi, T. London: Blackwell, pp. 187–213.

Lacan, J. (1971). La significación del falo. In: *Lectura estructuralista de Freud*. Ed. Lacan, J. México: Siglo Veintiuno, pp. 279–289.

Lacan, J. (1981). *Aún*. Buenos Aires: Paidós.

Laplanche J. (1988). *Castración. Simbolizaciones. Problemáticas II*. Buenos Aires: Amorrortu.

Laplanche J. (1989). *Nuevos fundamentos para el psicoanálisis. La seducción originaria*. Buenos Aires: Amorrortu.

Laplanche, J. (2001). *Entre seducción e inspiración: el hombre*. Buenos Aires: Amorrortu.

Laqueur, Th. (1994). *La construcción del sexo*. Madrid: Cátedra.

Lyotard, J.-F. (1983). *Le Différend*. Paris: Minuit.

Mitchell, J., Rose, J. (1982). *Feminine sexuality: Jacques Lacan and the école freudienne*. New York: N.W. Norton & Co.

Morin, E. (1995). *Introducción al pensamiento complejo*. Barcelona: Gedisa.

Winnicott, D. (1982). Escisión de los elementos masculinos y femeninos en el hombre y la mujer. En *Bisexualidad y diferencia de los sexos*. Buenos Aires: Ediciones del 80.

5 What women want and what men want of women

Arlene Kramer Richards

Sigmund Freud famously asked: "what do women want?" He asserted that he did not know and that it would be up to women psychoanalysts to find out. I think it is wonderful that women have been and are working very hard on this. It seems to me that women want two things. First, women want equality. We want to be valued equally to men, we want equal pay for equal work, equality of opportunity for education and for advancement in our work, and equal justice under the law. Second, women want recognition and valuing of difference. We want child care, elder care, and health care. We want early childhood care that enables mothers to care for our children even if we are working outside the home. We want elder care that frees sisters, wives, and daughters from having to stay home to care for older family members. We want health care that includes freedom of choice about what we do with our own bodies.

Women want to be listened to. We want our ideas, wishes, fears, and moral judgements to be heard, thought about, and responded to. We want other women to do this and we want men to do this also. We want to participate in every level of social and political governance. We want equal representation and equal responsibility.

Ironically, Freud did just this in his private life. He educated his daughter to be a psychoanalyst. He even handed over responsibility for the International Psychoanalytical Association to her rather than to any of his sons or male disciples. He encouraged many other women to be psychoanalysts. He encouraged at least one of his women patients (Hilda Doolittle) to continue raising her daughter in a lesbian relationship. He even encouraged her to continue her love affairs with men as well.

In his professional life, he made his lifework listening to women complain about their dissatisfactions. He listened to women. But he also thought about what they told him. He tried to create a theory that would account for their unhappiness, give them respect and self-respect for their wishes, and strengthen their moral values. He made a lot of mistakes, but in the end, he did spend his life trying to understand.

He thought about what it was that all men had and all women lacked: a penis. For him a penis was the greatest source of pleasure and sexual frustration the greatest source of pain. So, he concluded that women must suffer great pain

DOI: 10.4324/9781003180036-7

in being deprived of that. It is, I think, noteworthy that he wrote his last and definitive paper (1931) about what women want after his treatment of Hilda Doolittle. That was the paper in which he concluded that penis envy was bedrock. In other words, he thought once a woman understood that her unhappiness was due to penis envy, she would be cured of neurosis.

Doolittle wrote home to her lover during her analysis that Freud told her that all women, not just homosexual women suffered from penis envy. One way to understand that is that he was normalizing her wish and thereby alleviating her self-condemnation for her envy of men. The effect of the interpretation was that she was relieved of her inhibition and became the great poet and prolific writer that she did become. It is easy to see how he would take that as confirmation of the correctness of the penis envy interpretation of women's desire.

But another way to see it is that he was raising her self-esteem by alleviating her shame about her being a lesbian. He was saying that not only lesbians have penis envy; all women do. He was affirming in action the idea that she was worth listening to, that her words mattered to him, and that her ideas mattered to him. The outcome of this, I believe, is that he drew a wrong conclusion from a clinically useful intervention. That wrong conclusion haunted psychoanalysts and psychoanalytic theory for generations.

Another way psychoanalysis has investigated what women want has been by considering the Oedipal complex in females. Freud's (1933) last idea was that the little girl loved her mother best just as the little boy did. But then the little girl changed her object of her affections to her father. He accounted for this change as a response to the shock of seeing a penis. He reasoned that the little girl wanted it, resented her mother for not giving her one, and turned to her father as a potential love object who could give her a baby as a substitute for a penis.

But we now believe that little girls enjoy their genital and most little girls experienced great pleasure from it. So, the idea that seeing a penis caused envy of the male and rage at her mother for not giving her one no longer held water.

How do we now see the way the little girl comes to love a man? Infant observation has shown that little girls flirt with others by about six months of age. They play peek-a-boo with a stranger and the most usual stranger is the father. Thus, they do not turn away from mother in disappointment, but turn to the other with interest.

Socialized to know that most families have a mother and a father, little girls try to learn how to be feminine, how to act like what their bodies have signaled to the larger world that they are. Their bodies are softer and lighter than boys' bodies.

Dressed as girls, cuddled and held as girls, little girls know their gender by about two years old (Fast, 1984). Between 18 months and three years old toddlers focus on separation from their mothers. When they reach the developmental level of being comfortable that they can be on their own without a mothering person in sight they work on developing gender roles, practicing playing house, wearing adult looking costumes, imagining themselves as they want to be when they are grown up. From then on girls strive to be girlish, look to the outer world for confirmation of their gender, and play act being wives and mothers. By the time they find out that fathers are important in producing babies, they wish for a man to give them the fulfillment of their female sexuality, gender, and social role. This beginning is put aside when children concentrate on school learning, sports, and getting along with other children.

That is the "just so" story of female development. That is a normative developmental story. But there are many, perhaps infinite, variations. Some girls become "tomboys," preferring boy games and competition with boys. Some feel themselves to be in the wrong gender, feeling that they are really boys despite their female bodies. And we know that some girls become lesbians, being sexually aroused by other females, loving women, not men. And there are girls who believe that they are boys in girls' bodies but love men.

And we know that development as lesbians does not necessarily happen when girls are raised in homes with two mothers. Almost all lesbians are raised by heterosexual women and many have fathers in the home. This finding suggests that lesbians may be women who did not find a third person to engage their attention and love away from their mothers. This hypothesis fits with the idea that one lesbian theorist herself posited decades ago. She posited from her own experience and those of the women she knew, that lesbians want mother love even when they are themselves grown up.

We do not know why this variant on being a woman develops, nor do we know how early this happens. Similarly, we do not know why some biological females develop male gender feeling themselves to be boys in a girl's body. We do know that gender dysphoria may be fluid until puberty with many "tomboys" becoming female identified at the age of first menstruation. This suggests that hormones have something to do with females feeling ourselves to be female. It also suggests that gender role may have something to do with this development since some lesbians enjoy masculine looks, clothing, activities, and still feel themselves female.

But we do know what men want. They want to differentiate themselves from women. This happens early in male development. By six most boys want to play boy games, play with other boys, be daring, be admired, be paid attention, and not be sissies. When girls do the same, boys are often offended. It attacks their sense of being different from girls. So, they react with distain, or worse. And they attack boys who do not distain girls. They want boys to be boys and girls to be girls. Hence patriarchy.

What do women want? If women want men then what women want gets complicated by what men want. If girls and women want to be wanted by men, they are limited in what they can want by what men want them to be. The justification for female sexual mutilation is that men are said to want such mutilated women. The same justification was used for female foot binding in China. And the same justification has been and is offered for inhibition of ambition, giving up on math skills, avoiding the sciences in favor of language development, and many other forms of female inhibition or mental mutilation.

So, what women want is complicated by the contradictions between what we want for ourselves as people and what men want from us as sexual partners. All of the traits regarded as feminine in our society and in most other societies now and in the past are inhibitions. To be feminine is to be passive, weak, flirtatious, demure, nurturant, safe, home-loving, shy, retiring, kind, and self-sacrificing. Feminine is not pursuing glory, riches, distinction, or leadership. Young women and girls are more desirable sexually than mature women in many societies. Sex trafficking involves young women and children. Feminine is writing at home, in secret, taking time off to bake a cake, paying attention to the children, fitting one's own needs into the corners of time left from taking care of the husband, family, and household tasks.

So, we want to be equal with men and also to be desirable to men. But being equal to men means being active, strong, reliable, self-confident, courageous, willing to be out in the world, persistent, able to put one's own needs first, and willing to get our own way. These are the opposite of the feminine traits so desirable to men. Being equal to men involves pursuing glory, riches, distinction, and leadership. The contradiction between these sets of values led feminists of the 1970s to believe that only a lesbian life could afford women real equality with men.

We compromise all the time, but we live with the constant tension between wanting equality with men and wanting to preserve the sexual desirability and motherhood that are female and often mutually contradictory (Langer and Hollander, 1992). I believe that this is true universally. Some social arrangements make it easier to combine both. One of these is hiring a nanny to care for the young child. This generally involves getting a third world mother to leave her own children with relatives while she takes care of the professional or business woman's child. The inequity and frequent exploitation of the nanny make this choice distasteful to some women, me among them. Another option is taking a young student, usually foreign, as an *au pair*. This involves giving her room and board in exchange for babysitting after school and often driving to and from school. This option has the disadvantage of having an inexperienced teenager or young adult in charge of children who may take advantage of the young woman to do things the parents would not allow. Another choice is day care with the disadvantage of bringing a young child into an environment where she will be exposed to illnesses and often bring them home to the family as well. And it puts the child in care of low paid, often tired and resentful people. Yet another choice is having the grandparents or other relatives live with the family to care for the young. But grandparents in our society are likely to be busy with their own careers or social lives. Some social arrangements make it more difficult, but the contradiction between equality and difference seems to me the bedrock that Freud misattributed to penis envy.

Within these broad categories of equality and difference there are many weights of many values. For example, a story in the New York Times published on 14 September 2019, tells of how coal miners losing their jobs in Appalachia adapted to the loss of their roles as wage earners. Their wives went to school and became nurses, thus supporting their families. Neither the reporter of the story nor any of her sources considered the alternative of the men going back to school, becoming nurses, and continuing in their roles as breadwinners. The men chose to stay at home and do housework.

To me, this illustrates the deep and early learned value of not doing girly things being much more important than the later in life imperative to support the family. The newspaper story emphasized the men's reliance on female family members to help them with the at home chores. Clearly the men were not un-ambivalent about doing child rearing, shopping, preparing food, cooking, cleaning, repairs, and other chores. Yet their work at home was what their wives had been doing without help when they worked in the mines. The men required more help with the housework than their wives had done. Presumably this was because they found it more difficult to do this work than their wives had done. Ambivalence uses energy, they clearly were ambivalent about staying at home.

The economic change has led to a change in women's values. One woman who went to work said: "Women now, they got a little taste of freedom," Ms. Bowling said. "Men has been able to do whatever the hell they want for so long while women has had to sit in a chair and keep their legs closed and be nice and polite. Now they don't have to."

Men, on the other hand, find the change more difficult: "The way of life is changing so bad," Mr. Rose said. He grew quiet. "You'll get overwhelmed if you think about it too hard."

The change Mr. Rose finds so hard to think about involves change in gender roles that modifies and even contradicts what little boys learn early and reinforce in themselves and each other throughout their later years. Boys do not do girly stuff. Real men are not nurses; real men work hard with their muscles and their hands. Real men carry guns, shoot, dig, build, excavate, produce hard objects. Men who do fashion, hairdressing, nursing, teaching nursery school, and other "soft" jobs are not real men. They are considered sissies. They are as devalued as the women in their society have been.

Another hypothesis, suggested by Delia Battin (2019) about why men do not become nurses in such a situation is that men want to be nursed, longing for the mothering they enjoyed in infancy. I believe that in this scenario men have pushed away the mothering that they shunned in favor of masculine self-sufficiency and therefore still long for but must abjure in favor of macho independence.

In sum, while what women want is attuned to what men want women to want; what men want is to be lord of the manor, with a woman attuned to her man's every wish. And to the extent that this is true, patriarchy is entrenched while matriarchy, or even equality, is a hard sell.

References

Battin, D. (2019). Personal communication.

Fast, I. (1984). *Gender Identity*. Hillsdale, NJ: Analytic Press.

Freud, S. (1931). *On Female Sexuality. S. E. 21*:223–246.

Freud, S. (1933). *Femininity. S. E. 22*:112–135.

Langer, M., Hollander, N. (1992). *Motherhood and Sexuality*. New York, NY: Guilford.

Robertson, C. (2019). *In Coal Country, the Mines Shut Down, the Women Went to Work and the World Quietly Changed. The New York Times* (14 September).

Part III

Gender relations today

Introduction by Paula L. Ellman

This section contains four contributions that are rich in perspective and consideration. The chapters offer variance in both their focus and method.

Adrienne Harris in "Women and Psychoanalysis across Generations and Diversities. What do Women want Now: Not Answers but Questions" brings us poetic evocative voices from herself along with four progressive-thinking analysts. Harris sets the stage for an opening of the mind to alternative perspectives on gender and self. She invites four analysts to think and write about "what do women want today" in this chapter. Each of the four invited authors avails themselves of an opportunity to create their own space for both thinking and feeling about what women want in the realm of gender conceptualizations, racialization, cultural oppressions, self-experience, and ideas about pandemic-revealing fissures in the social fabric. Each offers a unique contribution, such that reading their sections is like reading a poem, each transmitting potent affects along with revealing complex vantage points. We are swept along in this panoply with each author's invitation to enter her mind, depart from our customary ways of thinking, and experience something new and distinct. Harris then brings into her conclusion her appreciation for the unique voices of her colleagues, a declaration of her wish to find courage to look ahead to the unknown and recognition of the problems of racism and inequities that must be addressed.

Graciela Abelin-Sas Rose's paper "Gender relations today" begins with the stunning statistics on violence and abuse of women, and even the prevalence of femicides in Latin America. She brings to our awareness the negligence of many governments to take any action against the assailants. Abelin-Sas Rose calls attention to the identifications that women participate in the cultural misogyny such that pursuing protection and equal rights becomes near impossible. She traces the origins of misogyny developmentally in the failed separation process, and the resulting need to disparage and hate the maternal object. She takes us into her review of her analytic practice in NYC over the past 30 years. She offers her conceptualization of the presence of the "Scheherazade Syndrome," where women while outside of marriage are independent-minded, within the couple, remain subservient and fearful, beholden to the man's need to remain powerful and dominant. She brings her expertise in understanding the couple

DOI: 10.4324/9781003180036-8

to a description of the couple dynamic and the nature of her interventions in this dynamic. She notes the shift in the couple dynamic with the next generation of women, more assertive and less compromising. In visiting Freud's antiquated commentary on women, she turns to her clinical data suggesting the profound cultural changes that have ensued since his time yielding new oedipal configurations and object relations constellations. Abelin Sas-Rose integrates the impact of media noting gender relations phenomenology where patriarchal traditions shift. Using her clinical data, she recognizes more typical aspects of gender relations in the couple and yet notes a recent revision of the binary conceptualizations of gender to incorporate more fluidity. She discusses two clinical vignettes depicting tensions and conflicts within the couple with a focus both on the nature of gender in the couple and on the individual familial patterns of development.

Janice Lieberman in "What should a wife want?" introduces this question with a discussion of the film and novel "Wife" and offers a thoughtful consideration of women in the public domain whose position as "wife" to their well-known husbands squelched their own development and aspirations. Lieberman recounts her own personal history as an invisible wife earlier in her life. In bringing her lens to her practice with NYC women who are not dependent on two incomes, she describes a current trend of women looking to become "wives" in the traditional sense – of marrying one's Prince – living in a regressive way, what she terms as a state of "adult developmental arrest." Lieberman forewarns us of the regressive social pressures at play that also accompany pressures for independence and careers. She makes a call to psychoanalysts to attend to the intergenerational trauma around marital roles and the latent rage at being confined in the role as dependent wife and also addresses the potential for a countertransference of envy of the non-working infantilized wife.

Cecile Bassen in "The Persistent Impact of Stereotypes about Women" explores the cultural stereotypes we carry about women, how and if they have changed over time, and the powerful psychological impact they have on women's self-experience. There are three prominent areas of thinking about stereotypes that Bassen explores using observations on fairytales, popular films, and culture and even merchandise marketing. Bassen suggests that women gain definition through their appearance, where the emphasis is on youthfulness and thinness, certainly having powerful implications for the experience of aging. Appearance not only includes how one looks, but also how one behaves – as vanity and seductiveness are scorned. Bassen includes consideration of the stereotype views that a woman's life is not complete without a man, along with the woman is loveable only when she puts others ahead of herself. Bassen addresses these long-held perspectives as reflective of the gender bias that while changing, still in many ways persists today. She tells us that in 20 countries women continue to have less than half the legal rights that men have. Bassen centers her paper in the psychoanalytic exploration of the origins of the fear of the powerful female imago rooted in the child's early life helplessness in their dependence on the mother and early projective-introjective processes. Also meaningful is the daughter's negotiating concerns of usurping the mother's powerful position by asserting her own powerful place.

Both Abelin Sas-Rose and Lieberman draw from their longevity of their practices with New York City patients and their perspectives on the current pressures for traditional regressive roles for women. Also, Bassen reminds of the prolonged history of cultural stereotypes of women that are both imposed on women externally and carried by women internally. In contrast the voices that are present in Harris' paper are expressed by contemporary women who challenge the binary of gender relations and introduce the possibility of fluidity in gender offering an array of concepts of diverse gender identity. "What do women want today?" therefore becomes the questioning and upheaval of long-held beliefs on binary gender roles and the call to find one's own subjectivity is difficult to mentalize. These voices offer a post-structuralist theory of gender relations, "a search for gendered and sexual differences which exceed existing understandings of *difference* itself." The question here is reframed: "What do those on the oppressed end of the gender non-binary spectrum, want today?" and a view that includes the intersectionality of gender relations with race relations becomes imperative.

6 Gender relations today

Graciela Abelin-Sas Rose

How many women today are living under conditions that allow them to feel free and be free to exercise their wishes? The UN reports that every day 137 women are killed at the hands of their male partners and that 70 percent of all women in the world have experienced physical or sexual violence in their lifetime.

In Argentina in 2019, a woman was killed every 29 hours. Seventy-five percent of the murderers were family members, husbands, or ex-partners. Seventeen percent of these women had filed a complaint against the assailant and 11 percent were under court-ordered protection; a most distressing truth. In Mexico, 98 percent of femicides go unpunished. Femicide in Guatemala has reached numbers higher than 700 a year – and with such impunity that only four percent of the assailants are prosecuted. In the United States, in 2020, more than 270 women were raped or sexually assaulted every day (United Nations Office on Drugs and Crime, 2019). On July 3, 2020, *The New York Times* reported that during the lockdown 26 females between the ages of two and 82 were murdered in the United Kingdom – they were trapped with their abusers, with no escape.

Reports and statistics like these bring to light the widespread level of murderous hatred and violence toward women as well as a concept of women as slaves, as possessions of male masters who have total power over their decisions, their activities, and their right to life. Few governments protect women from this hatred. For some, in fact, it is acceptable. Let us also keep in mind that 200 million women alive today have undergone female genital mutilation, many of whom sanction that their own daughters submit to this same practice.

There tends to exist a presumption that, if women's minds were free from the cultural forces that disempower them and permit their being treated in such ignominious ways, women would want to obtain equal status with their male partners. Yet the reality is that many women have so internalized the discriminatory and misogynistic attitudes that pervade their culture, that they remain irresolute about asserting their right to equality even when cultural forces have changed. So, we are perpetually faced with the question: how many women are able actually to know what they want, immersed as they are in social

DOI: 10.4324/9781003180036-9

situations that ignore their rights and that teach and force them to accept those conditions?

The wish to dominate, to have omnipotent control over the other, is present in all of us. Fundamentally, it arises out of a deep psychical need to survive in the presence of an adult other. Possessiveness and domination are the consequence of fearing vulnerability and helplessness. We see it develop in children of both sexes, independent of the hormonal effects their bodies are bathed in. It often finds expression in attacks directed at physically or psychologically weaker individuals. We know that rivalries, competitiveness, and aggression are expressions of the wish to dominate and control the situation. The capacities to collaborate, to be open to the wishes and needs of the other, and to be concerned for someone else's needs, are developed slowly during childhood, and they require revision and improvement throughout our lives.

What is at the origin of this hatred of women, and why? Freud thought that the horror of the female genitals was based on the boy's perception of it as an image of castration, to which Ferenczi added that in its place the image of Medusa's head appeared. The horror of this "mutilated creature" found a solution by feeling triumphantly contemptuous of the female, thus overcoming the experience of this man/boy need and desire. If Klein (1937) taught us that there is no love without hatred, and if Winnicott (1949) agreed that otherwise there is indifference, we still cannot understand the pure hatred of women expressed through groups like "Incel" without referring to the catastrophic fear of being rejected and derided that is at the *origin* of those hateful and vengeful emotions.

For Kristeva (1982), with the mother being the foundation of the object relation at the junction of the physical and the psychological, she will easily become the *Abject Object*, the object to be destroyed as the precondition for mental activity to take place: "the object that draws me where meaning collapses." It follows that the capacity to mourn the loss of one's mother as a pre-symbolic object is necessary to acquire the capacity to represent. Thus, for the depressed narcissist, the incapacity to mourn the loss of the object and therefore the inability to engage in the process of separation precipitates the hatred of it.

> Now consider, what can we say about the condition of women in a society in which discrimination is legally forbidden and socially condemned?

It is with this perspective in mind that I will report my observations about a very particular population. The women and men I have seen in private practice in New York City live in a very progressive society, another world, where sexual discrimination has evolved away from hatred, devaluation, and enslavement. Even so, there have in the past been significant limitations. Although women are now free to get higher education, only since 1969 have they been accepted into Ivy League schools. Women still receive, in many instances, less pay than men for their work. In fact, in 2014, female workers constituted two-thirds of the minimum wage workers in the United States. Yes, they are free to be sexually active, to change genders, to choose partners, to live alone, to earn a living. But – only since 1960 have they been allowed to have their own bank accounts (Sanders, 2017). The passage of the Equal Credit Opportunity Act of 1974 granted single and married women the right to own credit cards without their husband's signatures (most single women were refused by most banks). Today, 51 percent of women consider themselves to be the "CFO" of their household. Women's freedom to exercise the inalienable right to choose to become a mother or not, decreed in law in the United States since 1973, is often tampered with in certain states. On the other hand, the struggle to equalize women's rights over the last 40 years has brought dramatic changes that have had a profound effect on the lives of current generations. Those changes, as I will illustrate, have had an impact even among privileged, upper-middle-class white women who economically have become as empowered as men – the population representing most of my patients.

Variations in gender relations before and after 1990

In the first decades of my analytic career, I treated many women that complained of depressive symptoms. Although outside their marital relationships they were productive, efficient, and successful, their sense of value relied very heavily on their partners' view of them – despite their partners being neglectful of their needs, their talents, and their autonomy. These women were unaware of this situation or how it affected the quality of their lives. I observed that, once committed to a relationship, they tended to lose their sense of autonomy and developed an insidious sense of insecurity about their values and wishes. Their interests merged with their partners' and they sacrificed their previous ideals to the extent that their own ambitions were sidestepped. If they took a more assertive stance, they felt that they were upsetting the generally approved role of dominance of their partners. They lived in fear of their partners' moods and judgments while believing their role was to alter those reactions, feeling remorseful if they failed.

I was puzzled by what struck me as a paradox: on the one hand, the wife was intimidated and submissive to her husband and, on the other, she was protective of what she perceived as his fragility. In more precise terms, this woman viewed her partner in two different ways: the despotic or dominant other and the vulnerable child in need of protection and care. The turn from the first to the second emerged when his irritation and anger made her notice that her partner felt disregarded and devalued by her not meeting his expectations. She seemed unable to maintain her own firm perception of reality against the intensity of his reactions. As a result, she tried to repair the imaginary harm she had caused: the man became a child in her eyes and she became a solicitous mother.

Why was she terrified of knowing and asserting her own perceptions, expressing her disagreements? I inferred that she perceived her own rights as hostile and violent: they transformed her into a "castrating witch." Trying to flee this role, she resorted to taking on its inverse: the image of a loving mother.

> I concluded that the woman and her partner adhered to the same belief – power belonged either to one or the other. It could not be shared or created in harmony, together.

Researchers in other fields offered data that supported my observations. Carol Gilligan, in her 1982 study on college students, found that women's sense of obligation and sacrifice superseded the ideal of equality. Women measured their own value by the amounts of responsibility and caring they possessed, defining their sense of identity in relation to their connections with other people. They avoided causing pain while being keenly aware of their own sense of vulnerability, dependency, and fear of abandonment. Some years earlier, Jean Baker Miller (1976) demonstrated that, for women, the total loss of a relationship was experienced as a total loss of self, putting greater value on their affiliations with others than on their own self-enhancement.

For these women, addressing conflicts or unhappiness with their partners seemed like a dead end: they encountered denial or resentment toward their demands. Consequently, they turned silent and depressed. I named this constellation of symptoms the "Scheherazade Syndrome" (2010). In so doing, I had in mind the fate of the beautiful maiden depicted in the book *One Thousand and One Nights,* a tenth century compendium of stories from India, the Arab world, Persia, and Judaic tradition. Scheherazade was depicted as a woman who lived in fear of losing her head every day. King Shahryar, betrayed and publicly humiliated by his wife, avenged himself every morning by killing a young virgin he had forced to share his bed at night.

Obsessed by the image of woman-as-betrayer who had disgraced him before his court, he found no other solution to his humiliation than to exterminate all women, lest one of them ever again expose him to it – to his castration. By telling a thousand and one stories, Scheherazade managed to elicit the king's curiosity and thus escape the death sentence that supposedly awaited her. Wisely deploying narrative techniques, at the end of each day, she obtained one more day to live: so that she could tell the ending of the story she had purposefully left unfinished. She elicited the curiosity of this child-man, whose compulsion to kill did not differentiate between one woman and the next. As a loving mother would do to alleviate her child's insecurity at bedtime, she created a world of fantasy and art. She succeeded in differentiating herself from the king's image of woman as a witch-like castrator and found a way to lead him out of his monothematic nightmare. And so, in a dreamlike process, the king, a sanguinary omnipotent baby, moved out of his narrow reality, relearned laughter and sorrow, and began to perceive the value of life, words, poetry, and love.

However, we must not forget that Scheherazade herself was in a "no exit" situation. She was forced to invest all her creativity in placating the king's vengeance while, at the same time, she was constantly threatened by the power he had over her. She knew that she would be sentenced to death unless she poured her energies into alleviating her partner's fear of degradation, of castration.

Looking at this folk tale from the eleventh century, or at these professionally successful women living in the twentieth and early twenty-first centuries in New York City, we find women who believe they will be sentenced to death, or, in a contemporary setting, sentenced to a lack of love, abandonment, or denigration, unless they cure their partner's sense of humiliation and castration. Paradoxically, however, trying to undo the man's sense of castration or failure through further submission confirms the man's illusion that a "powerful phallus" is obtained by "beheading" someone else. In this situation, where power dynamics characteristic of the dialectic between master and slave are established and reproduced, each side of the couple manifests elements of both master and slave. For instance, being the victim of an omnipotent, unruly child may offer the woman the position of virtuous rescuer of an immature being. In this way, both are authors of what will bring the demise of their coupledom. They disregard the fact that the imaginary powerful "phallus," can only be built as the result of the couple's deep and loving collaboration.

Regardless of the dire circumstances that I have described, all of the women I treated showed an extraordinary capacity for change. Most were able to transform the dynamics established with their partners. The few who could not were able to separate from them.

The patriarchal system to which these women submitted has been powerfully exposed by the feminist movement. The influence feminism has had in women's development was notable; so much so that when a new generation approached their prime of life, they faced vastly different problems. I noticed that the women of this younger generation were much more assertive of their independence. The typical younger patient I saw had to deal with a sense of uncertainty about her role. Although she was succeeding to differentiate herself from the standards of previous generations, there were few alternative models to follow. She developed excessive self-demands to perform exceedingly well professionally and domestically. No longer displacing her own ambitions onto her partner's success, she attempted to integrate a multiplicity of roles done to perfection, an almost impossible task. Overstressed, she demanded equality with "less willingness to compromise," expecting her partner to perform beyond his potential, – almost a reversal of roles from the previous generation. It appeared that, due to her own self-demands, she had difficulty tolerating frustrations and regulating her aggression toward her partner.

In contrast to the self-effacement and resignation of the previous generation, these women showed boundless ambition. Many feared that maternity could affect their self-sufficiency. In fact, many women took the risk of compromising their fertility in their search for professional success, as Chodorow (1978) demonstrated.

Freud's female patients

My female patients were different from those Freud wrote about in Vienna in 1933. Let us hear his impressions:

> The fact that women must be regarded as having little sense of justice is no doubt related to the predominance of envy in their mental life; for the demand for justice is a modification of envy and lays down the condition subject to which one can put envy aside. We also regard women as weaker in their social interests and as having less capacity for sublimating their instincts than men.
>
> The aptitude for sublimation is subject to the greatest individual variations. On the other hand, I cannot help mentioning an impression that we are constantly receiving during analytic practice. A man of about thirty strikes us as a youthful, somewhat unformed individual, whom we expect to make powerful use of the possibilities for development opened to him by analysis. A woman of the same age, however, often frightens us by her psychical rigidity and unchangeability.
>
> Her libido has taken up final positions and seems incapable of exchanging them for others. There are no paths open to further development; it is as though the whole process had already run its course and remains thenceforward insusceptible to influence—as though, indeed, the difficult development to femininity had exhausted the possibilities of the person concerned.

My clinical data

My experience contradicts the three major statements made by Freud in relation to women – namely, that their superego development was poor; that they were rigidly set in their ways quite early in life and therefore unable to change; and that they were more self-involved than men. Not surprisingly, I found my patients to be capable of intense moral and noble judgment, in great part to the detriment of their self-esteem. They were eager to search into their own internal worlds and yet they felt responsible for the well-being of their partners and other members of their families, often to a greater extent than did their partners. Their masochistic stance did not appear to be innate – that is, an instinctual vicissitude inherent in women – but a solution to complex infantile object relations that were then reproduced in adulthood. Could the contrast between Freud's observations and the ones I present be due to cultural changes over a few decades?

Gender norms in Western society have evolved considerably from Freud's (1925; 1931) Victorian age, to the 1970s, 1980s, and 1990s (when I collected data for my paper), and until today. These shifts have greatly influenced the ways in which women experience their roles. Feminism, while a work-in-progress, has become normative for the educated middle and upper classes and has affected gender roles for both men and women. As I stated before, today's young woman in urban America has ambitions of her own, no longer attained through, or tethered to, her partner's achievements. She feels entitled to those ambitions and is more likely to be aware of her needs. Her experiences have permitted her to be aware of her patterns of sexual excitement, her conditions for obtaining pleasure, her requirements for her partner's achievements in relation to her own, whether the partner is hetero- or homosexual.

Was Freud's depiction of female patients attributable to his immersion in the patriarchal and misogynist views prevalent during the Victorian era? Or alternatively, has the presentation and symptomatology of female patients radically changed because of gender-related cultural and historical changes?

These are difficult questions to answer, and my goal here is not to come to a definitive conclusion. However, it is worthwhile to posit that we may be witnessing an ongoing dialectical shift between culturally normative gender roles and the formation of female gender identity at oedipal and pre-oedipal stages. While Freud and many of his disciples saw his portrayal of women as describing innate characteristics resulting from an inevitable oedipal triangle, it is becoming clear that cultural changes are creating new oedipal configurations, new object relations constellations, and consequently changes in female subjectivity and identity. Female aggression, affirmation, and ambition are becoming compatible with a sense of deep-rooted femininity.

As I stated before, the patients I see are, for the most part, highly educated, urban professionals who live in New York City. Have these changes taken place in other American communities?

In an article that appeared in *The New York Times* in September 2019, Campbell Robertson reported on an interesting development that took place between the years 2010 and 2017 in a community in Kentucky when thousands of miners lost their jobs. The job losses precipitated the need for women to go to work to support their families. Husbands and wives had to adjust their expectations of family life to deal with their difficult economic condition. Many of the wives decided to finish college and get a nursing degree. This sudden and disorienting situation led many of the now jobless men into depression and drug addiction, as they now had to pick up the domestic chores that their wives had performed, and, in the process, losing their sense of manhood. However, when the situation shifted back to a more balanced one, most women decided to continue working, as their horizons had opened, and men accepted it. This is an example of how, in a few years, gender role expectations and the balance of power can shift in a surprising way. Robertson called his article "In Coal Country, the Mines Shut Down, the Women Went to Work and the World Quietly Changed." I can only assume that this change did not take place as quietly as it appeared to be. Even though the men were grateful for the women's work, their self-esteem was deeply affected, albeit temporarily.

Could examples like this one permit us to think that the patriarchal traditions transmitted through the centuries are becoming more amenable to change? Could men's fear of being dispossessed of the expected role of provider, of control, of power, be so rapidly surmounted? We remember how, during the Second World War, women in this country were urged to go to work in industries needed to sustain the war, albeit at a reduced pay from the men. Once the war ended, however, they were discouraged from continuing their work outside the home, as those jobs were required once again by the men. But could those changes have remained? Hopefully today, the influence of the feminist ideals can prevail and prevent such a reversal.

Important shifts are happening in the culture, yet the power of the patriarchal system is still in full force and effect. Its influence is felt through the fear of being influenced, to be feminized into "the weaker one," of losing potency, and of losing the right to possess and dominate. This patriarchal system, where one partner has the power to dominate and devalue the other, has swayed the behavior of both genders. I have observed many marital relationships where the woman presents as the one who controls, who dismisses the other, or shows intolerance for differences. In those instances, the protagonists have changed sides, but psychologically the patriarchal system is maintained. We are still under a system lacking an equitable, mutual, and creative collaboration.

Are difficulties in today's couples in the western world determined by their gender?

We should differentiate patterns in relationships where the constraints of the accepted inequality of rights between genders is predominant from the patterns in relationships in societies where women are no longer weighed down by those sociocultural norms. I have demonstrated the transitions taking place between different generations over some decades of psychoanalytic practice. For some women and men those transitions have been slow and helped by psychotherapy; for others, they have happened rapidly and dramatically. I have also compared my view of women with Freud's view of the women of his time (six decades earlier) and wondered if women were seen in a different light due to sweeping cultural changes or because the observer did not question the social norms under which they lived. In that direction, Leticia Glocer Fiorini (2015) has emphasized women as being defined as the "other," different, and enigmatic. She underlines the "subject/object polarity" being related by Freud to sexual difference: the subject, the observer, being masculine, active, in possession of a penis, while the feminine, the object, is passive, and does not have the penis – a definition of the feminine in terms of a negative.

In the last decade, I have heard both women and men complain about the experience of being emotionally and sexually ignored by their partners and disregarded in their opinions or in their wish for togetherness. It is not that gender differences are not important, but I have noticed that those conflicts were based not in gender-expected behaviors but on difficulties between the partners' temperaments, their dissimilar needs for intimacy, dialogue, or sensuous expression and often based on neurotic solutions to early trauma, unconscious guilt, complex recreations of family situations, or unconscious fear of being taken over and/or succumbing to dependency or regression. These differences, often misinterpreted in meaning and intention, lead to disillusionment, dissatisfaction, and blame, interfering with a fruitful dialogue, and stalemating change. Understandably, given the preceding cultural patterns, and the insistence of many self-help books' description of those fixed behaviors as gendered, couples have tended to label each other's behaviors as gender related and, consequently, almost insurmountable. However, in treatment, both men and women have been able to move away from this simplistic categorizing of each other's differences and develop curiosity and interest in the meaning, origin, and impact of those behaviors. And – to a great extent and sometimes with great effort – they were able to shift perspectives and attitudes, which greatly benefited their relationship.

The following clinical examples of individual treatments highlight the complexity underneath what appears to be a gender-related situation.

I first met Monique when she was 48, shortly after she had attempted to jump off the terrace of her hotel room in the south of France. She was in crisis as she had just learned that her husband was emotionally engaged with a much younger woman and was still mourning the death of her father who had passed away four months earlier.

During three years of intense and fruitful work, we learned that her father, a writer, who was reported to be a formidable tyrant, instilled in her the passion for reading and writing and that she felt estranged from her mother, whose interests were vastly different from hers. The most embarrassing and guilt-laden memory of her childhood revolved around sexual games that she played with her younger brother, whom she despised because he was mother's favorite. In contrast to Monique's brilliance, her brother had severe learning problems, was perhaps even intellectually and developmentally disabled. Monique blamed herself for her brother's defects, thinking her seduction of him resulted in his learning and developmental issues. As though to remind her forever for this "crime," Monique's husband-to-be found her sexual freedom with him unbecoming. He felt that her sexuality was not "lady-like" and her intelligence, oppressive. He further confirmed Monique's already established unconscious myth: that her influence on men could be malignant and her sexuality and her creativity dangerous.

Monique, in her desolation, was at first totally focused on being abandoned, rejected, and betrayed in favor of a hated rival. However, during the first few weeks of treatment, she began to recall that she had thought, shortly after her marriage, that she should have divorced her husband. His sensitivity and sophistication were far from matching hers. Consciously, her fear of being alone and her fear of being accused of rebelliousness by her parents made her maintain the unhappy marriage. We learned that her need to punish herself for her early sexual crime was probably a more powerful motive than the reasons she gave for maintaining the marriage. Although her despair and hateful vengeance were, at times, intense, Monique was able to surmount them and examine the structure of her marital relationship and its origins. In a rather short time, Monique reviewed conceptions of herself and others, and of family relationships. In so doing, she extricated herself from her lifeless marriage.

It often happens that, at a tender age, afraid of loneliness and desirous of nesting, a woman (probably men, too) foregoes her freedom. She may ally herself with unconscious repressive forces that limit her development, under the guise of "falling in love." Monique could now see all the signs of her unconsciously carefully planned entrapment. In this summary of our work, I am underlining the importance of Monique setting her mate up in the role of a castigating presence, one who looked down on her. She converted her husband into an idealized authority, while unconsciously denying his limitations. Love, a powerful force that should lead toward unforeseen enrichment, had, in Monique's situation, become a formidable obstacle to her expansion and creativity.

Jacqueline, now 54, at 20 years old married a man 15 years her senior, presented a comparable scenario. In fact, Jacqueline, a caring mother of two children, came to see me because she was thoroughly discontented with her marriage and was considering leaving her husband of 31 years. Her beloved father was terminally ill when she decided to marry a man she admired for his integrity. After several months of therapy, it was easy for us to understand that Henry helped Jacqueline regain the presence of her beloved father and gratify her wish to remain forever in the position of daughter. Clearly, the fulfillment of these wishes limited Jacqueline's capacity for expansion. Although Henry appeared from her descriptions to be tense, prone to anger, rivalrous, loud, and scrupulously controlling of the family finances, Jacqueline recognized that he was also highly responsible, accountable, and that, in his own withdrawn, silent, and moody way, he loved her.

She hated his superficiality and preoccupation with financial matters. The terror Jacqueline experienced when eliciting Henry's anger (which he expressed through silent withdrawal and tension) was clarified when we understood that if she became an adult, an independent woman vis à vis her husband, she was once again confronted with her father's death. Her terror and ensuing hatred were the result of an unconscious trade-off: better a daughter than a mature wife. The recognition of her need to remain a "daughter," enslaved to the authority of an often-capricious father-like character, appeared more evident to her as time went on.

Having the freedom to explore the world and being able to act on desire for adventurous realms of experiences and knowledge are very often interrupted in the name of a marital relationship or the need for a family. The enjoyment that these situations provide might bring genuine and total contentment to some, but for others, they become justifications for a process of arresting growth. Very often the tradeoff involves an unconscious pact. In Jacqueline's case, a wish to keep her father alive through her position of dutiful (in her marriage, subjugated) daughter, in Monique's case, the need to find, at the height of her productivity and expansiveness, a repressive force: a husband who berated her creativity and policed her sexuality which she herself considered criminal.

Under those unconscious circumstances, a burgeoning freedom of woman-hood becomes sealed, exactly at the point where it could be enhanced through marriage and motherhood.

In his book "El Psicoanálisis Interrogado" (*Psychoanalysis Interrogated*, pp. 67–70, 2014) Julio Moreno emphasizes the vertiginous changes that have taken place in the last 70 years in terms of the variety of modes of being, of relating, of self-experience, and of different subjectivities that have evolved from generation to generation compared to the changes that occurred in the preceding years. From harmonious transgenerational continuity, we have experienced extraordinary disruptions and radical changes, which distinguish the five generations since the Second World War.

In fact, at present, "gender" has been re-signified and distributed among partners to the point of being barely recognizable by traditional criteria. In our culture, "feminine" and "masculine" have always been a binary pair that define each other and refer to complementary qualities (e.g., passive vs. active, receptive vs. penetrating, etc.) as well as to complementary functions. But gender-related problems were much more evident a few decades ago than in today's marital relationships. While half a century ago diverging from those expected gendered behaviors created severe dissention, in today's couples this binary conceptualization of gender has been subject to radical revision and has been re-conceptualized as a continuum: roles are easily interchangeable in the household, and either sex can show a multiplicity of expressions of their masculine and feminine "traits" that are far from being categorically established.

Who, for example, holds the "feminine position" in a couple today? Are the "feminine" gender attributes of tenderness, empathy, and sensitivity restricted to the female in a heterosexual couple? Isn't the feminine present in both members of the couple? How are so-called "feminine" and "masculine" roles distributed in a couple? Or, when it comes to parental functions, how are they determined in a homosexual couple? Unquestionably, when it comes to an individual's object choice or object of desire, these days it seems clear that it is virtually independent of an individual's gender identifications.

Indeed I have noticed that, with increasing frequency, men are more free to present with the so-called "feminine attributes": more contemplative, passive, dependent, and attached; more empathic, emotionally tuned, tender, and interested in creating a family an following the emotional life of their offspring. This reveals a great variation from one individual to another that I suspect has existed in a veiled way long before the feminist movement, but which has certainly been intensified by it. Inasmuch as women have suffered the consequences of restricting expectations based on gender, the same has happened to men. The canonical belief that female equals feminine and that male equals masculine has led to a profound misreading of the complex and singular qualities of everyone.

Of course, what each member of the couple has fantasized and expected about her or his role in the couple will have a great impact on their ability

to tolerate the reality of everyday life. But gender, like other traits and ten-
dencies, is co-constructed in a couple. The sense of gender-roles needs to
be altered and expanded, even transformed, while creating a couple.

(Abelin-Sas Rose and Mezan 2019)

Below is a vignette that illustrates this point.

Claire and Steven faced a profound crisis in their long and mainly contented
marriage. For a year he had maintained a secret love affair with a professional
colleague. Upon learning of this situation, Claire was deeply shocked and in
utter disbelief. Her despair surprised Steven who had believed her to be so
independent and solid that she did not ever "need him" for her happiness. Over
the years he had felt that his emotional expressions gave his wife the impression
that he was weak and needy. He was the one who missed their oldest child the
most when he left for college. In fact, he had hidden his grief from her for fear
of her disdain and criticism.

Now in treatment, wondering how they could move forward, the couple
recognized that in the three years preceding the affair a dynamic of this sort
had intensified. Claire reported that she had felt distant and unable to connect
emotionally to her husband. She stated that she did not recognize herself in
that attitude. Was it the departure from home of their second child that made
it more conspicuous? Or, perhaps more pertinently, the death of Steven's
father? He described his father as a rigid and cruel tyrant with no capacity
for emotional resonance, who was extremely critical of Steven and his sisters.
Had Steven's father's death precipitated a profound and effective transference
from Steven to Claire, who was then unconsciously persuaded to play that
part? She did recount feeling "transformed" into an unfeeling and critical
wife. Certainly, the elements of this dynamic had been there before. Claire
tended to be exacting with words and deeds. She evidently became less so
in the middle of this great crisis that had shaken her sense of integrity and
identity.

Given the fact that he felt deeply undervalued, Steven had sought solace in
the arms of a colleague who admired and supported him, who experienced his
emotions as enriching her world and sought to learn from him. His self-esteem
felt greatly improved, and yet he never considered leaving the marriage until
Claire gave him an ultimatum.

This may well be a situation that we have seen many times, but the reason
that I bring it up is to show how the characteristics that we often attribute to
one gender over the other are here, as in many other marriages, crossing the
limits of those attributions. Steven was more emotional, more insecure, and
more accepting and tolerant than Claire, as well as being more self-reflecting.
However, they both realized that the world of feelings was not part of their
dialogue. It was a world that had not been explored by either one. Steven
now realized that he had deferred to Claire's point of view to define his self
and his own value: she was his weathervane. Claire also realized that she was
as disturbed by his surrender to her directives as Steven felt enslaved by them.

Finding that Claire needed him to sustain her stance of apparent independence was surprising to Steven. He had no idea of the important role he played in maintaining her sense of strength and neither did Claire.

Not having access to a world of feelings and self-reflection, this couple was unable to embrace and understand their different sensitivities or how to deal with situations that demanded an expansion of the gender roles they were familiar with. Mainly, Claire's expectations for the masculine role in the marriage demanded that her husband be an unemotional and secure pillar of strength, regardless of circumstances. Similar gender beliefs were present in Steven. As for many men over the centuries, he had been expected to feel ashamed of his vulnerabilities and deep emotions, to the detriment of his identity. He surrendered his self-expression to the requirements of his more controlled and controlling wife while secretly resenting the constraints on him. The outcome was a desperate need to find solace in a new relationship that offered him the freedom he had relinquished. The couple reached a new and lasting stability when these hidden dynamics were brought to light.

> Even though important cultural sociological changes have taken place, couples tend to use essentialized gender positions to explain their difficulties. That is, they tend to "genderize" their conflicts, which leads to a facile explanation of their problems, but does not offer them any avenue of change. It only limits their understanding.

This brief vignette illustrates the pitfalls of the tendency to interpret couple discord within that binary system which ignores the complexity of an intimate relationship.

Greg found Marianne, a divorced mother of a lovely little girl, to be charming and sophisticated. When they married, he moved into her apartment, thus joining a well-organized family. He had to embrace certain rules of behavior that were alien to him such as taking off his shoes when he came into the house, buying only organic produce, recycling, and cleaning the kitchen after an elaborate dinner prepared daily by his wife. He adored her and her daughter and his contentment became total when they had a child of their own. But, there was a problem. He had a temper and, if tired, he tended to interpret someone's disagreement with him as provocative and as justifying an explosion of anger. Those explosions were short-lived, and he apologized for the upheaval he created.

To Marianne, those were, understandably, infantile, and unacceptable. She experienced them as deeply disturbing; he was not the man she had married; he became a total stranger for whom she had no empathy. She felt that he acted like most men did, and she wanted out of this bullying prison. During his rages, Greg would say things that shocked her deeply such as that she was controlling and demanded his submission. Was that his real image of her? Marianne was confused especially since at other times Greg idealized her to such an extent that it felt uncomfortable.

Greg was shocked that she wanted out of the relationship. The mere fact that this crossed her mind made him doubt the seriousness of her commitment. Had he married a volatile female? It was quite clear to me that Greg felt easily sidelined. I had heard him say that he "folded" in relation to his having freely agreed to something he had first opposed. Negotiating and changing positions or abandoning a point of view to another was experienced by him as being enslaved, submissive.

I might have wondered if his sense of masculinity were at risk; if his concept of maleness meant that he should have the authority and the last word in all aspects of their lives. However, it seemed to me that the issue was not a gendered one but one that had to do with the fear of being taken over by someone else's will, which interfered with his accepting and embracing of their dissimilarities. In that sense he was losing the opportunity of learning from his wife new approaches to a variety of situations. For instance, in sessions, moving to a "meta" level of communication, he would often declare that what Marianne wanted to discuss was irrelevant or stupid. Those declarations bent the dialogue toward his defining the value of the subject rather than dealing with their differences.

In fact, I learned that Greg was the child of very contentious parents, and it was difficult for him to feel respected by them. They had trouble accepting that they did not always have a monopoly on truth. Instead of framing his behavior in an essentializing way, I noticed Greg's identification with parents that hampered his self-respect, a pattern he repeated with his spouse. Marianne was impressed by this discovery as well as compassionate about his lonely and difficult position in childhood. I also learned that Marianne's mother had abandoned a scientific career when she gave birth to her and that she explicitly and verbally attributed her depression to her giving up this career for motherhood, which instilled a sense of guilt in her young daughter – a practice that she continued to the present.

To me, Greg's criticisms of Marianne during his tantrums echoed her being accused of an original sin, the one of having been born. She felt so unjustly injured that she was unable to confront the infantile and fleeting quality of his complaints. At those times, his behavior erased his more positive traits. In her eyes, he became a violent bully she despised. I therefore concentrated on the historical data that created Marianne's specific sense of self and her need to be rescued from her existential sense of guilt and Greg's easily elicited sense of being disregarded and disrespected. Those historical situations recreated an entangled web of painful traumatic situations. Once they became aware and sensitive to those, this couple was able to regain their affectionate closeness.

Rather than emphasizing a gender issue, I put the emphasis on unconscious conflicts that originated in childhood, defensive stances, unsuspected identifications, arrested or displaced mourning, transferences, misreading of intentions, misinterpretations, and difficulties with dissimilarities. I examine intergenerational family relationships, the results of immigration, historical traumas that have affected previous generations, and cultural differences.

In other words, when we can move away from stereotyped roles it becomes evident that the problems of coexistence are often based on an array of issues other than gender-related ones, such as fear of merging or loss of an independent identity, or of the repetition of traumatic family patterns. It is the richness that emerges from elucidating those issues that stimulates profound changes in couples.

Gender relations vary greatly depending on the culture or the social group the couple inhabits. As I have mentioned before, women who live in societies that demean them and curtail their rights to equal treatment may have to struggle not only externally but internally to re-position themselves vis à vis men's roles. Let us keep in mind that in 1959 Swiss men voted against giving women the right to vote in federal elections and in several cantons (Swiss states) women endorsed that decision. Their right to participate in federal elections was not obtained until 12 years later, in 1971. However, the struggle to change this law was first started in 1868! A hundred years of feminist work was needed for this evolution to take place. Unchallenged generational and gender roles are often experienced as safe models even though they are obsolete.

Today, in the Western world, the general trend is toward an inquisitive examination of the mores of previous generations. Additionally, cyberspace has opened a realm of social information and cultural questioning that has and may continue to elicit unexpected new developments. I believe that women and men today would like to be understood in their singularity, much beyond their gender, as complex and forever-developing human beings while a responsive embrace of their evolving otherness is essential to retain a pleasurable intimacy and commitment.

References

Abelin-Sas Rose, G. (2010). "Are women still in danger of being misunderstood?" In *Freud's Femininity*. London: Karnac, pp. 144–159.

Abelin-Sas Rose, G., Mezan, P. (2019). "The feminine in the couple today." International Psychoanalytic Meeting.Chodorow, N.J. (1978). *The Reproduction of Mothering*. Berkeley, CA: University of California Press.

Freud, S. (1925). *Some Psychical Consequences of the Anatomical Distinction between the Sexes*. S. E. *19*:248–260. London: Hogarth Press, 1955.

Freud, S. (1931). *Female Sexuality*. S. E. *21*:225–246. London: Hogarth Press, 1955.

Freud, S. (1933). *Femininity*. S. E. *22*:112–134.

Gilligan, C. (1982). *In a Different Voice: Psychological Theory and Women's Development*. Cambridge, MA: Harvard University Press.

Glocer Fiorini, L. (2015). *La diferencia sexual en debate*.Buenos Aires: Lugar Editorial.

Klein, M. (1937). *Love, Guilt and Reparation*. New York: The Free Press.

Kristeva, J. (1982). *The Powers of Horror: An essay on Abjection*. transl. L.S. Roudiez. New York, NY: Columbia University Press.

Miller, J.B. (1976). *Toward a New Psychology of Women*. Boston, MA: Beacon Press.

Moreno, J. (2014). *Ser Humano*. Buenos Aires: Letra Viva.

Robertson, C. (Sept. 15, 2019). "In Coal Country, the Mines Shut Down, the Women Went to Work and the World Quietly Changed." *The New York Times*.

Sanders, R. (2017). "The History of Women and Money in the United States in Honor of Women's History Month." One Advisory Partners blog post.

The New York Times (July 3, 2020). "U.K. Domestic Abuse Soared Despite Warnings." *The New York Times*.

United Nations Office on Drugs and Crime (2019). Global Study on Homicide 2019. Unites States National Human Rights Commission on Mexico.

Winnicott, D.W. (1949). "Hate in the Counter-Transference" *The International Journal of Psycho-Analysis, XXX* (Part 2):194–203.

7 Women and psychoanalysis across generations and diversities

What do women want now: not answers but questions

Adrienne Harris, Kirsten Lentz, Shubha Herlekar, June Lee Kwon, Romy Reading, and Julie Leavitt

INTRODUCTION

Adrienne Harris

Having participated in several COWAP-initiated conferences on Gender and subjectivity (broadly speaking) I began to collect my thoughts in response to Margarita Cereijido's invitation to contribute to a book organized through an International Psychoanalytical Association (IPA) committee: Committee on Women and Psychoanalysis. The book they propose is to be called: What do Women Want Today?

I decided to open up the project, indeed to make it a polylogue. I invited colleagues whose age and training and focus on gender and subjectivity, very broadly conceived, would be both linked and distinct. I wanted us to think across generation, orientation, passions, self-definition, and passions. I set up three questions for all of us to consider.

1   What are your current ideas about the way gender, sexuality and human subjectivity function in a relational context? What texts and ideas have influenced you? What clinical dilemmas most interest you?
2   What are the ways that you, as a woman analyst practice self-care? How are work and life projects in tension and integrated in your experience? I have written about the difficulties therapists of many kinds have in self-care. There may be particular strains on women in this regard as well.
3   How does ambition operate in your understanding of your work and your professional development? Again, ambition is often a complex structure for women.

To my immense delight, all these writers read these instructions and wrote in their own unique idiom, achieving so much more than I could have imagined.

DOI: 10.4324/9781003180036-10

My contribution

As I currently think of gender and its interlocution with other aspects of our subjectivity; class, race, culture, sexuality, and generation, I try and stand in a complex site, where these experiences are both fluid and fixed. In homage to ideas of Jacqueline Rose (2016), I feel we need to see that gender is often a matter of *suffering*. We are captured and interpellated and defined by the exacting requirements of how to be/do/perform/enact our subjectivities. We call it interpellation, a force in which the State, engaging in various social forces of conformity and authority demand our dutiful attention. Erving Goffman put it in a funnier but no less lethal way in his book *Stigma: The Management of Spoiled Identity*. "In an important sense there is only one complete unblushing male in America: a young, married, white, urban, northern, heterosexual Protestant, father, college educated, fully employed, of good complexion, weight, and height, and a recent record in sports" (Goffman, 1963, p.128).

We are all casualties of these socio-political interventions. The news is delivered with humor, with deadly violence, with contempt. Fanon (2008) defined this problematic for black men with the term "phobogenic." In the racism environment – he writes of Europe, we can see this in America, the black male body is phobogenic, that it is desired and feared and the consequences of this are, as we are attesting to in the protests around Black Lives Matter, catastrophic, murderous.

So we live in deep contradiction around gender. There is remarkable fluidity in the lived experiences of many. Gender nonbinary, trans, cis. Our useful metaphors are "rhizomes," or strange attractors, from nonlinear dynamic systems theory. These structures or assemblies are complex, emergent, unpredictable and our theories range across many variables: intrapsychic, intersubjective, transactional, fluid, emergent. Perhaps we might call up Winnicott's (1971) amazing theorizing of the intrapsychic and the intersubjective, the between, the playful emergence of transitions between self and other that become complexities within subjectivities.

I have been thinking and worrying about women's ambition for probably half a century.

It was not actually an easy matter in the context of second wave feminism to find a safe place for women's ambitions. Very often within the radical movements I was part of in the 1960s, gender politics remained highly restrictive. Women across many generations in the 20th century struggle with ambition, with being envied, with the dangers of aggression and assertion (Harris 1997, 2002).

I have seen women's (and my own) anxieties over achievement and competition as a problematic encounter with envy and disapproval from others. Riviere famously wrote of this problem, calling femininity a kind of masquerade. I would call it a retreat to melancholy forms of gender, a strange enactment of a caricatured femininity in order not to unsettle others regarding a woman's talents, efforts, achievements. She wrote of this in 1929 and now a century later it can still ring true.

In my writing on self care (Harris, 2010, I have been interested in how difficult self care is for all analysts. But as I think about this matter in regard to woman, I am interested in how woman professionals practice self care, divide, and/or absorb reproductive as well as productive labor. I became interested some time ago in the particular pathway of ego precocious children negotiate disorganized attachment situations. Lyons Ruth (2003) has described patterns for what she terms Tend/Befriend which preserves some children from the dysregulating effects of disorganized attachment patters. Is there a gender divide here? How does self care coordinate with care of others?

This is my set of wishes and worries, an analyst in late middle age.

Listen now to these voices.

WOMANHOOD, QUEERNESS, AND THE SOCIAL MISFIT

Kirsten Lentz

Though my body implies it, I don't actually think of myself as a woman. I don't mean to suggest that living in my embodied gender, I would be better described as trans, non-binary, or gender-queer. Or that I somehow magically exist outside of gender's reach. I appear to all the world as a cis-gendered, white, heterosexual woman. And so, I am required to be one most of the time. In my clinical work, I have found that this experience – of feeling oneself misaligned with the identity category one's body signifies – is not singular or unusual, but rather is shared by an array of social misfits whose presumed identity is accompanied by a sense of misrecognition.

That said, my body and its significations confer upon me various kinds of social privilege and power. This cannot be stated strongly enough. Even my own suffering is shaped by *white* femininity and its structures of feeling. Whiteness invisibly universalizes itself, and in so doing, systematically erases those it constitutes as "others" – a fact that women of color have been emphasizing since Sojourner Truth's "Ain't I a Woman?" speech in 1851 (Robinson, 1851). Moreover, since I am cis-gendered and, at least in my current self-presentation, I am not legibly queer, I also benefit from the physical and emotional safety this appearance affords, even if it renders parts of me invisible in a way I would not choose. And so I proceed with some humility and with a profound unknowing about the way my experience, forged in privilege, may or may not intersect or align with those of people whose races/nations/ethnicities are different than mine.

In 1995, Judith Butler wrote:

> I use the word 'foreclosed' to suggest … a preemptive loss, a mourning for unlived possibilities … When certain kinds of losses are compelled by a set of culturally prevalent prohibitions, then we may well expect a culturally

prevalent form of melancholia, one that signals the internalization of the ungrieved and ungrievable homosexual cathexis. And where there is no public recognition or discourse through which such a loss might be named and mourned, then melancholia takes on cultural dimensions of contemporary consequence.

(Butler, 1995, p. 171)

I am interested here in the internalization of ungrieved losses when something central to the self can't be named, consciously known or formulated because it is not culturally recognized. Butler speaks here of the "homosexual cathexis," which is apt and applicable, even for those who would not identify as "homosexual," but whose experience somehow includes it.

I'll call her Desi. A depressed young woman sits on the couch in my consulting room. Cis-gendered, white, and already a successful visual artist at 27 years of age, she presents for treatment with an "identity crisis." "Queer" is the term she tentatively adopts for herself, but using this name fills her with guilt. How can she claim it, she wonders, when her own sexual experiences up until now have largely been with men? She loves her boyfriend profoundly and also yearns for more experiences with women. She cycles around and around the same painful question: how can she feel herself so fundamentally to be a *queer* person when the gender of her object choices has not, to date, "proven" it?

As I listen, I find myself remembering Eve Sedgwick's observation that our culture suffers from a "linguistic poverty" when it comes to describing human sexual diversity. Sedgwick bemoans the "tiny number of inconceivably coarse axes of categorization" we have to work with: e.g., male/female, gay/straight (Sedgwick, 1990, p. 22). In trying to expand beyond these, she composes a Kinsey-esque list of variations in sexual experience. One of the many line items is: "Many people have their richest mental/emotional involvement with sexual acts that they don't do, or even don't want to do" (Sedgwick, 1990, 25). There's a glimmer in this sentence of what Desi describes to me. But even Sedgwick's capacious list can't give a name to the self-understanding my patient tries to locate.

In sessions, Desi recounts her many failed bids to belong to a queer cohort. Her queer friends are wary of her, subtly assuming her "straightness," even though she's come out to them as queer. She describes micro-aggressions she cannot even name as such. She feels her friends' suspicion, their sense of her as inauthentic, parasitic. Worse, she agrees with them. "I'm not walking the walk," she murmurs. Internally, she feels a strong pressure to break up with her boyfriend and take on a girlfriend in order to earn her place in a queer context. But given the strength of her bond to him, this is an impossible, painful choice. The queer community, and Desi's internalization of it, has no concept of and no place for her difference.

As analysts, we all come to this work with some kind of unconscious project, an "errand," as Maurice Apprey has put it (Apprey, 2014). And, thinking relationally, we can also say that in an uncanny way, analysts draw particular patients to their practices – patients who are working through problems that are not random and not unrelated to their own. Though I can't know the extent of it, I know that one of my errands issues from a lost sense of personhood that I feel in the radio static of my lived experience as a gendered and sexualized person. It is not surprising then, that my daily work circles around how subjects come into being, the way people assign themselves identities, and especially the way cultural narratives about gender and sexuality can both open up and close down thought and meaning-making. I sit, listening for the incongruities, silences and mishaps that may elide experience.

In various and diverse ways, many people have trouble with the identity categories that have been assigned to them, particularly when it comes to "being" a "woman" or a "man," a "straight" person or a "gay" person. Similarly, some people who have chosen new designations, such as "trans," "non-binary," and "pansexual," can still find themselves woefully misconstrued, their experience reified or oversimplified, even by those within their chosen communities. These troubles should not be underestimated; they can be the source of profound suffering. We all ardently need to have a sense of ourselves and a self-narrative that can be recognized and mirrored by others. In the absence of this, we can find ourselves leading lives that feel melancholic or false.

Francisco González, in 2013, wrote,

> In the beginning, then, [there is] a negative designation: a sign that represents by absence, a tick of discontinuity in the flow of things … This gap is a breach in the figuration and naming of things, and the registration of this gap is a slow coming to consciousness of an opacity in the social mirror, of its failure to reflect some vital element of the self … We have likewise developed something of a convention in the literature of speaking of "proto-gay" children … "Proto" is a way of acknowledging a formation of sexuality that has not yet quite fully set, one that remains in the realm of preconception, not yet consummated.
>
> (González, 2013, p. 115)

González's language here attempts to name the space left by the lost signifier for the unknown self. Here it is a "tick," an absence, a trace of the gap it leaves.

If a person wrestles inside a subjectivity that is only dimly perceptible, but otherwise culturally unintelligible within their historical context, they inhabit what I call a "liminal subjectivity." Such a person may have difficulty mentalizing their own suffering, because suffering typically issues from a recognizable identity position, with its attendant, better understood narratives of trauma. But to be unknown or alien to the social body is to be elusive even to oneself and therefore to be lonesome.

And yet psychoanalysis marches forward, typically assuming identity categories that already exist. This is one of many reasons that poststructuralist cultural theory has so much to teach psychoanalysis and ought to be primary to its study. Poststructuralism questions the nature and substance of subjectivity and of "identity." It draws attention to the way subjects are social and historical, made and not born. Recognizing this would mean that the work of psychoanalysis is not to organize its subjects into already existing categories, but to make available a liminal space of becoming that exceeds them.

In 1970, Louis Althusser wrote:

> I shall then suggest that ideology 'acts' or 'functions' in such a way that it 'recruits' subjects among the individuals (it recruits them all), or 'transforms' the individuals into subjects (it transforms them all) by that very precise operation which I have called interpellation or hailing, which can be imagined along the lines of the most commonplace every day police (or other) hailing: 'Hey, you there!' ... . The hailed individual will turn 'round. By this mere one-hundred-and-eighty-degree physical conversion, he becomes a subject.
>
> (Althusser, 1984, pp. 130–131)

What an evocative image for the historical moment in which so many cell phones record the many racial interpellations that end in violence and often death.

"Hailed" is an interesting term for us here. If the concept of interpellation describes something at a cultural level, to be "hailed" is more personal, more deeply experiential. What is being asked of us by others in the minutiae of everyday life as a consequence of our embodied "appearance?" And what then are the subtle or not so subtle acts of interpersonal violence that ensue?

I used to be a woman. It was delightful. I came out as a lesbian when I was 18, and felt myself to be very much a woman who loved women. I had shaved my head, but for a long strand of bangs hanging into my eyes. In this most androgynous state, lent to me by the aesthetics of the 1980s, I felt womanly. I remember one of my first adult lovers. She and I were subjects interpellated, not only by patriarchy, but also by a countercultural, gendered discourse that had taken shape during an era of "cultural feminism," an historically specific type of feminist thought which essentialized and idealized biological womanhood, and which most certainly defined it within an implicitly white framework. In a scene bordering the parodic, I remember us, sitting naked in her bed on a sweltering August night, eating mangoes alongside her slumbering German Shepherd. She was an artist who built abstract sculptures that resembled labia.

Alongside its delights, we also suffered the threats that often come with being visibly lesbian. As we walked home at night, drunken frat boys threw bricks at us from an apartment building balcony. Near misses. Another group of white men, seeing us holding hands, circled and trapped us in broad daylight. What were they going to do?! Beat us? Rape us? Terrified, we dropped to the ground, narrowly escaping between their legs. Experiences like these gave us greater conviction that we were, indeed, "women."

In 1929, Virginia Woolf wrote:

> It was thus that I found myself walking with extreme rapidity across a grass plot. Instantly a man's figure rose to intercept me. Nor did I at first understand that the gesticulations of a curious-looking object, in a cut-away coat and evening shirt, were aimed at me. His face expressed horror and indignation. Instinct rather than reason came to my help; he was a Beadle; I was a woman. This was the turf; there was the path. Only the Fellows and Scholars are allowed here; the gravel is the place for me. (Woolf, 1929, p. 6)

Woolf describes the temporality of interpellation here, many decades before Althusser could give another voice to it. She points to the temporal gap, the moment of coming to self-consciousness, that lies between the moment of interpellation and the realization of one's place in the symbolic world.

My mother, of Nordic ancestry, was born in America during the great depression and was raised in poverty after her father abruptly and mysteriously abandoned the family. Nevertheless, she grew up to break every rule against women's ambition that existed at the time. She graduated from a prestigious university in the early 1950s and then forged her way into graduate school in a field fiercely guarded against femininity: mathematics. In the final moments of her degree program, when she was to complete the last hurdle – a thesis paper – she was given a topic by her male professors which was intended to shame her into abandoning the field. She would have to mathematically tabulate women's menstrual cycles. Thus hazed and humiliated, she left without her graduate degree. And retreated into motherhood.

I was in graduate school when Judith Butler's book, *Gender Trouble: Feminism and the Subversion of Identity* hit the shelves and blew people's minds. Butler argued that "being" a sex or gender is "fundamentally impossible" and that the "appearance of being" is only achieved through "a performative twist of language." The repetition of this performance, she argued, creates the appearance of gender as an essence, a biological fact (Butler, 1990, pp. 18–19). Many people I met seemed both awed by and also hostile toward Butler's mind. The usual complaint was that her prose was too abstruse, her diction too high-toned and philosophical to be understood. But I think this anger arose less from her writing style, and more from the fact that she was trying to materialize a human subjectivity that was as yet culturally inconceivable. And to do so required difficult prose.

Alongside other feminist theorists at the time, Butler contributed to this new kind of thinking that would soon come to be called "queer theory." At its center was a diversification and "multiplication" of "perversions," to use Michel Foucault's terminology (Foucault, 1980, p. 36). Suddenly there were no longer two genders and two sexualities, but many. And though trans identities were, as yet, unavailable – still in a proto-stage of emergence into cultural intelligibility – there was certainly more on the menu. "Queer" became a new, and less reified, kind of personage.

"Queerness" came along at a moment when both "lesbian" and "woman" were faltering for me. My own sexual and gender identity needed something more diffuse, something that felt closer to the accumulation of varied gendered and sexual experiences and expressions that had shaped my life since I was a child. Queerness gave a name to what felt unnamable in me. "Woman" felt bankrupt, old-fashioned, ill-equipped to be descriptive of my experience. "Lesbian" seemed other-worldly and inaccurate for me personally. And while "bisexual" might have been a reasonable identity peg upon which to hang my hat, the category felt humiliating, alien. It didn't seem available at a phenomenological level, as an experience that could be *lived*, certainly not in a communal way. But here, into the fray, came queerness: a generous, inclusive category, one peopled by various perverts eager for friendship, and defiant of reductive assumptions. In short, in 1990, queerness offered a utopia (Muñoz, 2009). And to be understood as "queer," without the rigidity of older gendered or sexual moorings, was thrilling.

And yet, over the course of the decades following the birth of "queerness," I have gradually become aware of its limitations as a category that can actually support the diversity of its lived experiences. While queer *theory* has blossomed and grown in directions rich and productive, the *social experience* of queerness has reverted into a more familiar phenomenology. As quickly as the sexual binarisms were dismantled and proliferated, they soon congealed again into distinct pairs: now one simply became "queer" or "straight." To put it in other terms, a queer exceptionalism developed which began to police entrance into its fold. It was perhaps too soon for sexually marginalized communities to metabolize and make operable a truly queer way of life that might have emerged from the theory. Like González's "proto-gay desire," queerness was perhaps a victim of its historical precocity (González, 2013).

Desi finds it hard to remain awake in sessions. Her eyelids are perpetually heavy. She yawns. She frequently misses sessions. We talk often about her difficulty remaining present. She says she's not finding a connection to me. She can't put her finger on it, but maybe I don't have the "lightness" or "humor" that she needs. Ever diligent, she tries to stay in treatment. But eventually she decides to take a break, during which time she is able to use our work together and to revise her sexual life in more fulfilling ways. When she returns to treatment several months later, she soon resumes her fight with sleep, missing most sessions except for the last when she tells me that she is too frustrated with herself (and perhaps, unconsciously, with me) to continue.

Boggled by the mismatch she perceived between us, and by the deeply experienced unconscious resistance she had to the work, I struggled to understand how I might have contributed to Desi's inability to make use of me. Am I not funny? Am I too heavy? Did my own private identification with her plight – no doubt enigmatically transmitted – freight or misapprehend her? Even after self-searching and supervision, I never found an explanation that was truly illuminating. But what I can say is that, in an uncanny way, Desi's alienation from her sexual community, and then also from therapy, echoed my own history of alienation from sexual and gendered identity categories and communities. It still seems so deeply poignant that the two of us could not find a place of belonging with each other in the consulting room. Instead, we enacted what I've been trying to describe here. History was not ready for an "us."

Freud's bafflement about "the dark continent" of womanhood, most of us agree, is both a product of its historical moment and a sentiment that led to some of the foundational errors of psychoanalysis, grounded as it is in sexism, racism, and xenophobia (Freud, 1926, 212). But, uncomfortably, I'll confess to sharing some of Freud's confusion. *What is a "woman" anyway?* My privilege affords me the luxury of this question, since historically I have not been excluded from the category, as Black and trans women have often been. But then again, these were the very warriors who blasted open the question of womanhood in the first place.

Since modern psychoanalysis now has had access to decades of feminist, queer, and poststructuralist theory, as well as critical race theory and theories of postcolonialism, I think we can address "what women want now" as a fictional question in need of a science-fictional answer. What we need now is an attempt – by psychoanalyst practitioners most immediately – to lean into an understanding of radical *alterity*, a search for gendered and sexual differences which exceed existing understandings of *difference* itself. Perhaps this striving will seem like an impossible ideal. But isn't this in keeping with what we, psychoanalysts, were exhorted to do by Freud himself when he asked us to listen with "evenly suspended attention?" I'll quote him now, noting the telling difficulty of his pronouns: "[If the analyst] follows his expectations, he is in danger of never finding anything but what he already knows." (1912, p. 112).

WHERE MY FEET TAKE ME...: INTRO

Shuba Herlekar

My gratitude to Adrienne for the nature of this invitation and how it has allowed me to spread my wings. I knew that psychoanalytic ideas alone would not be sufficient for all that I see and want to think about. I sensed that the standard Western academic format might stifle what I need to hear inside of me.

Could I be brave enough to let myself know one layer of what women psychoanalysts like me want: to see psychoanalytic writings decolonized and more accurately reflect the realities of our lived worlds?

The late afternoon I sat to write this piece, I had finished a long clinical day "being" with patients on various tele-formats. Through it all, hoping my presence could be felt enough as I sat with them in their suffering, steadily recognizing that my back and body were aching by the end of the last hour.

As I closed my laptop and stood to stretch, I heard a woodpecker "tap, tap, tapping" on the oak tree outside my office window, and heard the squirrels rustling across branches as they chased each other. Turned on the music app on my iPhone to listen to one of my favorite songs – Otis Redding's *Sittin' on the dock of the Bay* – a couple of times, the trance reminding me of different times I'd notice particular inflections, or how phrases meant something so different to me at different ages.

Grabbed a notebook, pen, and baseball cap (imprinted with the logo of a favorite vacation spot in Mexico, made in Bangladesh) to step outside to work in the sun. Seeing the golden grassy hillside still fills me with joy – dotted with wildflowers, interwoven with so many types of trees and bushes that I now know are connected with underground root networks that have their own ways of communicating with each other. Just nearby a covey of California quail – babies and parents – hop out from the tall grasses and skitter across the planted garden area. I smile as I see them bob in unison, together making their way through their day. A small flash of frustration as I re-notice the drip irrigation system tubing, hailed as one of our water-conservation attempts, chewed up and rendered useless by the deer and gophers who've lived on this land much longer than we have. With background noises of the hillside birds and animals and the teenaged animals in our family room enjoying a 2019 redux of comic book characters created in 1939, I wrote this piece.

> The posthuman present is both the record of what we are ceasing to be: the actual, and the seed of what we are in the process of becoming: the virtual.... .
>   It is a flow pointing in multiple directions.
>
>   Rosi Braidotti (2019) Tanner Lectures at Yale University
>   *Here I offer a metta meditation for our zoe/geo/techno-mediated,*
>   *necro-political time:*
>   *May we all grow in our capacities to see with compound eyes and to act from a*
>   *stance of ethical loving-kindness.*

My "Little Engine that Could" self has been climbing the mountain of responsibility and feels like it's entering the last stations of recognizable maturity. The list with checkmarks:

•   Multiple academic degrees with a "doctor"ate in tow, thanks to my parents love and sacrifices

- Marriage to a partner I love, two fantastic children, house, dog
- 25+ years clinical work with patients I respect deeply
- Connection to a professional community that embraced me as their first person of color graduate psychoanalyst
- Heartfelt and nourishing friendships that keep me alive

If I am lucky enough to live, learn, and love for 30 more years – *for what should I yearn?*

My Hindu voices say grandkids; sanyasa spiritual life-stage where you relinquish householder obligations; my American-dreamed parts offer images of retirement, travel, adventures, self-determinations – sprinkled with some next-level academic strivings, perhaps?

Somehow these lovely notions don't seem adequate for all that the world needs from us now.

WHAT MY FEET LEARNED WALKING ON KARVE ROAD (1979)

Though I was born in Jamaica, Queens, New York, and lived most of my life in Northern California, for a few years my parents (and I) returned home to India to be with our extended family. We lived in the town of Poona (now called Pune), in the state of Maharashtra, on Karve Road.

Our apartment was about a mile away from the Hingne Stree Shiksan Samstha – a home for widows – established by the progressive Karve family. I would walk down this busy thoroughfare to go to different shops and markets with my Mom. Vegetable stalls, flower marts with garlands of jasmine, tuberose, and marigolds hanging at their entryway. On lucky days we would walk all the way down as the road would turn and curve, sometimes to the bookstore, and then on to Vaishali restaurant next to Fergusson College, where my Mom and her friends would gather during their college days. I loved all of it.

Sometimes I'd hear whispered revelations from my aunt or uncle telling me that when my grandparents would argue, my Aji (maternal grandmother) would threaten to leave the family and live in the Hingne house – a threat on many levels to my respectable Brahmin family. I knew the words were ominous, but not exactly why… I didn't understand what would be wrong with wanting to live and learn there… and could not fathom the intricacies of shame and societal dejection that the widows were "supposed" to feel as they continued in life without their husbands.

Recently I found myself curious about the Karves and wanted to find out more. I learned the extent of their family's progressive values were deeply intertwined with believing that girls/women had the right to education, at all levels, as a means to self-reliance and freedom from societal limitations – and about the ire they drew from respectable society at the time. It came as no surprise to discover that the first woman anthropologist in India, Irawati Karve, was the founder's daughter-in-law, had been supported in completing her doctoral studies in Germany in the 1930s, and returned to teach at Pune University (amongst others) and do fieldwork throughout India, for a long and productive career.

Heartwarming to hear that Irawati Karve had also attended Ferguson College, 30 years before my Mom.

Saddened to remember that my Mom was invited to begin lecturing at Pune University – just a few months before my parents decided to move back to California instead.

Poignant to feel drawn to pioneering courage – capacities in my Aji's young adult life as she married for love and earned a bachelor's degree psychology in Lahore in 1930s – and to then watch as she never recovered from the traumas of the Partition, which shattered her external and internal worlds.

Writer, organizer, educator, and spoken work artist Walidah Imarisha, in her Introduction to *Octavia's Brood: Science Fiction Stories from Social Justice Movements* (2015) wrote:

> Visionary fiction encompasses all of the fantastic, with the arc always bending toward justice. We believe this space is vital for any process of decolonization, because it is the most dangerous and subversive form there is: for it is where all other forms of decolonization are born. Once the imagination is unshackled, liberation is limitless.

Writing in this summer of 2020, in the middle of a pandemic, another racial radicalizing reckoning, and the painful anticipation of a presidential election, we together at PINC (the Psychoanalytic Institute of Northern California) are working. To decolonize our curriculum. To denature our whiteness-based culture. To dare to imagine a psychoanalytic world where our Round Table looks more like a meeting of the United Nations than knights of King Arthur's Camelot.

We do not know how our work will go.

What do I think women want now?
FREEDOM of mind, body, and chosen connection

Outro

We cannot be visionary if we are not rooted in our histories. Without the layerings of the past, visioning seems hollow. What has been possible for me to dream, accomplish, hope to make happen in the world emerges from my transgenerational emotional *terroir*, motored by both maternal mitochondrial longings and fierce wishing for what I want my children to count on from the world. With this first foray into a new kind of writing for me, there's a visceral unbinding and light-hearted enthusiasm I long to know more about.

Perhaps it's best to leave on a note of challenge, inspiration, and mystery from one of many who blazed this liberatory path – Black science fiction writer Octavia Butler. In her novel *Parable of the Sower* (1993) she wrote these oft-quoted lines:

All that you touch,
You change.

All that you change,
Changes you.

The only lasting truth
Is change.

God is change.

It will be a personal challenge for me to swim in an internal caesura that allows me contact with both the *freedoms* I so desire, and, the profound actualities that Ms. Butler's words help us to see. I wonder how adaptation and unshackling speak to each other, in daily life? Can I keep my hand on the heart of my pain and yet be inspired by the transformations that are yet meant to be?

2020: THE INNOCENCE IS BLACK AND BLUE

June Lee Kwon

June 2020, Elisa

She tells me that her Black male friend has been beat up by white strangers in midtown Manhattan. The friend is hospitalized with serious injuries and he is refusing to report anything to the police as he does not want any potential media attention regarding his hardship. She starts wailing on my tablet screen. Her cry comes through my headphones, it is ringing in my ears, echoing in my face. Her Florida sun kissed cheeks flush red, and her tears bullet down to her chin. She had just settled into her friend's summer home after months of lone lockdown in her Brooklyn apartment, which was a few blocks away from refrigerated trucks full of dead bodies. She wipes her tears and tells me her parents fled from Hong Kong and sold her childhood home due to continued protest and chaos. A hysterical siren pierces through my window. I lay awake at night reading news and hearing sirens.

Breonna Taylor

After more than 20 bullets were shot by policemen, we were told an innocent 26-year-old Black woman named Breonna Taylor was killed. Her name has joined a row of Black men's names killed by policemen and vigilantes in 2020, and once again, it is time to #sayhername.[1] Numerous memes, including her name, blossom all over internet like wild poppies.[2] Some men are emboldened to make creative slogans incorporating her name for their business[3] and brand identity.[4] A white actress posts a nude photo of herself and claims that she uses the power of her sideboob to call attention to justice for Breonna Taylor, and she is swiftly condemned by the crowd.[5]

Artists create Breonna Taylor portraits. Daisies and roses blossom around her and she is held noble by backdrops of pink, blue, gold, and turquoise. Her brown eyes gaze poised and shine dignified with pride. Female celebrities post selfies wearing t-shirts of her portrait. Her portrait is on the Vanity Fair cover. Oprah Winfrey makes a magazine cover and billboards with Breonna's portrait.

This is how we fight for her honor and hold her life worthy. We keep her trending, visible, and advertised. Her wide brown eyes, baby cheeks, chocolate colored skin, soft shoulders, and bosom sell her name beautifully and make all of us look good. She is put to work. Breonna's Law bans policemen from entering unannounced.

Kyle Rittenhouse

On 23 August 2020, white policeman Rusten Sheskey pulls Black man Jacob Blake by his shirt and fires seven bullets in his back. Kenosha, Wisconsin burns with a fiery cry, "Black Lives Matter," "Black Lives Matter." A group of people show up with guns at night and a 17-year-old white boy named Kyle Rittenhouse from Antioch, Illinois, joins them with his rifle. The photos from the night show a boy with smooth white cheeks and soft baby pink lips looking

"Disentangling from the Gender Binary: Insisting on What Lies Beyond"
Romy Reading

> The quality of light by which we scrutinize our lives has direct bearing upon the product which we live, and upon the changes which we hope to bring about through those lives.
>
> Audre Lorde

I am seeking to find a certain "quality of light," one by which I can find a connection to the question posed, "What do women want, today?" But the landscape is murky, turbulent, muddled. And the only signage that I can see is weathered, words carved into wood – "man" and "woman." The signs point into opposite directions, one veering right, the other to the left. Do I follow the one declaring "woman"? I sense that if I do I will surely get lost, never arrive, if there is even a point of destination to be reached. So with a flashlight in hand I will head off in a different direction. The bifurcation spells danger … And I have been down that road one too many times!

The flashlight – queer theory, theories of intersectionality, and the illumination of poets – and likely more. I will be sure to name anything else that may guide me along as this unfolds.

Oh yeah … I can't forget to share … Audre Lorde gave vast encouragement to ALL to tap the reservoir of "our non-european consciousness," a source of knowledge and power that does not abide by the rules of *logos* or follow the structure of linearity. She prods and primes us, with her title "The Master's Tools Will Never Dismantle the Master's House," to give up the familiar discourses and methodologies that we are so apt to follow without question. What a provocative dare!

"I dare you; I double dog dare you!!" a gleeful entreaty. And a frightening imperative to consider. And, and, and! She offers a great comfort too. Permission to **not** invent a new idea, "For there are no new ideas. There are only new ways of making them felt …" And perhaps not even "new ways" are necessary, but simply different ways, different from what we habitually do. That is "good enough."

Aha! So we can give ourselves permission to venture away from familiar formats and discover something new for ourselves?! This is certainly one thing that this cisgender woman wants today.

In the shrouded terrain (outside of the gender binary) a great weaving, swimming, mass of intersecting thoughts emerges, a bright bolus of ideas. We have encountered these terms and constructs before – fluid, not-fixed, non-linear, dynamic shifting system, "gender performativity" (Judith Butler's groundbreaking phrase) – each points to the non-binary aspect of gender.

Yet here we are again – Back in the 0/1 … with the question as it is worded. It's a "strange attractor" (the non-linear dynamics thinkers gave us this phrase) pulling us back to a particular system of organization that wants to bridle the liminal, fix in place that which de-centers, and translate the enigmatic (Laplanche – I will return to his contributions). I know I'm not saying anything new here; many have articulated these ideas and given us elegant theories. And yet we seem to repeatedly re-instate the gender binary? Why do we struggle to fully live an ethos of non-binary understanding when we approach questions of gender? We "get it" and then we lose it (myself included). And I recognize that in the very act of trying to capture the liminal we are bound to slip and quickly grab hold of a familiar anchor. It's easy bedrock to rely on. But I want to encourage us to let ourselves slide a bit so that we do not fall into the trap of simply paying lip-service to gender fluidity. Can this become our new bedrock and starting point?

Ok so let me give it a try … What do those on the oppressed end of the gender non-binary spectrum, want today? A sobering queer intellectualism that stifles a bit. Maybe a both/and approach might help? One that honors the *conventional reality* of masculine/feminine, men/women (a phrase used by Buddhist thinkers which refers to the reality we can directly and easily experience) AND one that centers the liminal soup of gender fluidity, the plurality of gender identities. The term plurality brings me to another concept that I want to weave in – Intersectionality.

This explication requires a more formal approach:

The concept of intersectionality was born out of Black feminist thought, dating back to 1851, when Sojourner Truth repeatedly declared, "Ain't I a woman?" in her speech at a national woman's right convention in Akron, Ohio. She needed to reassert her gender identity to her fellow activists who had become fixated on her race. They, not unlike us, fail to maintain a grasp on plurality of identities – the intersectionality of the ways in which one experiences intersecting forces of oppression. Later Black feminist activists in the 1960s, 1970s, and 1980s (Angela Davis, Audre Lorde, Combahee River Collective, and bell hooks) carried forth the ideas of intersectionality. In 1989, Kimberlé Crenshaw, a legal scholar, introduced the concept in a paper which described how the US law elides the unique combination of racism and sexism by treating them separately (Crenshaw, 1989).

I give this brief history in order to counter erasure. In my early exposure to intersectionality in graduate school I had learned that it began with Crenshaw. The elitism of academia can blind.

Now activists and scholars from across fields speak about intersectionality. Of key importance, intersectionality emphasizes the unique effects of the intersection of social forces of oppression **and** privilege, which shift based on context. It's not simply a listing of multiple identities. Yes, once again the emphasis is on fluidity and complexity.

I feel a cognitive strain as I try to hold on to this complexity, like trying to grab hold of water. It's there. I see that it is there; but it defies possession. Laplanche (phew … I am keeping my word and bringing him back) understood this dilemma deeply. When theorizing about the formation of the sexual unconscious (which for him *is* the unconscious – no distinction) and the ego, he articulated how essential our "translations" are to psychic functioning. They comprise the ego and demonstrate our attempt to organize the enigmatic messages from the sexual unconscious of the other. Yet there always remains an enigmatic residue – an untranslatable charge that defies symbolization and will be housed as the receiver's sexual unconscious. This charge can propel "de-translation," helping us to enter a state of not-knowing, a liminality out of which something new can emerge (must emerge or else we risk becoming psychotic). Fantastic! We all want to have new ideas emerge and YET we love the containment of known translations – two of our favorites are the gender binary and the social construction of whiteness/race.

So it requires a psychic surrender in order to find moments of de-translation?! The implication is not that we should completely cast aside these translations. We couldn't if we tried and a terrifying shattering of ego and psyche are the not the point. These constructions are "strange attractors," norms that shape and act on us. We can never fully step outside of them – but we can try to get a foot, an arm, the right side of the brain – or the left – to stretch past their edges.

So I'll try again to queer the original question: (Queer as a verb refers to the critique and dismantling of, not only heteronormativity, but also the multiple systems of hierarchy and disparity – generous heaps of de-translation and deconstruction).

What do you want today for ALL the oppressed female-identified in our world, for those designated as other than MAN?

A path is emerging … I can move. It's not optimal – the words are too small, they can't capture. They never fully do – but I can see new signage in the clearing. Others are walking by my side. Everyone has a light source, each with a distinct "quality of light." And I hear many answers to the question. And I answer as a White-presenting, Latinx, queer, Buddhist, mixed-class, cisgender female-identified person. I inhabit both privileged and subjugated positions depending on the who, what, when, and where that constitute the given moment. Too many times I have consciously and/or unconsciously housed myself within the identity that is easily intelligible and manageable for others (and me). In doing so I have been dislodged from the "phobogenic" (homage to Fanon) parts of myself. Not today.

These answers are calls to action, entreaties for awareness, and a reclamation of desire and subjectivity.

They are aspirational wishes.

May we …

> Continue to fight against gender-based violence – the retaliatory hate and rage of injured masculinity seems to know no limits
>
> As women in positions of privilege, include the desires and experiences of those who do not hold these positions – This is no time for "the friendly face of cheap alliance" – Audre Lorde
>
> Fight to stop sexual harassment and its effect of bewilderment that induces despairing confusion and feeds the perpetrator's sadistic perversion (Thank you, Virginia Goldner for your analysis of the dynamics at work in harassment)
>
> Have parity of pay!
>
> See that care for others at the expense of the self is not our mandate (especially true for therapists)
>
> Believe that confidence and ambition are not dirty words. They are connected to Eros (not only Logos)
>
> Dismantle the gender binary so that we are not reifying patriarchal constructs
>
> Find solidarity between trans/cis/queer/gay/lesbian and hetero women
>
> Preserve the right to choose which labors our bodies will perform
>
> No longer collapse gender and avoid seeing the effects of sexism and patriarchy in our lives

Vanquish complacency in order to keep each other awake and speaking

I hope that as you read this incomplete list that you were adding your own desires and demands.

WHAT WOMEN DON'T NEED NOW: MISOGYNY BETWEEN WOMEN

Julie Leavitt

> When a White woman cries, Black people die.
> Overheard by the author at a colloquium on "Coloniality," 2018

Introduction

"What do women want now?"

Such a complicated question! First, at the interface between the one posing it and the one contemplating it: here, both "white women," (Dr. Harris and myself): both self-identified "feminists," both psychoanalysts. Problematics of identity generalizations notwithstanding, that this essay lives in tension between this particular pair matters: the ways we share elements of lived experience, the ways we don't, and all the assumptions in between.

And who's listening? Given the "great question"[6] framing this book, I imagine it will by and large be *white* women. But bear with me: my intention is not to dismiss the critical presence of women of color here (whether their actual presence as with some of my fellow authors of this chapter, or their present absence). In fact I hope to harness the attention of all women – indeed all feminists – to strategize how, in this time of great momentum around examining racial inequities and social divides, we can forge generative contact and mobilize coalition-building between white women and women of color. This is my charge, to assert to white women in particular that this will require first that (as white women) we identify and confront the ways in which we have in so many ways been blind to the existence of, the experiences of, the needs of, the "wants" of, the women of color living alongside us.

Unpacking and historicizing signifiers

Before going further though, it is important to briefly name the generalizations already implied in the question "what do women want now?" itself. For example, to whom does "*women*" actually refer "*now*" – in the 21st century – given late 20th century Copernican-turn gender deconstruction, performativity, trans/gender non-binarism, etc. And are we talking about individual women? "*The* women" as a collective? "Women" as a generalization? What about differences re: age, race and economic/educational class, body-ability, and place-in-the-world: cultural place, and social positioning vis à vis capitalism/class elitism, the patriarchy, social privilege? Holding these critically worthy factors in mind, the *disparate* experiences of misogyny and sexism[7] toward people who are perceived as, socialized as and related to as "female" is sadly relevant: the (interpellative *and* concrete) laws that, *inequitably among women*, constrict and compromise rights, freedoms, safety, bodies … and yes, sexualities. The *who* and the *when* of this question as such get complicated very fast.

And then there's the "Want" of women: is this desire in the psychoanalytic sense? Something about female sexuality per se, and if so, sexual identity or sexual behavior? And *whose* sexuality or sex – as in who truly owns and governs women's sexuality? Who also, women's bodies? It seems that in so many ways much of psychoanalysis has followed [led?] sociopolitics in pushing female heterosexuality into tight corners of acceptability, toward invisibility – or at best, into a mirage in a two-way mirror reflecting male sexuality in the male gaze. Through that lens, the "power" of female desire is forever binarily locked into "feminine v. masculine" desire. And female-queer desire? Psychoanalysis and sociopolitics struggle to find its way there much at all, beyond another two-way mirror – the one that refracts it in juxtaposition to that vanishing female heterosexual desire just mentioned.

This anchors the psychoanalytic legacy of the question at hand – Freud's question – which, per Ernst Jones,[8] Freud asked M. Boneparte at some unknown time. Indeed, from Ernst Jones' telling (where reference to this question originates) it is clear that Jones could not but contextualize Freud's query about women's desire within the frame of Freud's desire. Here is the context, from Jones' intimate biography of Freud (Jones, 1955):

> If judged by it alone Freud's attitude to women would probably be called rather old-fashioned… it might perhaps be fair to describe his view of the female sex as having as their main function to be ministering angels to the needs and comforts of men. His letters and his love choice make it plain that he had only one type of sexual object in his mind, a gentle feminine one. While women might belong to the weaker sex, however, he regarded them as finer and ethically nobler than men; there are indications that he wished to absorb some of these qualities from them.
>
> There is little doubt that Freud found the psychology of women more enigmatic than that of men. He said once to Marie Bonaparte: **"The great question that has never been answered and which I have not yet been able to answer, despite my thirty years of research into the feminine soul, is 'What does a woman want?'"**
>
> Freud was also interested in another type of woman, of a more intellectual and perhaps masculine cast. Such women several times played a part in his life, accessory to his men friends though of a finer calibre, but they had no erotic attraction for him. …
>
> Freud was quite peculiarly monogamous…

And what of Boneparte's response? Of that, there is no record.

Therefore, it's necessary here to introduce other questions: Who actually cares about women's *own – articulated or inarticulable – desire?* Does theinquisition *qua women* really matter in terms of actual opportunities for change? If so, how is change possible?

Although general and provocative, I don't mean for my questions here to be rhetorical. In fact I am trying to counter the question itself – originally born, in psychoanalysis anyway, from a man's curiosity, gaze, and intellectual query – by drilling down to what this question might actually mean for women, about women, from women, now. Let me interject here a spoiler about the historical underpinnings that pave the way to where I'm ultimately headed: that it is ana- lyzable that this same man, the father of psychoanalysis, referred to women's sexuality as "the dark continent." The intersectionally elided significance here is critical.[9]

Now: care of self = care of collective

In 2020 US, we are living in a time of acute danger – of malignant-capitalist/ authoritarian aims by government leaders and with extreme vulnerability to global conditions like advancing climate change and serial pandemics. With that, communities are dramatically confronted with the mass social disruption and ills both revealed and exacerbated by the impacts of these dangers. What has been revealed is in so many ways linked to pre-existing, pernicious race-, class- and gender-inequities: pre-existing disparities of poverty, lack of safe housing and health care, hate-based violence, state violence and domestic violence, grave cultural hostage-taking by people with the immediate means to commit gun violence. "On the ground" is where US society finds itself: forced, at last, to face our 400 year history for indigenous genocide; Afro-Black enslavement; entrenched nationalism and its twin, reactive xenophobia; the resultant and ongoing pain and oppression of marginalized peoples; and real social/cultural/ political breakdown (breakdown not just *into reality*, but *of social-cultural realities*). I rattle off these sociocultural-historical afflictions like so many others do, but they bear naming again and again: as a country and a global society we need to examine, account and atone for them. As Audre Lorde reminded us, while feminist movements prioritize social injustices afflicting women, to avoid a mono-culturalism that asserts a dominant (white) agenda, it is critical that these movements consider forces complexly (we would now say intersectionally), not solely as gender inequities. "Whatever the core problems are for the people of [any particular] country," Lorde wrote,

> must also be the core problems addressed by women, for we do not exist in a vacuum. We are anchored in our own place and time, looking out and beyond to the future we are creating, and we are part of communities that interact.[10]

This has to include painstaking self-inquiry and grief work for individuals and the collective. We are long overdue in facing the question of "self-care" not only with self in mind: we must think care-of-self in terms of care-of-collective, and work of mourning in terms of collective mourning.

From that perspective I then ask, what is the status of "white women" with regard to sharing the category "woman" with other, non-white women, espe- cially regarding how care-of-collective implicates socio-political positioning in white supremacy and patriarchy. Have white women really spoken "in a different voice" from the white-patriarchal order, to conjure a feminist call from the past?[11] In the political mainstream of 21st century US, are white women's voices really that different from white men's? Are white women in fact positioned, if unwittingly, to being potent spokespeople for the continued strength and posture of neoliberal-capitalist, patriarchal, white-supremacy, which works to divide us, especially? Philosopher Kate Manne wrote in 2018, "Misogyny works to disrupt female solidarity, especially among white women."[12] How might this complicity reinforce whiteness/racist structures in psychoanalytic institutes and societies?

Patriarchy X White feminism = perverse pact = "Becky"

These are the questions I have been having to face in the past few years, awakening to the realization that my feminist "self-care" was born out of activism against patriarchal oppression, wherein I was oblivious to the "perverse pact"[13] between that oppressive system and white feminism. Those questions center on interrogating how I am a member of the collective of not just white women but *all* women in the US and globally, the white contingent who finds ourselves *not having ever actually heard and understood* the social concerns around racist oppression by whiteness structures specific to, and articulated by, our sisters of color. For example, I was not listening when I read "Killing Rage" by bell hooks in the 1990s, in which she wrote of the:

> "many barriers preventing black females and white females from forming close ties in white supremist capitalist patriarchy," namely that, "individual white women tend to be more unaware than their black female counterparts of the ways that the history of racism in the United States has institutionalized structures of racial apartheid that were meant to keep these two groups apart."[14]

This pact has worked for the patriarchal order that structures my life… and in so many ways, hasn't the patriarchal structure worked for me? Well in so many immediate, positively reinforcing, greedy ways, yes; in actuality, no! In fact, it is not working for me precisely because I haven't been working to undo my complicity with white supremacy for the *common good*. It has harmed and it is harming – our sisters, the feminist cause, and any possibility for a true, inclusive, potent coalition whose aims include (human) survival on this planet.

This "perverse pact" is the nidus for the now popular "Karen" meme in COVID-time social media, and her (because she is always [white] female) pre-COVID big sister, "Becky." I touch on this because it captures the complex conundrum of white women who, wedged between their privilege in whiteness and their oppression by patriarchy, are prone to a peculiar vulnerability/victimhood that incites them to follow a form of feminism described as "carceral feminism," which reinforces culturally sanctioned societal and state violence against people of color, especially Black and Brown people.[15] In short, Becky(/Karen) is a white woman who, through her aggressive demands, publicly embodies and enacts rhetoric, emotionality and behavior that "upholds whiteness at the expense of people of color's humanity, dignity and expertise" and which "shuts down the potential for racial understanding."[16] As the "policewoman of all human behavior" she colludes with law enforcement as the "[hardly] petty enforcer who patrols other people's behavior," especially people of color. The Becky/Karen archetype has been especially painful for middle-aged white women like myself. Not only because it (albeit stereotypically and in a [at times violently] misogynist way) nails "how whiteness entangled with dynamics of gender, femininity, and innocence embodied in the white woman negatively impacts people of color";[17] but as well, because it is leveled toward White women by Black people especially, who have no doubt suffered the real, harmful consequences of such behavior, but with a force that suggests a funneling of all manner of rage and mistrust toward (always already) racist White people onto White women.

Where is the love?

In 1995 bell hooks included in her book *Killing Rage: Ending Racism* a chapter poignantly entitled "Where is the love: Political bonding between black and white women."[18] In it she wrote powerfully and presciently about the history of relations between black and white women in the US, calling for feminist action and change:

> Studying this powerful history within feminist circles, it was clear to individual black and white women that sisterhood could not emerge between us if we did not assume accountability for our roles in either sustaining racist thinking and action or nurturing conflict by holding onto mistrust and contempt. We had to take our understanding of the history of our social relations and relate it to our contemporary lives. …bonds were made only by those individual women who were willing to interrogate themselves honestly.
>
> Unfortunately, the vast majority of white and black women in feminist movement did not commit themselves to forging bonds. … the overall failure of feminist movement to challenge racism, sexism, and class elitism in ways that would make it possible for women to bond across difference does not mean that feminist thinking is not needed. … such bonding [between black and white women] is possible only if the two groups are willing to undergo processes of education for critical consciousness that supports changes in thinking and behavior.

hooks movingly urged black and white women to "decenter the obsession with male regard and make significant the regard in which women hold one another":

the moment white and black females refuse to compete with one another an important intervention happens: the existing sexist/racist structure is disrupted. If that will to compete is replaced with a longing to know one another, a context for bonding can emerge.

Knowing one another better and cultivating mutual acknowledgement and respect, she pointed out, would allow this coalition to

play a major role in ending racism. As long as white and black women are content with living separately in a state of psychic social apartheid, racism will not change. If women willingly allow racist/sexist [and I would add class elitist] thinking to shape our relationships with one another, we cannot blame patriarchy for keeping us apart. Interrogating female xeno-phobia (fear of difference) must be a significant part of future struggles to end racism and sexism.

This was a message I refused in the nineties, out of ignorance and, well, an "obsession with male[/gender] regard." As a white lesbian-turning-queer I was too preoccupied with deconstructing gender as a stealth tact toward leveling the playing field with men, to be able to take up hooks' invita-tion to end racism. I remember having enormous difficulty getting through her books. They left me feeling impotent to engage with anti-racism work, because I didn't actually have any significant, ongoing, trusting alliances with black women. I blamed this on a massive social race-segregation that was too big to confront (in fact, too easy to ignore), when instead it was my resist-ance that was too big, my refusal to commit to doing the painstaking work of confronting my unconscious *allegiance* with the patriarchy through my deep dependence and embeddedness in white supremist social conditions/conditioning.

hooks' observations are critical for psychoanalysis. We surely know that the vast majority of the women in the field are White. How many of us commit to forging feminist movement with other women in the field at all, never mind between ourselves and women of color in the field? How many white women in the field think about race at all? Surely more now than even six months ago – certainly in the US, probably globally as well.

Returning to Lorde's plea above, for women to address the needs of women as a community, I am called upon to think about how I as a white woman have to find a way to live between the unfair advantages and privileges and the entitlement that breeds in my attitudes and presumptions of "safety" and "deserving" I have as a white person, with the real effects of structural mis-ogyny that both entrap me and hold me in place (of malignantly compla-cent comfort); that speak over me and through me, degrade me and my voice, erase me by my own hand which has until too recently blindly refused to link misogyny and racism as one nefarious, social complex. This is a particular brand of "intersectionality," the critically useful concept Kimberley Crenshaw developed in the early 1990s to describe the exponentially deleterious effects of multiple subordinated identity categories on black women (but which was by then already understood by black women, including bell hooks, whose moving accounts of their lived experience illuminated the intersectional forces that constantly reinforced their intersectional "subjection"[19] by undermining their efforts toward liberated subjectivities). This is unconscious misogyny that lives in white women to ensure our supremacy within female circles. This is the part of the "Becky/Karen" meme that resonates – ever painfully so. I cannot simply discard the "Karen" meme as a sexist slur, until I myself have committed to undoing the misogyny that I unwittingly commit against black women in that complex where racism Trumps sexism – in other words where these two aims of oppression collude in "white feminism."

Conclusion

The intersectionality of racism/whiteness elided in the white feminist movement insidiously privileges white-prioritized feminist politics over race politics in the fight against patriarchy. In real time, this amounts to the projection by white women onto black women of internalized misogyny/misogynist identification, misrecognition, ungrievability and envy of beatifically expressed feminine sexuality[20]; myths about Black male sexuality as a displacement for hatred of the patriarchal power and disgust of white men.

How can the white feminist movement be accountable in reckoning with these ultimately racist psychological maneuvers? Further, how do white women radicalize? What are our vulnerabilities? Where is our power? How do we name the ways that we are oppressed and that we oppress, and the relationship between those two forces? How do those forces, in their vicious cycle of cause and effect, in fact implicate and mobilize each other? Whereas Black women "radicaliz[ed] because of the ways their multiple identities opened them up to overlapping oppression and exploitation,"[21] white women have had a stake in the white heterosexual male patriarchal power structure, so have been more susceptible to the enticements of capitalism because they have – by simultaneously if unwittingly caving to structural misogyny – reaped the privileges garnered from capitalist consumerism and "safety." This, tragically, has historically made it worth leaving Black women behind. It has also meant leaving behind the basic radicalism of feminism itself, which was built on fundamental values of activism for the sake of the collective and in the spirit of coalition-building. This is where "collaboration" may be offensive to women of color, because it implies asserting your own priorities and power at the table rather than relinquishing power and one's own set of priorities, and sometimes one's voice (for the sake of listening to the lived experiences of others), for the sake of the whole – to imagine radically different needs and desires that need to be taken into consideration.

Notes

1 Workneh (2015).
2 Romano (2020).
3 Tampa Bay Rays (2020).
4 Imani (2020).
5 Sanchez (2020).
6 From Jones (1955), see text reference.
7 Manne (2018, p. 20), author of *Down Girl: The Logic of Misogyny*, distinguishes misogyny from sexism this way: "sexism is the branch of patriarchal ideology that *justifies* and *rationalizes* a patriarchal social order, and misogyny as the system that *polices* and *enforces* its governing norms and expectations. So sexism is scientific; misogyny is moralistic."
8 Jones (1955, p. 468).
9 A reference to Kimberly Crenshaw's concept of "intersectionality," in which she describes the exponential deleterious effects of multiple subordinated identity categories on black women (Crenshaw, 1991).
10 Lorde (1992, p. 64).
11 Gilligan (1982).
12 Manne (2018, p. 263).
13 Harris (2018).
14 hooks (1995, p. 217).
15

> Carceral feminism is an ideology which upholds the criminal punishment system as the sole or primary arbitrator of gender violence justice and leverages the credibility of feminist movements to widen the scope of state powers. This is done by increasing prison and police funding, expanding definitions of criminalized behavior, and advocating for longer prison sentences. However this analysis ignores the central role of the state itself in producing rather than addressing gender and sexual violence (Holmes, 2020).

16 Matias (2020, p. 5).
17 Matias (2020, p. 1).
18 hooks (1995, pp. 220–222).
19 A reference to the use of the term "subjection" in Hartman (1997).
20 For an immediate experience of such envy (read: awe and appreciation!), I turn to Beyoncé in her music video "Formation": www.youtube.com/watch?v=WDZJPJV__bQ – Accessed 28 July 2020, 3:15 PM.
21 Manne (2018, pp. 33–34).

References

Agamben, G. (2005). *States of Exception*. Chicago, IL: University of Chicago Press.
Althusser, L. (1984). *Essays on Ideology*. New York, NY: Verso.
Apprey, M. (2014). A pluperfect errand: A turbulent return to the beginnings in the transgenerational transmission of destructive aggression, free associations: Psychoanalysis and culture, *Media, Groups, Politics*, 66, 16–29.

Braidotti, R. (2019) Posthuman knowledge. www.youtube.com/watch?v=0Cewn VzOg5w

Brown, A.M & Imarisha, W. (2015). *Octavia's Brood: Science Fiction Stories from Social Justice Movements.* Oakland, CA: AK Press.

Butler, J. (1990). *Gender Trouble: Feminism and the Subversion of Identity.* New York, NY: Routledge.

Butler, J. (1995) Melancholy gender – refused identification, *Psychoanalytic Dialogues*, 5(2), 165–180.

Butler, O. (1993). *Parables of the Sower.* New York, NY: Four Walls Eight Windows.

Crenshaw, K. (1989). Demarginalizing the intersection of race and sex: A black feminist critique of antidiscrimination doctrine, feminist theory and antiracist politics. *University of Chicago Legal Forum*, 1:8.

Fanon, F. (2008). *Black Skin, White Masks.* Grove Press-Revised Edition: New York.

Foucault, M. (1980) *The History of Sexuality: Volume 1: An Introduction.* New York, NY: Vintage Books.

Freud, S. (1912). Recommendations to physicians practicing psycho-analysis. *S.E.*, 12: 109–120.

Freud, S. (1926). The question of lay analysis. *S.E.*, 20: 183–250.

Gilligan, C. (1982). *In a Different Voice: Psychological Theory and Women's Development.* Cambridge, MA: Harvard University Press.

Goffman, E. (1963). *Stigma: Notes on the Management of Spoiled Identity.* Englewood Cliffs, NJ: Prentice-Hall.

González, F.J. (2013). Another Eden: Proto-gay desire and social precocity. *Studies in Gender and Sexuality*, 14(2), 112–121.

Harris, A. (1997). Envy and Ambition: the circulating tensions in women's relation to aggression. *Gender and Psychoanalysis*, 2, 291–325.

Harris, A. (2002). Women's envy: disowned excitements. Paper presented at the Austin Riggs Center. 8 March 2002.

Harris, A. (2009). You must remember this. *Psychoanalytic Dialogues*, 19(1), 2009.

Harris, A. and Sinsheimer, K. (2010) The Analyst's Presence and Finetuning Boldies. In Anderson, F. (Ed.) *Bodies in Treatment* Taylor and Francis.

Harris, A. (2018). The Perverse pact. Paper at Program on Race. BIPSE. 16 April 2018.

Hartman, S. (1997). *Scenes of Subjection: Terror, Slavery and Self-Making in Nineteenth Century America.* New York, NY: Oxford University Press.

Holmes, C. (July 12, 2020). Carceral Feminism, Femonationalism and Quarantine. *Abolition Journal.* https://abolitionjournal.org/carceral-feminism-pandemic/ Accessed 22 July 2020, 4:37 PM.

hooks, B. (1995). *Killing Rage: Ending Racism.* New York, NY: Henry Holt and Company.

Imani, Z. [@zellieimani]. (2020, June 23). Drink Water. Use Seasoning and Arrest the Cops Who Killed Breonna Taylor. [Tweet]. *Twitter.* https://twitter.com/zellieimani/status/1275412715633283072?lang=en

Jones, E. (1955). *Sigmund Freud Life and Work, Volume Two: Years of Maturity 1901–1919.* London: The Hogarth Press.

Lorde, A. (1992). *A Burst of Light: Living with Cancer.* Toronto: Women's Press of Canada.

Lorde, A. (2017). *The Master's Tools Will Never Dismantle the Master's House.* New York, NY: Penguin Books.

Lyons-Ruth, K. 2003. Dissociation and the parent-infant dialogue: A longitudinal perspective. *Journal of the American Psychoanalytic Association*, 51: 883–911.

Manne, K. (2018). *Down Girl: The Logic of Misogyny.* New York, NY: Oxford University Press.

Matias, C.E. (2020). *Surviving Becky(s): Pedagogies for Deconstructing Whiteness and Gender.* London: Lexington Books.

Muñoz, J. (2009). *Cruising Utopia: The Then and There of Queer Futurity.* New York, NY: New York University Press.

Riviere, J. (1929). Womanliness as a Masquerade. *International Journal of Psychoanalysis,* 10: 303–313.

Robinson, M. (1851). Women's rights convention. Sojourner Truth. Anti-Slavery Bugle, Salem, Ohio, 21 June 1851.

Roche, L. (2014). *The Radiance Sutras: 112 Gateways to the Yoga of Wonder & Delight.* Boulder: Sounds True.

Romano, A. (2020, August 10). "Arrest the Cops Who Killed Breonna Taylor": The Power and Peril of a Catchphrase. *Vox.* www.vox.com/21327268/breonna-taylor-say-her-name-meme-hashtag

Rose, J. (2016). Who do you think you are? *London Review of Books,* 38(9): 3–13.

Sanchez, C. (2020, July 1). Lili Reinhart Regrets Using a Topless Photo to Demand Justice for Breonna Taylor. *Harper's Bazaar.* www.harpersbazaar.com/celebrity/latest/a33022961/lili-reinhart-topless-photo-breonna-taylor-apology/

Sedgwick, E.K. (1990). *Epistemology of the Closet.* Berkeley, CA: University of California Press

Tampa Bay Rays, [@RaysBaseball]. (2020, July 24). Today is Opening Day, which means it's a great day to arrest the killers of Breonna Taylor. [Tweet]. *Twitter.* https://twitter.com/raysbaseball/status/1286632257076289536?lang=en

Woolf, V. (1929). *A Room of One's Own,* New York, NY: Harcourt, Inc.

Workneh, L. (2015, May 21). #SayHerName: Why We Should Declare that Black Women and Girls Matter, Too. *Huffpost.* www.huffpost.com/entry/black-women-matter_n_7363064

Winnicott, D.W. (1971). *Playing and Reality.* London: Tavistock.

8   The persistent impact of stereotypes about women

Cecile R. Bassen

According to Cambridge Dictionary (2020), a stereotype is "a set idea that people have about what someone or something is like, especially an idea that is wrong." Google describes it as "a widely held but fixed and oversimplified image or idea of a particular type of person or thing," and gives the following example: "the stereotype of the woman as the carer" (definition provided by Oxford Languages, 2021).

Inaccurate generalizations about a group of people create expectations about members of the stereotyped group. Even though most of us recognize the harmful impact of stereotypes and consciously reject them, they tend to persist on both conscious and unconscious levels. Researchers have noted that this is particularly true of positive stereotypes, which tend to fly under our anti-bias radar because they seem acceptable. However, even positive stereotypes have negative consequences, creating expectations which are likely to reinforce stereotypical behavior (Czopp, Kay, and Cheryan, 2015). Members of the stereotyped group have to contend with others' expectations that they will fit widely held stereotypes, as well as their own. They experience anxiety about failing to live up to positive stereotypes, as well as fear of acting in ways that confirm or conform to negative stereotypes.

Peggy Orenstein explored the problematic impact of gender stereotypes on girls in her 2011 book titled *Cinderella Ate My Daughter*. She wrote

> …what I want for my daughter seems so simple: for her to grow up healthy, happy, and confident, with a clear sense of her own potential and the opportunity to fulfill it. Yet she lives in a world that tells her, whether she is three or thirty-three, that the surest way to get there is to look, well, like Cinderella.
>
> (p. 9)

When Orenstein's 3-year-old daughter became enamored by the idea of being a princess after playing Sleeping Beauty with her older female cousins, Orenstein realized that there was no way to prevent her from being exposed to gender stereotypes by friends, extended family, and mass media. Orenstein began to investigate marketing to children, and she was horrified by what she saw at the

DOI: 10.4324/9781003180036-11

annual Toy Fair in New York City: a blue banner in the pre-school boys' section of the Fisher-Price showroom said "ENERGY, HEROES, POWER," while a pink banner in the girls' section said "BEAUTIFUL, PRETTY, COLORFUL"! (pp. 51–52).

Orenstein and many others have noted that companies create and market gender stereotyped toys because they sell well. They appeal to many children, and to parents who are interested in reinforcing a clear gender identity in their children. Other parents find it hard to refuse to buy toys their children clamor for, especially when saying "no" to Disney princesses and Barbie dolls may make them even more desirable.

Gender stereotypes tend to appeal to young children because they provide an unambiguous, black and white picture of the way the world works, and a clear sense of what to expect. Children often distort or misremember information when it fails to conform to their stereotypes. Orenstein cites one study, which found that over half of 5- to 9-year-old children who watched a TV commercial in which a boy played with a doll and a girl with a truck later recalled the reverse! (Note 57, p. 202).

Many young girls enjoy pretending to be a fairy tale princess who is singled out and chosen for her beauty, and find the idea of being awakened with a kiss exciting. But like many parents, Orenstein worked on broadening her daughter's ideas about what it means to be a girl. She was relieved when her daughter got tired of pretending to be Sleeping Beauty because "all Sleeping Beauty ever does is sleep" (pp. 143–144), and outgrew her Disney princess phase by the end of kindergarten.

There has been significant progress rejecting the stereotype that "energy and power" are male attributes which are inappropriate or out of reach for girls and women. However, the image of women *as* beautiful objects of desire is persistent and powerful. We respond strongly to girls' and women's appearance throughout their lifetimes, and girls learn that being beautiful is desirable from an early age.

This emphasis on beauty has been perpetuated through fairy tales and myths for centuries. Fairy tales both reflect cultural beliefs and serve to reinforce them. They embody stereotyped views of women that have been passed down and internalized for generation after generation. Maria Tatar and other scholars of folklore have documented that many iconic fairy tales are universal, existing in multiple versions throughout the world. They retain a basic plot structure despite rich cultural variations, and have persisted for centuries despite changes over time. For instance, the fairy tale we know as Cinderella originated more than 1,000 years ago, and it has hundreds of variants around the world with the heroines going by many different names (Tatar, 1999). Tatar has suggested that fairy tales are "arguably the most powerfully formative tales of childhood" (p. xi).

Think of the fairy tales you grew up with. Many fairy tales divide female characters into two distinct categories: good girls and wicked women (witches and evil stepmothers). This is true of both "Cinderella" and "Snow White," two iconic fairy tales with many striking similarities including the stereotypes they convey about women. In both tales, a beautiful young girl with a dead mother is badly mistreated by a selfish and evil older woman. The heroine has done nothing to merit this mistreatment, but her innate grace and beauty arouse spiteful envy. She endures her plight virtuously and passively, without hostility or even complaint. Her salvation and happiness rest on winning the love of a prince, who has the power to rescue her. The heroine is rewarded for her selfless beauty, while narcissistic striving is characterized as selfish and ugly (like Cinderella's stepsisters) or blatantly evil (like Snow White's stepmother) (Bassen, 2014).

As many feminists have pointed out, "Cinderella" and "Snow White" reinforce problematic gender stereotypes with their emphasis on beauty, the virtues of passive endurance and selflessness, and the love of a powerful man as the solution to powerlessness (Gilbert and Gubar, 1979). Yet, despite this, they remain so much a part of our cultural zeitgeist that parents continue to read them to their children, and variants of both tales are frequently made into movies. One website I visited lists 48 films based on "Cinderella"; over 35 of these were made since 1990! (Ranker Film, 2020).

The storylines of both fairy tales revolve around three familiar and problematic gender stereotypes:

1   Women are defined by and valued for the way they look.
2   A woman's life is incomplete without a man.
3   Women are only likable and lovable when they put others first.

Taken together these three stereotypes reinforce the assumption that a woman is completely defined by her relationship to others, by her roles as wife and mother. The artist Louise Bourgeois depicted women subsumed by the identity of housewife in drawings, paintings, and sculptures she titled "Femme Maison" throughout her career; these women are part body and part house, frequently portrayed with houses where their heads should be (Morris, 2007).

There have been significant social and cultural changes in much of the Western world since the mid-20th century – especially in the assumption that adult women will spend their lives as housewives. The majority of women in the United States with even very young children work for pay; and the share of all mothers of children younger than 18 who are breadwinners (unmarried working mothers or mothers who out earn their partners) or co-breadwinners (married mothers who bring home at least 25% of their household's income) has more than doubled since 1967 (Glynn, 2019).

Yet children continue to be captivated by "Cinderella" and "Snow White." Are the gender stereotypes embedded in these fairy tales as persistent as the fairy tales themselves? To what extent, and in what ways, do these stereotypes continue to have an impact on girls and women today?

Women are defined by and valued for the way they look

While the fantasy of being "the fairest of them all" appeals to many young girls, the tendency to define girls and women by the way they look becomes a burden as girls encounter reality and begin to worry about their appearance. For too many girls and women, real and imaginary flaws in their appearance become a lifelong preoccupation and source of narcissistic vulnerability. Constant reminders and reinforcement of external definitions of beauty make it difficult for women to work through feelings about the way they look, triggering anxieties about not being attractive enough or thin enough.

Like the other gender stereotypes, the internalization of external expectations about beauty tends to create an unattainable ego ideal, leaving women with painful feelings of inferiority. While this is something all women tend to struggle with, it is more of a burden for women whose facial features, skin color, and/or body type differ significantly from whatever is idealized as beautiful in their culture. The idealization of youthful beauty heightens women's anxiety about aging, with fears of becoming invisible and undesirable. In addition, women struggle with criticism and self-criticism for internalizing widely accepted gender stereotypes – as if they could and should be immune to cultural norms and expectations.

The fear of being unattractive and undesirable serves as a significant motivation for cosmetic surgery. According to the American Society of Plastic Surgeons (2019), $16.7 billion was spent on 1.8 million cosmetic surgeries in the United States in 2019; 92% of these cosmetic procedures were performed on women.

As women obtain higher education and pursue professions, they have more opportunities to define themselves as individuals, independent of appearance. However, the statistics for cosmetic surgery in 2019 illustrate the degree to which the tendency to value women by the way they look continues.

A simple example illustrates how the impact of this stereotype is determined by a complex combination of external and internal factors. One of my patients was honored by an invitation to speak about her work to a national audience of professional colleagues a few years ago. She spent a considerable amount of time deciding what to wear, and worried about how her hair looked throughout her presentation, distracted by the fact that her image was being projected onto several large screens. Her preoccupation with how she looked was heightened by her awareness of being a woman in a male-dominated field. She commented that she doubted that any of her male colleagues would have worried about their clothing: they just had to put on a suit. I am sure that my patient was correct in assuming that her colleagues would notice her appearance. At the same time, her response also reflected her life-long concern with her appearance, fueled by growing up with a mother who made frequent critical comments about her body. Lastly, my patient struggled with how to look attractive but also professional, without looking as if she paid too much attention to her appearance.

This raises another aspect of the gender stereotype about beauty. Women who are perceived as paying too much attention to their appearance are subject to criticism for being vain. Cinderella's stepsisters are mocked, and Snow White's stepmother is vilified for her insistence on being "the fairest of them all." Girls and women also learn that while they are valued for the way they look, they are likely to be seen as responsible if their appearance leads men to experience them as sexual objects. We are all familiar with women being blamed and blaming themselves for being seductive, and with depictions of women as the evil Seductress, beginning with Eve.

Another aspect of this gender stereotype is our tendency to label certain emotions as ugly: envy, jealousy, greed, resentment, and even anger – especially in women (Sinkman, 2013). Fairy tale heroines like Cinderella, Snow White, and Sleeping Beauty are depicted as innately beautiful, innocent, good-natured, and blameless, free of all these "ugly" emotions that are attributed to ugly stepsisters, evil stepmothers, and witches.

The result is that women are defined by the way they look, according to a narrow culturally imposed definition of beauty that extends beyond physical features to traits that are seen as appealing, and traits that are rejected as ugly. A few years ago, "resting bitch face" became a popular meme, portraying women who fail to smile enough as bitches. The Urban Dictionary describes resting bitch face as "a person, usually a girl, who naturally looks mean when her face is expressionless, without meaning to" (www.urbandictionary.com). One columnist noted that plastic surgeons perform frequent "grin lifts" on women seeking to turn up the corners of their mouths, as well as Botox injections to relax bitchy-looking wrinkles between their eyebrows, despite the fact that a more accurate description would be "Resting 'This Wouldn't Bother You if I Was a Guy' Face" (Grossman, 2019).

One final comment on this stereotype: We empathize with the wish to be attractive to others, but tend to be uncomfortable with the wish to be attractive for its own sake. We find beauty coupled with warmth and romance appealing, but describe beautiful women who are not interested in men as "ice queens." This stereotype is intertwined with the assumption that women are defined by their relationships, instead of as individuals, and that attracting a mate is (and should be) the central goal for all women.

A woman's life is incomplete without a man

Iconic fairy tales like "Cinderella" and "Snow White" are based on the notion that a woman's happiness in life rests on winning the love and devotion of a desirable man. The stereotype that a woman's life is incomplete without a man combines the appeal of romance with the assumption that women need to depend on men because they cannot create a good life on their own. Fairy tales reinforce a rigid gender dichotomy where activity and power are the province of men – something that women only obtain through the men that they marry. When selfless beauty is idealized in women but assertive striving is characterized as selfish and ugly, the only appealing option is marriage to a successful man.

Unfortunately, this stereotype reflects the reality of women's lives for much of history, due to restrictions on women's freedom to support themselves and live independently in many cultures. Although this remains true in many parts of the world, women's lives in first world countries have changed a great deal. Yet, even when it became increasingly possible for American women to live independently in the 1950s and 1960s, the belief that women's lives were incomplete without a man lingered. Being a spinster or "old maid" continued to carry a negative connotation, and people still joked about women going to college to get their "Mrs." Degree.

However, there has been a revolution in what is socially acceptable and economically feasible in much of the Western world since then: single and divorced women living on their own, or living with a man without getting married; bisexuality and homosexuality; and women becoming single mothers, or having and raising children with a female partner or female spouse. While most heterosexual women still long to find the man of their dreams and may feel that something important is missing without him, it is no longer taken as a given that a woman's life is incomplete without a man today in America.

As I noted earlier, fairy tales both reflect cultural beliefs and serve to perpetuate them. Several recent film adaptations of "Cinderella" and "Snow White" including *Ever After* (1998), *A Cinderella Story* (2004), *Mirror, Mirror* (2012), and *Snow White and the Huntsman* (2012) demonstrate how much this stereotype has changed. Although all four films depict a selfless, beautiful heroine oppressed by her selfish and evil stepmother, Cinderella and Snow White are now active, resourceful heroines who rescue others in need, rather than needing to be rescued. These heroines triumph by virtue of their own resourcefulness; they no longer need to be rescued by a man.

Two newly created fairy tales go one step further, by rejecting romance. In *The Paper Bag Princess*, a best-selling children's book first published in 1980, the heroine rescues her fiancé from a dragon, then leaves when he criticizes the fact that she is dressed in a paper bag and goes off to live on her own (Munsch, 1981). In the film *Brave* (2012), the heroine refuses to accept her parents' insistence that it is time for her to marry. Merida insists that she has no need for a husband, competes against the suitors vying for her hand, and wins.

When women are free to live independent and active lives, traditional gender roles and the relationship between the sexes need to be re-imagined. We live in a time of transition, where this is both an opportunity and a complex challenge. The new and updated fairy tales I've mentioned illustrate the extent of this challenge. When the heroines of these stories end up with the prince, it is often because they have rescued him. (*Ever After* and *Mirror, Mirror* are comic updates of "Cinderella" and "Snow White," respectively, which rely on role reversal: the heroine, who is strong and resourceful, rescues and then marries a hapless prince.) They rarely depict a resourceful heroine with an equally resourceful love interest – which leaves us with the impression that a powerful woman will end up with a hapless partner or end up alone, and that it is hard to imagine relationships in which women and men are equally strong.

It is clear that freeing women from restrictive gender roles threatens the status quo, throwing male prerogatives and male gender roles into question. Despite the fact that it is now culturally acceptable for women to be active and independent in much of the Western world, attachment to the status quo makes it hard to question fixed assumptions about male and female roles and abilities, and to recognize and acknowledge gender bias.

Women continue to experience discrimination in the workplace including unequal pay, and lack of equal opportunities for promotion and for leadership roles. A large body of research documents numerous ways in which gender stereotypes continue to adversely impact women at home and at work (DeWolf, 2017; Eagly and Karau, 2002; Glynn, 2019; Grant and Sandberg, 2014, 2015; Sandberg and Grant, 2015). Unfortunately, much of this research is consistent with the disturbing finding that most social groups tend to be perceived as warm or competent, but not both. Women (along with older people and the mentally handicapped) are frequently stereotyped as being high on warmth but low on competence! (Czopp, Kay, and Cheryan, 2015).

Nicholas Kristof (2015) referred to unconscious bias against women that flies under the radar as "misogyny without misogynists." It remains difficult to alter pervasive but unconscious forms of gender bias. What has changed significantly is the degree to which blatant bias is confronted and called out, instead of being tolerated in silence or with a shrug.

One relevant example: the author of an opinion piece published in the Wall Street Journal in shortly after the 2020 presidential election addressed Jill Biden as "kiddo," and objected to her use of the title "Dr." (which reflects the fact that she has an Ed.D). He wrote that it "sounds and feels fraudulent, not to say a touch comic," and suggested that she "forget the small thrill of being Dr. Jill, and settle for the larger thrill of…(being) First Lady" (Epstein, 2020). As soon as this Op-Ed was published, it was widely condemned as misogynistic (Treisman, 2020).

As things stand now, however, barriers to women's autonomy remain. It is noteworthy that the Equal Rights Amendment remains controversial and was never ratified by a sufficient number of states to be enacted, despite being passed by both houses of Congress in 1972. A 2020 study of legal protections for women in 194 countries (concerning freedom of movement, work, equal pay, marriage, child rearing, business ownership, asset management, and pensions) found that women in 20 countries have less than half the legal rights accorded to men, while on average women world-wide have three-fourths of men's rights. Only eight countries guarantee full equal rights to women and men; the United States was not among them (World Bank, 2020).

Barriers to acknowledging women's competence, and to allowing women opportunities to develop and demonstrate competence, leave external glass ceilings in place. This makes it harder for women to develop confidence about their abilities, so that they remain vulnerable to internal glass ceilings.

Women internalize the same gender stereotypes as men, leading them to make unconscious assumptions about other women and themselves. In their series of Op-Ed pieces on "Women at Work" in the New York Times, Adam Grant and Sheryl Sandberg noted that both male and female managers favor men over equally qualified women in hiring, compensation, performance evaluation, and promotion decisions. They also cited a comprehensive analysis of 95 studies on gender differences that showed that although men are more confident at leadership skills, women are actually more competent (Grant and Sandberg, 2014). Harriet Wolfe (2019) has noted that internalized misogyny can hold women back from aspiring to leadership positions, instead of recognizing that psychological abilities typically described as feminine (including careful listening, receptivity, and capacity for containment) actually characterize good leaders.

Unfortunately, the field of psychoanalysis has contributed to the belief that women are incomplete and inferior to men. Freud took male development as the norm in creating his phallocentric theory of psychosexual development, and he believed that women were defined by their lack of a penis and by penis envy. Freud's theories led him to conclude that women's sense of morality is inferior to men's (1933) – a view that he never repudiated. He was unable to question the gender stereotypes he had internalized, or to recognize that much of what he believed to be bedrock was actually culturally determined. Fortunately, psychoanalysts since Freud have created a robust body of literature exploring women's psychosexual development in all its dimensions; and contemporary analysts understand women, and the role of women in our psychic lives, quite differently than Freud did.

Contemporary psychoanalytic developmental theory helps us understand the third enduring stereotype about women:

Women are only likable and lovable when they put others first

As I've already noted, the belief that women are only likable and lovable when they put others first is central to the message conveyed by iconic fairy tales, where selflessness is idealized and rewarded. The variant of "Cinderella" which we know best, recorded by Charles Perrault in 1697 (and subsequently used in the 1950 Disney film), ended with an explicit moral: grace (defined as goodness and selflessness) is priceless and will win a man's heart; but "if you wish to shine and gad about" you will get no help from godparents and "your life will never have great events" (Tatar, 2002, p.43). In other words, selfless beauty is lovable, but narcissistic striving is not.

Despite changes in what is culturally acceptable for women in much of the Western world, we continue to expect women to attend to the needs of others as much or more than their own, both personally and professionally. We remain intensely ambivalent about assertive striving in women, and are quick to equate it with being selfish and pushy. We tend to confuse and conflate assertion and aggression in women, instead of differentiating the two (Harris, 1997, 2002).

Women continue to carry the brunt of unpaid work within the home, including caring for children and performing household tasks, despite the fact that 70% of married mothers with children under 18 worked outside the home in the United States in 2017 (DeWolf, 2017; Glynn, 2019). As Grant and Sandberg noted in their Op-Ed series on "Women at Work" (2015), expectations for men and women in the workplace also differ. Women are expected to be helpful, and expect themselves to help others; as a result they tend to do the lion's share of office housework, in ways that do not bring them recognition and which hold them back from activities that do bring recognition. Women also tend to experience a double-bind in professional meetings: they often go unheard when they speak, but are likely to be judged as aggressive for speaking too much if they persist in trying to be heard (Sandberg and Grant, 2015).

Recent film versions of "Snow White" capture our ambivalence about women who assert themselves by depicting two diametrically opposed forms of assertive striving in women: assertion on behalf of others is idealized, while assertion at others' expense is vilified. In *Mirror, Mirror* (2012) and *Snow White and the Huntsman* (2012), this dichotomy is heightened. Both films depict a power-hungry Queen whose villainy devastates her entire kingdom and harms everyone in it; and a heroine who is active and resourceful on behalf of others, freeing the kingdom from a monstrous ruler. These updated fairy tales make it clear that the belief that women are only likable and lovable if they put others first is closely tied to our fear of powerful women.

Fear of the power of women is long-standing and deep-seated. In *Women and Power* (2017), the classical scholar Mary Beard notes that Aristotle considered women's speech wicked and dangerous, and ancient Greeks did not allow women to speak in public. Many have noted that female politicians tend to inspire significantly more intense dislike, mistrust, and demonization than male politicians (Chira, 2017). Although as Harriet Wolfe (2019) has suggested, qualities we think of as feminine are valuable assets for all leaders, women in leadership positions find themselves resorting to feminine gender display in an attempt to avoid being perceived as unlikable (Eagly and Karau, 2002; Williams, 2019**).**

Two recent Academy Award winning films based on newly minted fairy tales depict the dangers of a young woman asserting herself. Both *Brave* (2012) and *Frozen* (2013) center on strong and resourceful young women who unwittingly harm others, then struggle to undo the harm they have caused. "Let it Go," the hit song from *Frozen*, has been described as a tribute to "girl power." However, the heroine sings it when she feels like a pariah after inadvertently displaying her magical powers. She has fled from her kingdom, and she is completely alone. The song's lyrics make it clear that a good girl tries to keep her power hidden inside her, instead of seeing what she can do; she follows rules and doesn't test limits. When Elsa does let go of her constraints, there are devastating consequences: she accidentally engulfs her kingdom in an eternal winter, and also freezes her sister's heart.

The young heroines of *Frozen* and *Brave* eventually find a way to reverse the harm they have done through the power of love. These films convey a cautionary message: that girls and women need to learn to control their emotions and to be careful about how they assert their power to avoid harming others – especially those that they love.

Both films spoke to a generation of girls, and countless girls listened to "Let it Go" over and over again, memorizing the lyrics. Their popularity suggests that the dilemma they pose speaks to a deep-seated concern that girls and women continue to struggle with: is there a way to be assertive and be yourself without alienating or harming others?

The psychological origins of our ambivalence about powerful women

A significant part of our persistent discomfort with women who fail to smile and are powerful or assertive can be traced to universal feelings in early childhood: how wonderful it feels when mother smiles, and how awful it feels when she doesn't. As many have noted, there are deep-seated and long-lasting psychological consequences of infants' helplessness and children's prolonged dependence on their primary caretaker, who is most often their mother (Benjamin, 1986; Chodorow, 1978; Dinnerstein, 1976; Elise, 1997; Harris, 1997, 2002; Kulish and Holtzman, 2008; Raphael-Leff, 1984).

Janine Chasseguet-Smirgel (1990) described the early roots of our discomfort with powerful women, which she attributed to the negative maternal imago. She wrote:

> I believe that a child, whether male or female, even with the best and kindest of mothers, will maintain a terrifying maternal image in his unconscious, the result of projected hostility deriving from his own impotence … This powerful image, symbolic of all that is bad, does not exclude an omnipotent, protective imago … varying according to the mother's real characteristics. However the child's primary powerlessness … and the inevitable frustrations of training are such that the imago of the good, omnipotent mother never covers over that of the terrifying, omnipotent, bad mother.
>
> (p.107)

As many developmental theorists have noted, the young boy tends to react to feelings of powerlessness and dependence by wishing to assert his power, to be the one in charge, especially if this is reinforced by the belief that being powerful like his father will win his mother's love (Chasseguet-Smirgel, 1990; Chodorow, 1978; Dinnerstein, 1976; Tyson and Tyson, 1990).

In contrast, the young girl's fear that her wish to take her mother's power for herself will endanger her relationship with the mother she both needs and identifies with, frequently leads to her repressing or disguising her aggressive feelings and rivalrous wishes (Tyson, 1982, 1989). Inhibition of a subjective sense of themselves as aggressive agents often becomes a pervasive defense for girls (Harris, 1997; Hoffman, 1999; Kulish and Holtzman, 2008). As Dianne Elise (1997) put it: "Not only can a girl's anger get in the way of her relationship with her mother, her relationship with her mother … can get in the way of her anger" (p.512).

Even assertion becomes problematic when a girl is raised by a mother who believes that women are only likable and lovable when they put others first. Mothers who have not resolved their own conflicts about asserting themselves have difficulty tolerating assertion in their daughters. The young girl's fear that asserting her own wishes and feelings will threaten her relationship with her mother and make her unlovable is subsequently generalized to others, and reinforced by gender stereotypes.

In essence, childhood experiences lead young boys and girls to fear the omnipotent bad mother, and to long for a mother who will always put others first. In addition, many young girls defensively inhibit assertion and aggression to avoid threatening their relationships with their mothers. Both factors contribute to this stereotype being perpetuated for generation after generation.

Unfortunately, the belief that women are only lovable when they put others first makes it difficult to enjoy and sustain intimate relationships. One woman I worked with spoke often of doing "backbends" to please others. Several women I have seen in my practice habitually put their partner's wishes and feelings first, then become increasingly upset when this is not reciprocated, and end up enraged. This reinforces their fear of being unlovable, leaving them stuck in a no-win position. For women who find it difficult to be themselves in relationships and to make space for their own feelings and needs, being alone can feel like a relief.

Jane Fonda described her difficulty with relationships in a documentary named *Jane Fonda in Five Acts*, which makes it clear how deeply all of the gender stereotypes I've discussed tonight have affected her (Lacy, 2018). The film is organized around five different chapters of Fonda's life, with the first four chapters named for the man who dominated that phase – Jane's father, then each of her three husbands. Fonda describes how she completely remade herself for each man, trying to be whoever he wanted her to be, beginning with her father who criticized her weight and made her feel that how she looked was all that mattered. Looking back at her life at the end of her 70s, Jane is clear that she spent much of it being "too worried about pleasing." She wishes she had been brave enough not to have plastic surgery, but she was too concerned about her appearance. It was a profound turning point when she realized that "I don't need a man to make me okay." She has come to realize that she is "most myself when I'm with my women friends," and says that she is the happiest she's ever been, living alone in her fifth act. Fonda was born in 1937; the film also makes it clear that there are factors in Fonda's life history that left her especially vulnerable to internalizing and embodying gender stereotypes. However, many girls are still raised in circumstances that make it more likely they will internalize gender stereotypes, and more likely to choose partners with stereotyped expectations.

Of course, some women are less affected by gender stereotypes; they are more comfortable asserting themselves, and are able to create and sustain intimate relationships where they can be both affiliative and assertive. However, this can become more challenging once they have children. Then, the complex process of becoming a mother is exacerbated by the gender stereotypes which they and their significant others have internalized. This is especially true for professional women, who discover how difficult it is to pursue a demanding career while protecting time for their children. Some women struggle with unrealistic expectations, fostered by a new gender stereotype: women can have it all if they just believe in themselves and their ability to do it all, and "lean in." Many women feel trapped in an impossible balancing act: unable to be at work or with their children as much as they would like, they feel they are missing out at both, and fear they are failing at both. Some women, who did not previously feel conflicted about working, worry that their career aspirations are harming their children. They struggle with the expectation that they should be putting their children first; and may find it difficult to tolerate their children's anger because it exacerbates their fears of being a bad mother in their children's eyes and in their own. The stereotype that women are only lovable when they put others first can be much harder to reject as the mother of young children. School and day care closures due to the pandemic have exacerbated the dilemmas mothers of young children struggle with, and forced hard choices on many women. The fact that so many more women than men lost their jobs during the pandemic, or voluntarily left work to care for children, also demonstrates the extent to which significant differences remain between men's and women's roles in both the home and the workplace (Ewing-Nelson, 2020).

The likelihood of further change

We live in an era where there is more acceptance of fluidity in gender roles. We encourage girls to be active, resourceful, and independent; and no longer see energy and power as male attributes, which are inappropriate for girls and women, despite our discomfort with powerful women. As women defer the age at which they marry and have children, they have more opportunities to define their identities before becoming wives and mothers. All of this leads me to believe that over time, women are likely to be defined and valued by many characteristics beyond the way they look, and are less likely to see themselves and to be seen as incomplete without a man.

Several factors may help facilitate further change. There is a growing body of academic research on the nature and impact of stereotypes, and on ways to combat gender stereotypes and gender inequality (Czopp, Kay, and Cheryan, 2015). Increased attention is being paid to the factors that interfere with women being promoted to leadership roles (Eagly and Karau, 2002). Although the United States has never had a female President, we recently elected a female Vice President for the first time in our history. The more experience we have with women as competent leaders, the easier it becomes to question both internal and external glass ceilings.

There is increased awareness of the negative impact of gender-stereotyped marketing, especially marketing directed at young children, and steps are gradually being taken to change this. In 2017, several major corporations joined with UN Women (the United Nations entity for Gender Equality) to create the Unstereotype Alliance, which seeks to educate people on how advertising perpetuates biases (www.unstereotypealliance.org/en). An increasing number of countries have passed laws prohibiting gender-stereotyped advertising (Safronova, 2019). Positive ad campaigns seek to change the meaning of doing things "like a girl" (Procter and Gamble), and our ideas about "real beauty" (Dove). Even Barbie dolls are changing: Mattel has gradually introduced 200 careers for Barbie over the past 60 years, and introduced four different body types in 2016 (Lakritz, 2020).

As I noted earlier, changes in traditional gender roles for women mean that gender roles for men and the relationship between the sexes also need to be re-imagined. This presents a formidable challenge. However, although traditional male gender roles come with power and privilege, they also involve their own gender straightjacket: boys and men are pressed to "man up," and taught to minimize or inhibit their affiliative wishes (Pollack, 1998). There is increasing awareness of ways in which traditional masculine gender roles are problematic for men, as well as for women. Various initiatives have begun to address this including an organization named "A Call to Men," which coined the term the "Man Box" to describe problematic male stereotypes. Their website states "In the Man Box, men are expected to be strong, successful, powerful, dominating, fearless, in control, and emotionless … . (and) women are viewed as objects, as the property of men, and as having less value than men" (2021). The American Psychological Association released its first set of "Guidelines for Psychological Practice with Boys and Men" in 2018, noting that guidelines are needed because socialization to conform to traditional "masculinity ideology" has been shown to "limit males' psychological development, constrain their behavior, result in gender role strain and gender role conflict, and negatively influence mental health and physical health" (p. 3).

Although we are a long way from eliminating gender stereotypes, increased acknowledgement of and attention to their negative impact is an important step in the right direction.

References

A Call to Men. (2021). Healthy manhood. Retrieved January 31, 2021, from www.acalltomen.org/healthy-manhood/.

American Psychological Association, Boys and Men Guidelines Group. (2018). APA guidelines for psychological practice with boys and men. Retrieved from www.apa.org/about/policy/psychological-practice-boys-men-guidelines.pdf

American Society of Plastic Surgeons. (2019). Plastic surgery statistic report. Retrieved from www.plasticsurgery.org/news/plastic-surgery-statistics

Bassen, C. (2014). Happily ever after: Depictions of coming of age in fairy tales. In L. T. Pasquali and F. Thomson-Salo (Eds.) *Women and Creativity* (pp. 237–254). London: Karnac Books.

Beard, M. (2017). *Women and Power: A Manifesto.* New York, NY: Liveright.

Benjamin, J. (1986). The alienation of desire: women's masochism and ideal love. In J. L. Alpert (Ed.) *Psychoanalysis and Women: Contemporary Reappraisals* (pp. 113–138). Hillsdale, NJ: The Analytic Press.

Cambridge Dictionary. (n.d). Stereotype. Retrieved December 19, 2020, from https://dictionary.cambridge.org/us/dictionary/english/stereotype.

Chasseguet-Smirgel, J. (1990). Feminine guilt and the oedipus complex. In C. Zanardi (Ed.), *Essential Papers on the Psychology of Women* (pp. 88–131). New York, NY: New York University Press.

Chira, S. (2017, June 26). Nancy Pelosi: Washington's latest wicked witch. *The New York Times.* Retrieved from www.nytimes.com/2017/06/26/opinion/nancy-pelosi-washingtons-latest-wicked-witch.html

Chodorow, N. (1978). *The Reproduction of Mothering.* Berkeley, CA: University of California Press.

Czopp, A.M., Kay, A.C., Cheryan, S. (2015). Positive stereotypes are pervasive and powerful. *Perspectives on Psychological Science,* 10:451–463.

DeWolf, M. (2017, March 1). Twelve Statistics about Working Women. *U.S. Department of Labor Blog.* https://blog.dol.gov/2017/03/01/12-stats-about-working-women

Dinnerstein, D. (1976). *The Mermaid and the Minotaur.* New York, NY: Harper & Row.

Eagly, A.H., Karau, S.J. (2002). Role congruity theory of prejudice toward female leaders. *Psychological Review,* 109 (3):573–598.

Elise, D. (1997). Primary femininity, bisexuality, and the female ego ideal. *Psychoanalytic Quarterly,* 66:489–517.

Epstein, J. (2020, December 1). Is there a doctor in the White House? Not if you need an M.D. *Wall Street Journal.* Retrieved from www.wsj.com/articles/is-there-a-doctor-in-the-white-house-not-if-you-need-an-m-d-11607727380

Ewing-Nelson, C. (2020, October 2). Four times more women than men dropped out of the labor force in September. *National Women's Law Center.* Retrieved from https://nwlc.org/resources/four-times-more-women-than-men-dropped-out-of-the-labor-force-in-september/.

Freud, S. (1933). Lecture 33 Femininity, In *New Introductory Lectures on Psychoanalysis and Other Works. S. E. 22*: 112–135. London: Hogarth Press.

Gilbert, S.M., Gubar, S. (1979). *The Madwoman in the Attic.* New Haven, CT: Yale University Press.

Glynn, S.J. (2019, May 10). Breadwinning mothers continue to be the U.S. Norm. *Center for American Progress.* Retrieved from www.americanprogress.org/issues/women/reports/2019/05/10/469739/breadwinning-mothers-continue-u-s-norm.

Grant, A., Sandberg, S. (2014, December 6). Women at work: When talking about bias backfires. *The New York Times.* Retrieved from www.nytimes.com/2014/12/07/opinion/sunday/adam-grant-and-sheryl-sandberg-on-discrimination-at-work.html.

Grant, A., Sandberg, S. (2015, February 6). Women at Work: Madam C.E.O., get me a coffee. *The New York Times.* Retrieved from www.nytimes.com/2015/02/08/opinion/sunday/sheryl-sandberg-and-adam-grant-on-women-doing-office-house-work.html.

Grossman, S. (2019, January 10). The Insidious sexism of 'resting bitch face.' *The Week*. Retrieved from https://theweek.com/articles/815496/insidious-sexism-resting-bitch-face

Harris, A. (1997). Aggression, envy, and ambition: circulating tensions in women's psychic life. *Gender and Psychoanalysis*, 2:291–325.

Harris, A. (2002). Mothers, monsters, mentors. *Studies in Gender and Sexuality*, 3(3):281–295.

Hoffman, L. (1999). Passion in girls and women: Toward a bridge between critical relational theory of gender and modern conflict theory. *Journal of the American Psychoanalytic Association*, 47:1145–68.

Kristof, N. (2015, February 22). Straight talk for white men. *The New York Times*. Retrieved from www.nytimes.com/2015/02/22/opinion/sunday/nicholas-kristof-straight-talk-for-white-men.html.

Kulish, N. & Holtzman, D. (2008). *A Story of Her Own – The Female Oedipus Complex Reexamined and Renamed*. Lanham, MD: Jason Aronson.

Lacy, S. (Director). (2018). *Jane Fonda in Five Acts*. HBO.

Lakritz, T. (2020, August 9). Here's what Barbie looked like the year you were born. *Insider*. Retrieved from www.insider.com/how-barbie-dolls-changed-evolution-2018-3.

Morris, F. (Ed). (2007). *Louise Bourgeois*. London: Tate Publishing.

Munsch, R. (1981). *The Paper Bag Princess*. Toronto: Annick Press.

Orenstein, P. (2011). *Cinderella Ate My Daughter: Dispatches from the Front Lines of the New Girlie-Girl Culture*. New York, NY: HarperCollins.

Pollack, W. (1998). *Real Boys: Rescuing Our Sons from the Myths of Boyhood*. New York, NY: Random House.

Ranker Film. (2020, November 23). The best Cinderella movies. Retrieved from www.ranker.com/list/the-best-cinderella-movies/ranker-film.

Raphael-Leff, J. (1984). Myths and modes of motherhood. *British Journal of Psychotherapy*, 1(1):6–30.

Safronova, V. (2019, June 14). Gender stereotyping banned in British advertising. *The New York Times*. Retrieved from www.nytimes.com/2019/06/14/style/uk-gender-stereotype-ads-ban.html

Sandberg, S., Grant, A. (2015, January 12). Women at work: Speaking while female. *The New York Times*. Retrieved from www.nytimes.com/2015/01/11/opinion/sunday/speaking-while-female.html.

Sinkman, E. (2013). *The Psychology of Beauty*. Lanham, MD: Jason Aronoson.

Tatar, M. (Ed). (1999). *The Classic Fairy Tales*. New York, NY: W.W. Norton & Company.

Tatar, M. (Ed). (2002). *The Annotated Classic Fairy Tales*. New York, NY: W.W. Norton & Company.

Treisman, R. (2020, December 13). Op-Ed urging Jill Biden to drop the "Dr." Sparks Outrage online. *National Public Radio*. Retrieved from www.npr.org/2020/12/13/946068319/op-ed-urging-jill-biden-to-drop-the-dr-sparks-outrage-online.

Tyson, P. (1982). A developmental line of gender identity, gender role, and choice of love object. *Journal of the American Psychoanalytic Association*, 30:61–86.

Tyson, P. (1989). Infantile sexuality, gender identity, and obstacles to oedipal progression. *Journal of the American Psychoanalytic Association*, 37:1051–1069.

Tyson, P., Tyson, R.L. (1990). *Psychoanalytic Theories of Development: An Integration*. New Haven, CT: Yale University Press.

Williams, J.C. (2019, August 16). How women can escape the likability trap. *The New York Times*. Retrieved from www.nytimes.com/2019/08/16/opinion/sunday/gender-bias-work.html.

Wolfe, H. (2019, February 9). Female leadership: Difficulties and gifts. Plenary Presentation. American Psychoanalytic Association Meeting, New York.

World Bank. (2020). *Women, Business and the Law 2020*. Washington, DC: World Bank. doi:10.1596/978-1-4648-1532-4. License: Creative Commons Attribution CC BY 3.0 IGO.

9 What should a wife want?

Janice S. Lieberman

A quote from Shakespeare's "As You Like It"

> Men are April when they woo. December when they wed. Maids are May when they are maids, but the sky changes when they are wives.

I would like to explore the role of "wife," problematic even in this advanced year of 2021. I was inspired by Glen Close's role as "wife" to a Nobel Prize winner in Literature in the 2018 film "The Wife" (based on the (2003) novel by Meg Wolitzer), the "wife," as portrayed by Glen Close, was overlooked, ignored, patronized, forced to play second fiddle to her most difficult, narcissistic husband. She was manifestly quite bitter about it. Was she envious of him? Was this a classic case of penis envy? Why could she not just enjoy the luxury hotel, the designer clothes and expensive jewelry, the pomp, and circumstance of the Nobel awards in glorious Stockholm, and just brush away the micro-aggressions of being ignored and patronized? At the end of the film, we have the answer: *she* had actually written all of the books for which *he* was acclaimed.

After having won a Golden Globe award for her portrayal of the wife, in her acceptance speech, Glen Close (2019) cited in Rieden (2019) espoused her theory that the film probably took 14 years to get funding because of its title and its negative connotations! There are those who believe that she did not win an Academy Award for this performance due to disdain for the title "The Wife"! She spoke of the denigrated role her own mother took in her marriage: "I'm thinking of my mom, who really sublimated herself to my father her whole life. And in her '80's, she said to me: 'I feel I haven't accomplished anything my whole life." Close concluded: "We have to find personal fulfillment. We have to follow our dreams."

Close is describing what I consider to be a reflection of "adult developmental arrest," to be referred to later on (Ceron, 2019).

In the novel, Wolitzer artfully paints a picture:

> Everyone knows how women soldier on, how women dream up blueprints, recipes, ideas for a better world, and then somehow lose them on the way to the crib in the middle of the night, on the way to the Stop and Shop, or

DOI: 10.4324/9781003180036-12

the bath. They lose them on the way to greasing the path on which their husband and children will ride serenely through life.

She goes on sarcastically and with irony: …

But it is their *choice* (some) might say. They make a choice to be that kind of wife, that kind of mother. Nobody forces them anymore; that's all over now. We had a women's movement in America, we had Betty Friedan, and Gloria Steinem with her aviator glasses and frosted parentheses of hair. We're in a whole new world now. Women are *powerful*.

(p.183)

Wolitzer went on:

Everyone needs a wife, even *wives* need wives, Wives then, they hover. Their ears are twin sensitive instruments, satellites picking up the slightest scrape of dissatisfaction. Wives bring broth, we bring paper clips, we bring ourselves and our pliant, warm bodies. We know what to say to the men who for some reason have a great deal of trouble taking consistent care of themselves or anyone else.

(p.184)

A recent biography of Susan Sontag written by Benjamin Moser (2019) claimed that *she* was the author of her first husband Philip Reiff's seminal work *Freud: The Mind of the Moralist*. This is a story that has many counterparts in many fields. Jackson Pollack's perhaps more talented artist wife Lee Krasner was virtually unknown. Only when he died was she able to do her artwork on a large scale, moving from where she worked in her small bedroom to the huge adjacent barn where he had worked. Their neighbor Elaine de Kooning was similarly in her husband's shadow. There are many counterparts in our field of psychoanalysis too, with some noted exceptions. The spouses of Ruth Bader Ginsberg, Elizabeth Warren, Kamala Harris, while accomplished in their own right, have stayed in the background.

I love to quote from Anne Tyler's (1995) novel *Ladder of Years*. Her heroine was a married woman who ran away from her husband and three adolescent children after spending the day at the beach with them:

Delaware State police announced early today that Cordelia B. Grinstead, 40, wife of a Roland Park physician, has been reported missing while on holiday with her family in Bethany Beach … a slender, small-boned woman with curly fair or light brown hair, Mrs. Grinstead stands 5'2" or possible 5'5" and weighs either 90 or 110 pounds. Her eyes are blue or gray or perhaps green … Her family members could not agree upon her clothing.

(p.3)

Talk about invisibility!

In my private practice in New York, I do not recall ever hearing a woman patient say that she wanted to become "a wife." "Married," "have a relationship," "have a family," "be taken care of," but never "wife." In recent years, with the legalization of gay marriage, I have heard many gay women proudly refer to their "wives." Hopefully these wives will not follow in the footsteps of traditional heterosexual wives!

Many years ago, after I had earned my Ph.D. in Psychology and had a two year old, I went with my then husband to live in Milan, Italy. I joined the ranks of the invisible, the home-bound. Wives and mothers left the house only in the afternoon to buy food or clothes or have their hair done. When I bought some groceries and asked that they be delivered, I was asked: "Tu sei sempre a casa?" "You are always at home?". The good wife. I understand from a Venetian woman that things have not changed very much. A feminist was born in those two years!

Let's consider some of the wives of famous men: Freud's wife Martha was "sempre a casa" and quite unlike his brilliant women colleagues. Shakespeare's wife Anne Hathaway was said to have been poorly treated by him. Romeo's wife died as soon as she became his wife, Lady Macbeth killed. The Shrew had to be tamed. Consider briefly the recent "stand by your man" positions taken by wives Hillary Clinton and Seema Spitzer. A number of women I knew, when asked at the time where they thought Hillary would be if she left Bill replied: "Nowhere." Germaine Greer (1999) in her book "The Whole Woman" noted that: "A First Lady must only be seen at her husband's side on all formal occasions, she must also be seen to adore him, and never to appear less than dazzled by everything he may say or do" (p.263). Michelle Obama, in her (2018) book "Becoming" echoes Greer: "First ladies showed up in the news, having tea with the spouses of foreign dignitaries; they sent out official greetings on holidays and wore pretty gowns to state dinners" (p.342). Brilliant Michelle used her time well with her gardening and children's health projects, staying far away from her husband's political work and adapting herself to *his* schedule.

Today's dilemma is such: the wife who does not play second in importance to her husband is still regarded by some as "castrating," a "ball-breaker," a "bad wife." The wife, even if the more successful breadwinner, is still cast as the caretaker: of children, both sets of aging parents, of the home, and especially, the husband. If not, she is not, in our social world, a "good wife." If her husband takes the role of "house husband," he is often publicly admired, but secretly disrespected.

You may have guessed at this point that I am speaking about relatively or very affluent women in marriages in which second incomes are optional, not necessary for survival. In marriages in which both partners must work, some of the same dynamics often exist, but the wife at least has a place in the world outside the home. In the recent pandemic many working wives chose to leave their jobs in order to oversee their children who were home from school while their husbands worked remotely from home. They also assumed much of the housework in what I consider to be a great setback for women, a regression to former roles.

In 2021, to my disbelief, I still see a certain number of young women coming to me for therapy who are seeking men to support them. Some come to therapy at the point at which they are about to enter marriages knowing that they will be forever financially dependent on their husbands and who have already abdicated any power in decision making about the wedding, the honeymoon, where they will live, etc. They idealize becoming mothers and hope to spend their days at home with little or no interaction with other adults except perhaps other stay at home mothers doing the same. Often they are in symbiotic relationships with their own mothers who are looking forward to assisting them with the children and keeping them company. The work they do will end as soon as the first child is born if not before. Some are school teachers, others trained to be lawyers, doctors, or financial experts. Their choices are welcomed by their future husbands, who are quite successful and do not need their financial assistance.

Their mothers and friends see these future wives as modern day Cinderellas who have won Princes who will take care of them forever after. They will be able to purchase as many golden slippers made by Christian Louboutin as they desire. Many of their husbands have erratic work schedules in which they often travel or return home late when not traveling. They want wives who will not complain and manage on their own when they are gone, wives who will cook and stock the house with food and look beautiful when they come home. If their wives have credit cards, their husbands question the charges and feel free to forbid future spending. They are truly child brides. To what extent do we or should we analysts challenge our patients' life choices when we can predict what the future will hold for them?

Many readers are probably having a hard time identifying with this trend. Those of you who are wives can leave your husbands to shift for themselves and attend a conference on a weekday or a weekend. I know of some who cannot. We psychoanalysts live in a kind of bubble among others like ourselves who share similar lifestyles and values. Many of us are not wealthy or married to wealthy men and have never considered not working. I will attest that today in 2019 we still have some women living and hoping to live the lives Betty Friedan (1963) wrote about and were depicted in the (2007–2015) TV series "Mad Men." I regard their choices to be regressive in this day and age. I see a difference from the late '70's, when I began my practice, when most of the women I saw were anxious to do the balancing act, to break out of the traditional roles their parents had been in, to change the balance of power they were experiencing with their husbands. This has come as a surprise to me. I want to note that the majority of my women patients today who are wives have pretty well-balanced power relations with their husbands. But the women I have just described have succumbed. I believe they are in a state of "adult developmental arrest" halted in their personal development.

I have also seen in psychotherapy and psychoanalysis a number of women in their 50's and 60's who were single, divorced, or widowed, all of them successful career women, who met, while in treatment, wealthy, successful, domineering men. They gave up their work to be "wives" to these men. They met up with the same fate as the younger women I spoke of: they became invisible at dinner parties, went on vacation only where and when their husbands wanted, and had to run all expenditures by them. Each lived in the shadow of their husband's first or second wives, who "stay at home women" were catering to their husbands' every need. Each reported feeling depressed, having low energy and fear of losing these husbands. Their suppressed rage at their husbands emerged and these late life marriages had to be renegotiated. Fortunately, they came to treatment. Many do not.

Think of the case of MacKenzie Bezos. Her husband Jeff Bezos left her for another woman after 25 years of marriage. She was given half of his wealth. There were many discussions about whether MacKenzie, who had given up her career as a writer to raise their children, deserved so much. Filipovic (2019) noted that:

> What divorces like this show us is how little we value the often invisible and unpaid labor that so many women do to enable their husbands to find professional success … Would (Bezos) been able to have a stable, happy family and build a prosperous company without the work of his wife?

Her giving up of her writing career was framed as a choice, but it was a yes "fargone conclusion."

Many years ago, I saw in therapy a lovely young woman, a lawyer in her early 30's, who met at a party a married lawyer from another city. He traveled to New York regularly and they began a passionate affair. One evening he arrived at her apartment with his suitcase, one of those two-sided kinds. He bent down and opened the wrong side: it contained his dirty laundry for his wife back home. The right side contained a bottle of champagne and a box of chocolates for his mistress. His stay at home wife had no ken of where he was or what he was doing. He was clearly bored with her but would never leave her. He was attracted to my lively patient, whose heart he eventually broke.

So, what should the role of the psychoanalyst be in 2021? I think we all need to be aware of the societal pressures that still exist that push women to be traditional wives. We want to believe that there are considerable societal pressures for them to have careers and to be independent women while married and having children. These exist side by side. I believe that no matter how difficult it may be, it is healthier for women to have careers, work they love, to be out of the home as well as inside the home, to know other working adults, to share responsibilities, decisions, and finances with their husbands. Not just in the U.S. but internationally. Take the example of Japan. According to Rich (2019):

the percentage of women who work in Japan is higher than ever, yet cultural norms have not caught up: Japanese wives and mothers are still typically expected to bear the brunt of the housework, childcare and help for their aging relatives, a factor that stymies many of their careers, Fed up with the double standard, Japanese women are increasingly opting out of marriage altogether, focusing on their work and newfound freedoms, but also alarming politicians preoccupied with trying to reverse Japan's declining population.

I do not think we should be silent when we see our women patients making decisions to opt out of the workforce for years; they may never have the possibility of returning. They may have to negotiate future marriages or re-negotiate the marriages they already have.

As psychoanalysts we must analyze our women patients' dependency wishes, their identifications, conscious, and unconscious, with mothers and grandmothers who took subservient roles at home. We must think in terms of intergenerational trauma around marital roles. We must analyze the latent rage of our women patients who have stayed in such roles. Similarly with our male patients, we must look at what they are doing with their wives. Do they believe that they are doing them a favor asking them not to work? Are they trying to get some more mothering? Are they secretly resentful that they are the sole breadwinners? I think of a couple I worked with: she was encouraged by him to do her sculpting and rented her a studio although she never sold anything. He constantly told her how proud he was of her. In their session one day, dropping his benign mask, he shouted: "You would be *nothing* without me!"

We women analysts could be prone to countertransference envy of our women patients who do not have to work, being free to go to the gym, have lunch with their friends, go to museums, to shop, and to look good at the end of the day. We must not overlook the psychological price paid for such freedom. We must remember that they are not Cinderellas, but Noras of the Doll House!

References

Ceron, E. (2019). "Try not to cry at Glen Close's Golden Globes speech." *The Cut* (January 7).

Filipovic, J. (2019). "Why MacKenzie Bezos deserves half of her husband's wealth." *The Guardian* (January 13).

Friedan, B. (1963). *The Feminine Mystique*. New York, NY: W.W. Norton.

Greer, G. (1999). *The Whole Woman*. New York, NY: A.A. Knopf.

Moser, B. (2019). *Sontag: Her Life*. New York, NY: HarperCollins.

Obama, M. (2018). *Becoming*. New York, NY: Crown Press.

Rich, M. (2019). "Craving freedom, Japan's women opt out of marriage." *The New York Times*

Rieden ,J. (2019). "How Glen Closes's mother inspired her performance in The Wife".
   Women's Weekly (online)
Shakespeare, W. (1599). "As you like it," Act 4, Sc.1.1 (153).
Tyler, A. (1995). *Ladder of Years*. New York, NY: A. Knopf.
Wolitzer, M. (2003). *The Wife*. New York, NY: Scribner.

Part IV

Psychoanalysis in the community

Introduction by Nancy R. Goodman

The two chapters in this section are particularly relevant to the ways that psychoanalytic thinking can be brought to understanding societal traumas, particularly concerning women. Nancy Goodman centers her observations on the impact of the psychoanalytic function of witnessing and what happens when it is present or absent. Adriana Prengler focuses on what it means that women have so often not had voice in communities throughout the world. Women are told it is not feminine to express themselves and ensure active places in their societies, families, and professions. While both chapters refer to events in the world, they also bring internal psychic realities and external realities together with reviews of psychoanalytic literature and models of the mind pertinent to enriching clinical practice with women. The overall problems of considering women as silent and of the effects of denying acts of misogyny making women invisible gains depth through the writings here about unconscious fantasy and trauma. Both authors have included creative imagery and ideas in their chapters illustrating the efforts and success of contemporary psychoanalytic writings about women.

What do women want? Let our voices be heard

Adriana Prengler begins her chapter with Homer's *Odyssey* and the statement he makes to his mother to not speak and to return to her quarters – using voice is to be for men. The taboo around women speaking and influencing is further illustrated with vivid stories about individual well-known women. Adriana gives historical context to the development of psychoanalytic thinking about women. While Freud offered women the opportunity to know the unconscious, he was also a man, the only boy in his family, who learned that his mother would rid the home of piano playing since he needed quiet to study. We learn that Margaret Thatcher took voice lessons to have a more male resonance and be taken seriously.

The unconscious representations of women have been recognized and expanded on by many female psychoanalysts helping to break the silence that was thrust on women because of fears about women's voices. The earliest insights of Anna O. to call her voice, essentially free associating, as "cleaning the

DOI: 10.4324/9781003180036-13

chimney" are followed by the new insights of women psychoanalysts such as Mariam Alizade, Emilce Dio Bleichmar, Francis Tustin, Francoise Dolto, and Annie Anzieu. With deep knowledge about the distortions that were built into our own theory, women are better known and their silencing more visible to be better challenged.

Psychoanalysis is based on the idea that children form images and stories from their body experience and from their recognition of differences between boys and girls, between men and women including the difference of their genitals. Adriana writes:

> It is difficult to deny the metaphorical analogy that exists between the structure of the genitalia of the sexes in relation to their mode of expression in the "psychic field." Her important observation is followed by her question: "Is female sexuality a dark continent", as Freud stated? Or are the enigmatic aspects—all the sensations, experiences and knowledge in need of more space to be expressed, heard, and shared?

The chapter ends with the wonderful recognition of individuality – "maybe we should ask: What does this woman want? What does this man want?"

Opening space for women to dream and symbolize when facing misogyny: the need for an active bystander witness

Nancy Goodman puts forth the idea that an active bystander witness is needed to acknowledge the horrors of misogyny for individual women and for society. If the mind is closed down from trauma and denial of the existence of trauma, a double layer of pain has been produced through the action of negation by passive bystanders. In the first part of her chapter, she brings together the experience of double trauma appearing in individual clinical presentations and for society. Active bystanding opens the mind to feelings, desires, fears, remembering, and the narratives of transgenerational trauma as well.

The mechanism of finding the active bystander witness is a necessity in regard to the many terrifying traumas occurring worldwide including in refugee camps and at the Border of the United States and Mexico. Women are particularly perpetrated against with rape, abuse, isolation, and harm to their children. In many places in the world, rates of femicide have increased during COVID when more women are stuck at home and have lost their jobs. Witnessing psychoanalysts have gone into communities, developed programs, and brought active bystanding to the victims of extreme and inhuman circumstances. The experiences of Haroula Ntalla, Gil Kliman, and Susan Siegeltuch represent courageous psychoanalysts who have taken clinical understanding of human sorrow and child development to places of disaster. Details of their efforts bring inspiration to our community. The active bystander makes a difference, becoming internalized as a witnessing object validating experience and all psychic realities.

In the second part of the chapter, Nancy presents the way dreaming becomes possible as space for symbolizing is open. She creates a metaphor from her visit to an art gallery in Prague where she saw a sculpture of a naked woman lying on a couch. The tension builds as she describes the fear that a guard would confiscate her camera for taking a photo. This projection evolves into discovery of the good object witness as the guard points to the title of the sculpture, "woman dreaming." She writes: "It is often the dream that has inspired women to come together and to fight for their basic human rights and for understanding of their full psychic internal world."

10 Opening space for women to dream and symbolize when facing misogyny

The need for an active bystander witness

Nancy R. Goodman

Women want to be able to dream, to acknowledge the symbolic stories of their minds and to recognize the wishes and fears that Sigmund Freud told us are the forces at work to form the content of dreams. Violence against women in communities around the world include for example: femicide, mutilation of genitals, verbal abuses, sexualization, physical abuse, shaming, and limiting of opportunities with the proverbial glass ceiling. These terrors infiltrate the psyche often becoming elements of unconscious fantasies concerning punishments for desires, wishes, and rage. When identifying with the action of misogyny, women's power to create is inhibited and fear is planted in the mind as a cruel presence. With these internal and external perpetrating objects, acts of aggression prevent opening of internal space for dreaming. To expand understanding of the way the female mind can become closed down in the face of terrible violence and to discover the way the mind can gain resilience and openness, I highlight the need for an active bystander witness. The felt presence of an object offering active witnessing is able to counter the extra layer of trauma that takes place when there is a turning away by others who will not acknowledge what is taking place thus forbidding female psychic realities. The first part of this chapter describes the importance of active bystanders for the individual woman and for society when harm is being perpetrated and no one wants to see. The second part delineates the process needed for women to be able to dream and have their internal life without fear.

Part 1: Women need the active witnessing bystander to mend the trauma of misogyny that had been made invisible by passive bystanders

Our contemporary world and communities are filled with incidents of misogyny at all levels of society and with neglect and aggression toward the most vulnerable including women in refugee camps, impoverished girls in need of education, and victims of sexual and domestic abuse. With COVID-19 raging around the world, there are reports of increased abuse of women who have less ability to remove themselves from dangerous situations. Governments are in the position of perpetrators when they cannot enact laws protecting women

DOI: 10.4324/9781003180036-14

and may in fact be implicated in acts of aggression toward women through denial of access to healthcare, birth control, and when rape is not defined as a crime.

Psychoanalysts define these external situations as factors producing trauma, psychic helplessness, shame, identifications with the aggressor, and transgenerational hauntings about the feel and imagery of unspeakable abuse and terror. External threats activate internal unconscious scenarios about women in women's minds, in men's minds, in our patients' minds, and in analysts' minds. Images of sadistic interactions with women can become sexualized and enter society as normative. The constant presence of misogyny causes trauma and helplessness interfering with girls' perceptions of themselves as agents of their own lives and prevents opening of space for dreaming, as presented above. Traumas of misogyny may be a single shattering event such as rape or ongoing intense bullying. Traumas often ensue from an accumulation of moments of dismissal, shaming, and shunning of the feminine as the girl is treated as invisible. Psychic life includes unconscious and conscious fantasies related to such abuses which then make up the scenes appearing on the stages of the inner theater of the mind (Goodman, 2017). In psychoanalytic treatment the feel and content of the traumatic realities of "then and there" will appear in the "here and now" of transference and countertransference. When the analyst receives the ravages of the mind, the unraveling of the trauma story, conscious and unconscious begins. In this way traumas are witnessed and intently listened to enabling symbolization, working through, and growth of resilience.

Need for the active witnessing bystander

In regard to the traumatic unconscious, both the overwhelming nature of the contemporary terrors and the historic primitive internal terrors; it is my premise that it cannot become known until there is a component of witnessing bringing the felt presence of an active bystander to the mind. I add this specific requirement to the concept of witnessing; that is, the need to feel the existence of the active bystander who will not turn away, who will be attentive and caring. It is important to bring the idea of the active bystander to psychoanalytic understanding of our witnessing function and of what makes it possible for the traumatized psyche to make contact with the therapist and ultimately with one's own conscious and unconscious mind. We as psychoanalytic therapists show our activity in listening, listening no matter what. In very nuanced ways, our patients hear when we are present and when we turn away and most importantly when we turn back to hear more. Within this active and receptive listening, images and scenes, and affects and enactments leading to description appear and evolve with the multiple determinants from infancy until now. Witnessing as active bystanders is powerful bringing about anti-trauma forces (Goodman, 2012) needed to mend the intersubjective destructions of severe trauma that has been met by passive bystanders.

What is an active bystander? How does it function to create a transformative internal object?

I first learned of the concept of active bystander from the work of Ervin Staub (Goodman and Meyers, 2012) a scholar of bystandership. He was a child Holocaust survivor who survived because of the actions taken by others to hide and feed him and his family. An active bystander is someone who will cross the street to help when they see you are in trouble. A passive bystander looks the other way and hurries away. Erwin Staub considers passive bystanding to be a crucial element in predicting a pathway to atrocity and genocide and considers active bystanding to function as a preventative. Translating his understanding to the realm of psychoanalysis, the presence of an active bystanding posture in psychoanalytic listening is healing, titrating the powerful presence in the mind of a traumatizing internal object who never acknowledged the events nor emotional truths of the traumas. When women are victims of misogyny, rape, and devaluing, they often speak of the worse wound coming from lack of acknowledgement by those who should have known and could have helped.

I want to be clear, the passive bystander is someone who is present and seemingly available, but will not actually see and hear; and, does nothing. This is an act of dismissal and abandonment resulting in shame, rage, and a sense of being devalued. The placement of passive bystanders in the mind is like brain washing, gas lighting, and results in disorientation and despair. The mind is captured by what Rosenfeld calls an inner gang. This co-opting of the mind brings the death instinct near and keeps away authenticity and creativity. How is one to know what is real, or even if one is real. Basically, the one being confronted with the passive bystander is invited to develop a fantasy of being eternally de-realized. Andre Green refers to such devastations as the internalized "dead mother"; Leonard Shengold refers to soul murder. I am referring to implantation of the passive bystander and an array of fantasies about one's worthlessness. It is the sense of the passive bystander, in reality and in the mind, that is so damaging. It can take a long time for the analytic attitude to seem real when the passive bystander has been embedded and it takes fortitude for the analyst to work at what Darlene Ehrenberg (1992) calls the intimate edge between patient and analyst confronting and experiencing together the absolute belief that someone will make the other's pain invisible. When there is contact with the patient's unconscious belief of never being real, the analyst may also feel dismissed and unreal and must survive this devastation over and over and speak to the immediacy of this destructive process as it takes place in the narrative and enactments of the therapy hours.

Clinical significance of absence and presence of active bystanding

We confront the clinical significance of both passive bystanding and active bystanding in our offices. If there has been a turning away to a child's trauma, the psychic reality of internal life contains a representation of the passive bystander leading to continual intensification of suffering and despair. Using the sense of the psychoanalytic internal theater (Goodman, 2017), we can imagine the psychic residues of an internal passive bystander who makes communication impossible keeping the trauma in a "black hole" of nothingness, a dead place in the mind. The absence of an actively attentive witness creates a double layer of pain, the original trauma and the absence of reception for it. The mother's or father's or society's turning away engenders a fantasy that seeing and knowing will break the taboo against it. There will be punishment for defying the pressures of denial. When the psychoanalyst listens actively, shows attentiveness, and willingness to provide what Bion calls alpha functioning for beta bits of anxiety, there can be an awakening in a new space of contact. The therapeutic active witnessing position breaks through the fog and the patient can feel their own unconscious coming into being. Through the action of witnessing, we are allowing the event and the subjective experience of it to be fully known – to be transferred into holding and containment as a new psychoanalytic object takes hold. In the micro-communications of transference and countertransference contact is made and transformation takes place. The presence of the active witnessing bystander opens new space making it more possible for unspeakable mysogyny to become thinkable and representable sometimes in direct descriptions and sometimes in metaphoric images.

Some clinical examples of the absence of the active bystander

I learn about the internal passive bystander from many of my female patients whose mother or father or teacher or neighbor or clergy, or former therapist looked away when various forms of abuse were taking place in plain sight or in disguised unconscious enactments. It is so difficult almost impossible for these patients to believe that we are not also allied with betrayers who would not truly want to see their truths or what was happening to them in their traumas.

There are a myriad of ways that the intense blinding of being with the passive bystander comes about. There can be a damaged internal boundary between oneself and others when traumas and psychic helplessness of childhood are not registered with anyone else. Without the internal representation of an active bystander, a system of unconscious fantasies develops which are filled with the certainty that someone will use someone often presenting first with body pain and aches (Ellman and Goodman, 2017). No one will function, as the ego. Wishes for pleasure, happiness, and success are dangerous; because there is no one to hold to the existence of reasonable limits. The internal passive bystander would allow incest and murder. Unseen women can be terrified of all wishes for intimacy due to the solid presence of a shadow of boundless punishments.

I hear stories of alcoholic fathers who fluctuated between abandoning and sexually overstimulating their daughters. When drunk, Ms. M's father would exhibit his penis and her mother would just smile. She was painfully aroused and terrified of her body sensations and sexual fantasies. Another patient's mother would be intoxicated and ask Ms. A. to rub her breasts. Both of these women are creative and capable and severely inhibit any kind of excitement in themselves. Many female patients have been stamped with an overly erotized sense of themselves. But, the most intense internal pain arises because no one validates what is happening, nor tries to stop it. Girls and women are often left with a sexualized sense of themselves as they identify with the perpetrators. In treatment, the psyche wants to seduce and blind the analyst to prove there is no hope for an active bystander. A number of my patients have had the experiences of being invited into fusions with mothers; and, it was fathers, in the role of passive bystanders, who did not claim the need for a boundary, would not function as the necessary third. In my psychoanalytic treatments of women patients in China, there is often transgenerational presence of the historic one-child policy in which babies, particularly girl babies were aborted or left to die. A kind of survivor guilt takes hold in the psyche interfering with feelings of success, of creativity, and about becoming pregnant and having a baby. The events have attained unconscious meaning along with the "rule" to not speak of these things. It takes time to build an idea of permission to be creative and procreative and to feel, know, and internalize the active bystander witnessing function of the analysis itself.

Creating a sustaining image of the active bystander for the individual woman and for society: contributions of psychoanalytic thought and courageous witnessing psychoanalysts

Explorations into how psychoanalysis finds unconscious fantasy (Ellman and Goodman, 2017) reveal how scenes in the mind enliven knowing, understanding, and are often discovered through enactments of patient and active witnessing analyst as they listen to the unfolding of psychic realities in analytic sessions. Defining the transference/countertransference interactions through building of descriptions of what is taking place in the room is a process bringing about holding and containment of meaning and clearly presenting the idea that this is a place where you are with a witness. A major function of psychoanalytic treatment is the finding and creating of these unconscious scenes and images, from what is hidden in the mind, repressed, and unsymbolized. In our writing on *Finding Unconscious Fantasy in Narrative, Trauma and Body Pain* (2017), Paula Ellman and I highlighted how enactment processes lead to narrative and symbolization.

In my thinking, it takes active bystanding witnessing to accomplish the work of symbolizing the traumas of misogyny. Through this witnessing the truths of trauma are discovered often with verbal clarification of visual scenes awakened in the room. The importance of the visual scene was present when Freud told his patients to discover their mind by looking out of the window of a train and saying what they see. In relation to the traumatic, the scene is also essential. Dori Laub in his work with Holocaust trauma and all severe trauma asked that those giving testimony in video archives or as patients in his office to speak about what they see as if they were opening a family album and reviewing the old photos. Our function as psychoanalysts involves being this active presence providing the sense of active witnessing to enable the internalization of an active bystander object. This was recently reinforced for me when I presented a question to Marianne Leuzinger-Bohleber during the IPA podcast on Immigration and Refugees. I asked how we handle our countertransference of helplessness to patients' helplessness about the terrible situation for refugees and all that is aroused in their minds. She, quite passionately, spoke if the importance of our offices where we let people know we are listening and their experience is valuable and that this empowers them. This is the feel of the active witnessing bystander.

At the Border of the United States and Mexico, children, even infants, are being separated from their mothers and fathers, held as prisoners in cages, sleeping on cold cement floors with the potential of being disappeared forever – to never be re-united. We know the harm being done and how it is being sanctioned and labeled, mislabeled, as a "refugee policy." Irvin Staub also tells us that calling perpetrations by ordinary language is also one of the techniques of creating a pathway to genocide and this perversion of language needs to be challenged such as when linking the term refugees with criminals, rapists, or invaders.

In regard to active bystanding at the Border of the United States and Mexico, we have photographers providing images resonate with the horror of the events, especially for children. As in psychoanalysis, we are drawn in by the evocative image, can see it with others and recognize the truths of it. Some images have become iconic and strike at the heart of the matter. The camera is a witnessing presence and the publicizing widely of these images is the active bystander position. In describing his work as a photojournalist, John Moore expressed the hope that "we can make people feel." His award-winning photo at the Border does this with the trio of a mother, little girl standing and crying, and the immigration officer detaining and separating the mother-daughter pair. Another photo that makes us feel is of an asylum seeking boy from Central America who is pictured running down a long empty hallway after being detained and directed to a shelter. He is so small and so alone. The photographer is Gregory Bull who took this photo on 11 December 2018. The long hall and sterile lighting is the world of passive bystandership. Traumatically, no one is interfering, no one is holding his hand. Fortunately, the moment is captured on film to be known and remembered and to activate further active bystanding. In Morton, Mississippi immigration authorities rounded up hundreds of workers including a little girl's father. We have a video of her crying openly and emotionally – repeating: "I need my Dad, I need my Dad, he is not a criminal. I need my dad, he is not a criminal." The cry that could have been silent is on her own video. Each of these visual representations reaches those who are motivated to witness. In psychoanalysis, we often create the scene that the patient needs to be known and verified as meaningful. The scenes are lasting and etched into the mind of the analyst as are the images of the photojournalists of trauma.

There are psychoanalysts who have become active bystanders in communities of desperation and their determination provides witnessing and the invitation to others to join their efforts and to see the truths often being obfuscated by the perpetrators. Haroula Talla presented, in my Pre-congress Trauma Group at the London IPA (2019) describing her remarkable work setting up therapeutic contact with refugees in her homeland of Greece. Haroula works tirelessly, in extremely difficult environments, to hear the trauma of women who have been raped, separated from their homes and families, are fearful for their children's safety and survival and are now living in refugee camps that are immensely unstable. She makes contact with these refugees offering herself as a listening witnessing active bystander. This is what women want in our modern world where so many women are under duress.

Gil Kliman is an innovative and dedicated psychiatrist and certified psychoanalyst who has founded organizations to help children in stressful situations such as foster care, loss of parents, and in areas of international crisis. The American Psychoanalytic Association (APsaA) recognized Dr. Kliman with the APsaA President's Humanitarian Award for his work in the community. When hearing of the children being separated from parents and being detained at the Border of the United States and Mexico, he became active to offer help to forensic needs of the families and children caught up in seeking asylum. In his words:

> … I am expanding Freud's theories, now including the drives of murder and cruelty so often expressed in wars and child abuse. My hope is that fuller psychoanalytic understanding of cruelty in the form of irrational wars and unspeakable abuses of children will improve conditions at the U.S. Border and in other international conflicts.
>
> (personal communication)

When I communicated with him he told me that telling the children and parents that he wants to record their stories makes them feel seen and more hopeful.

Susan Siegeltuch describes her experience with Dr. Kliman at the Border in her chapter that was award the Plumsock Prize from the Contemporary Freudian Society in 2020. The title, "Out from Behind the Couch: The case of a mother and her suicidal teenager in detention" tells the story of her being a witnessing active bystander. All of the traits needed to be in this anti-trauma position is found in her descriptions of a traumatized child and mother. Susan shows courage, determination, and the special willingness to become traumatized while taking in the horrible trauma of others. In her words:

> I had the good fortune, to be part of a team in August 2018 with Dr. Kliman to conduct evaluations at the detention center or jail in Dilley, Texas. It was there that I had the privilege and truly moving, though enormously difficult experience of being invited to sit in with him to serve as a translator when

we interviewed an 8 year old little girl who was frightened, traumatized, and sad – suffering with separation from her mother. It took all my control not to weep, never mind cry.

Susan has told me that there are nightmarish after effects of being an active bystander and that she feels an absolute need to be there.

In the interaction at the Border that led to her paper, Susan and Gil returned to Dilley, Texas, responding to an urgent request to evaluate a suicidal 15-year-old girl who had been detained for seven months and her mother. She tells me

It was difficult allowing that to sink in: seven months in detention including 1 week in isolation in a freezing-cold windowless room. We interviewed them as a pair and individually over the course of a day and a half. Dr. Kliman prompted this intelligent, accomplished, protective mother to use her voice to "speak to the nation" when she was released into the community.

Part 2: The need to dream and the fears around dreaming: removing impediments of the attacking passive bystander

In 2013 while in Prague during the IPA Congress, I visited an art gallery and had an experience illustrative of how fear of a persecutory object can bring certainty that female curiosity and desire (mine) will be met with punishment. In a spacious gallery, there was a statue of a beautiful naked woman on a couch that I saw as an analytic couch. How wondrous and synchronous to discover her during the days when thousands of psychoanalysts were arriving in Prague. I took out my cell phone and took a photo. A female guard, in uniform, was walking over to me and I developed fantasies that my delight and desire for a photo of the naked woman on the couch would result in confiscation of my cell phone (my psyche). Or perhaps even worse, because I must be breaking a rule, I would be in serious trouble in a country where the Nazis had marched and murdered and then the Communists. In the internal workings of my mind, there was a sadistic woman in uniform just waiting to notice the trespassing of my desire to look closely at the naked woman and to take her picture.

I view my quick terror imagining as a metaphor for the compromise formations that can vividly exist in the psyche of women and be reinforced by society for example when hearing chants of "lock her up" used against Hillary Clinton and the attacks on powerful female leaders such as Nancy Pelosi and Kamala Harris. Women can feel that their enthusiasms of mind and body will inevitably lead to disaster – there is a sadistic superego woman in uniform just waiting to attack. Will there be punishment, rape, isolation, and shame when the life forces of desire and believing in oneself are active? We know from our patients and the psychoanalytic literature on conflicts of femininity that women imagine attacks in multiple ways such as harm to genitals, mind, and capacity to have a baby. Watching the terrible images of immigrant women in refugee camps being unable to protect their children or the videos of forced removal of children from mothers and the border of the United States and Mexico can reinforce belief that women are helpless. In history and folklore, powerful women are often depicted as meeting their doom – witches are drowned, saints are burned at the stake, and contemporarily, women disappear through societal acts of femicide, girl babies are aborted or left to die as shown in the film "One Child Nation" concerning the one child policy in China.

One way to thwart the internal persecutory fear is to discover the unconscious meaning often held as a compromise for women who come to fear their own wishes leading them to some form of self-harm. When frightened of retaliations for assertiveness and having a living mind, women can become the doer of harm to self rather than wait for being humiliated by others. On the analytic couch, the unconscious fantasies are fleshed out allowing new space for thought and action as the unthinkable becomes thinkable.

When the persecutory guards in the mind disappear and are replaced by an approving object, the girl is freed to be curious and joyful. This is what happened in the art gallery. The approaching guard I saw as ready to punish became an encourager to help transform my fear. She was coming toward me gesticulating, speaking energetically, and had a smile on her face. She kept pointing straight ahead, had my projection been correct and was she designating me for being kicked out of the museum? I put aside my fear and followed her gesture – she was showing me another part of the artistic installation that was a large red mark in the shape of a comma under which showed the title of the artwork, "Woman Dreaming."

When women are not allowed to dream or are humiliated and bullied about their individual dreams, there is a robbery of their minds and a shutting down of creativity and thinking. It is often the dream that has inspired women to come together and to fight for their basic human rights and for understanding of their full psychic internal world. It is interesting to note how societal change and psychoanalytic change have often interconnected. The second wave of feminism brought about by the contraceptive pill and the growth of consciousness raising groups in the 1970s was accompanied by a psychoanalytic movement to honour female experience and development with expansions in the concept of primary femininity. Primary femininity states that little girls know they live in a female body and have fantasies about that body, what they have and what they do not have. Without penis envy as bedrock, new vistas of the feminine appeared in psychoanalytic writing, mainly by women. Women psychoanalysts gathered observations about female development to bring forth new ideas and new capacity for creating interpretations. This history of ideas is one example of what transpires when active bystander witnessing is at work.

What women want today and tomorrow

The active bystanders in our psychoanalytic community inspire us and encourage us to turn toward what needs to be known and to be active bystanders. Witnessing misogyny, violence, abandonment, physical abuse, mistreatment of children, rape, and all dehumanizing behavior helps individuals feel hope and find the capacity to tell their trauma stories and re-connect to others. Active witnessing and creation of a representation of a person who is unwavering in listening, knowing, and acting brings about internalization of an active bystander witness. In many ways this is a way to never again feel shunned, alone, and isolated as one's right to be seen and known gains power. When inner space opens for feeling and knowing, the dreaming mind is active – the woman on the analytic couch is then fully alive.

References

Ehrenberg, D.B. (1992). *The Intimate Edge: Extending the Reach of Psychoanalytic Interaction.* New York, NY: W.W. Norton.

Ellman, P.L., Goodman, N.R. (2017). *Finding Unconscious Fantasy in Finding in Narrative, Trauma, and Body Pain: A Clinical Guide.*. London: Routledge.

Goodman, N.R. (2012). The "Anti-Train": A metaphor for witnessing. In N.R. Goodman & M.B. Meyers (Eds.). *The Power of Witnessing: Reflections, Reverberations, and Traces of the Holocaust-Trauma, Psychoanalysis, and the Living Mind* (pp. 3–26). New York, NY: Routledge.

Goodman, N.R. (2017). The "Finding Theater": A schema for finding unconscious fantasy. In P.L. Ellman & N.R. Goodman (Eds.), *Finding Unconscious Fantasy in Narrative, Trauma, and Body Pain: A Clinical Guide* (pp. 22–34). London: Routledge.

Goodman, N.R., Meyers, M.B. (2012). *The Power of Witnessing: Reflections, Reverberations, and Traces of the Holocaust-Trauma, Psychoanalysis, and the Living Mind.* New York, NY: Routledge.

11 What do women want?

Let our voices be heard

Adriana Prengler

What do women want? And, why does that question sound so difficult to answer? Surrounding the mystery of this inquiry, we need to recognize that women's voices have been ignored throughout history, in culture and in literature. The numerous examples of ignoring women's voices are nothing less than an ancient tradition.

I begin by citing Mary Beard, a well-recognized British scholar and classicist, professor of ancient literature, who referred to one of the earliest examples of Western literature in which a man told a woman to "shut up" because her voice should not be heard in public. It is found in Homer's *Odyssey* from the eighth century BCE. *It concerns* Telemachus, the son of Odysseus and Penelope. It describes

> the story of his growing up; how over the course of the poem he matures from boy to man. The process starts in the first book with Penelope coming down from her private quarters into the great hall, to find a bard performing to throngs of her suitors; he's singing about the difficulties the Greek heroes are having in reaching home. She isn't amused, and in front of everyone she asks him to choose another, happier number. At this point young Telemachus intervenes: "Mother," he says, "go back up into your quarters, and take up your own work, the loom and the distaff ... speech will be the business of men, all men, and of me most of all; for mine is the power in this household." And off she goes, back upstairs. There is something faintly ridiculous about this wet-behind-the-ears lad shutting up the savvy, middle-aged Penelope. But, it's a nice demonstration that right where written evidence for Western culture starts, women's voices are not being heard in the public sphere. More than that, as Homer has it, an integral part of growing up, as a man, is learning to take control of public utterance and to silence the female of the species.
>
> (Beard, 2014, paragraphs 1 and 2)

Although nobody will be surprised by Beard's quote, there have been many women throughout history who were brave enough to challenge the established "common sense" of shutting up and thereby left their influence in the world.

DOI: 10.4324/9781003180036-15

That said, they needed to make extraordinary efforts to do so and they were efforts never requested of a man in the same position. Not only in efforts and creativity, but also in other aspects. For example, Margaret Thatcher, the first female prime minister of the UK, took vocalization classes to learn how to make her voice sound more serious, and like a male voice, unlike her own. She needed her voice to sound more masculine, to afford more opportunities to be listened to and respected as a public voice. She was called "the iron woman" or a phallus woman. It seems difficult to have a voice of authority if one sounds like a woman.

Studies of the male and the female have been present in psychoanalysis since the beginning of our profession. Traditionally, male sexuality has symbolically referred to power, activity, and completeness, while female sexuality has been defined by the penis that the woman does not have, by absence, and by the envy that this absence provokes.

It is difficult to deny the metaphorical analogy that exists between the structure of the genitalia of the sexes in relation to their mode of expression in the "psychic field." The anatomical differences of the sexes have their analogy in the psyches of the female and male. Man, by his anatomy, is oriented outward, toward what is seen, toward action, is associated with activity, strength, power, knowledge, reason, and leadership. For its part, the feminine, according to the anatomy of hidden sexual organs, refers to the internal, to the dark, to what is not seen but allows penetration. It is a continent that welcomes and receives, in a more passive and less action-oriented way; but, is directed toward intuition and affection.

But, this absence, this hole, this castration, the penis envy with a consequent substitution of a baby, are not enough to unravel the "mysteries" of female sexuality to which Freud referred in a letter to Marie Bonaparte.

The child wondering about the differences between the sexes expresses curiosity and the desire to know, to discover. This idea reminds us of the biblical story of Adam and Eve with their interest in the forbidden fruit from the tree of knowledge, which would lead them to the knowledge of the difference between the sexes and the awakening of sexual desire.

What did Adam and Eve want to discover by eating the forbidden fruit?

What does man want? What does woman want? Is female sexuality an enigma, a dark continent? Was it ever? Is it still? What remains? And is male sexuality as enigmatic for women as female sexuality is for men?

What has happened over the years to the answers to the questions and the associated concepts? How is the female and the male understood today?

Freud hoped that women would help unveil the enigma of female sexuality. In this hope, he shows us that he recognized the phallic model was not enough to explain female sexuality. And he was not wrong in this estimation.

Why was female sexuality so enigmatic to him? When we create a theory, we do not escape our own psyche nor our own history. Sigmund Freud was the firstborn of Jacob's third wife, Amalia. When Sigmund Freud was two years old, his little brother Julius was born, but died at 6 months of age, creating the fantasy in the mind of the little Sigmund, that his omnipotent desire to eliminate this little usurper from his path, had succeeded.

Five sisters were then born, and finally a youngest brother. None of them ever occupied, in the Freud home, the privileged place that Sigmund had, with his own room in the house, and for whom all the sisters had to be silent while the prodigious child was engaged in his studies. The young Sigmund even felt the right to ask that his sister's piano be removed from the home as her music disturbed him when he tried to concentrate on his studies. The piano was immediately eliminated from the Freud home.

My intention in recounting this story is to help us reflect on whether these early experiences of power could have structured, in Freud's mind, the germ that later, along with the stories of his patients, originated his theory of penis envy in women. Was it the organ of the penis that his sisters envied, or was their envy for the position of power that their older male brother obviously held? Perhaps the power was what they envied, not the penis, and perhaps it was the **voice** of Sigmund's desire, which seemed to be attended to by his parents as if it were the divine word. I suspect his sisters' possible feelings of inferiority might have nothing to do with castration and penis envy, but rather with the feeling of submission and inferiority evoked by the family dynamics, including the introjected social-cultural environment which disqualified them and silenced their voices.

And what was the relationship between Freud and his wife Martha? Was it possible for Martha to express her erotic desires as well as her desires in other areas? Or perhaps in that Victorian home of the late nineteenth century, as in so many others, women did not have a voice with power to express their desires, their worries and their ambitions?

Is female sexuality a dark continent, as Freud stated? Or are the enigmatic aspects – all the sensations, experiences, and knowledge in need of more space to be expressed, heard, and shared?

While Freud suggested the absence of the penis as a source of early anxieties in women, Mariam Alizade (2008) put forth another idea. She said that not having a penis seems to "facilitate in women the diffusion of the eroticism throughout the whole body surface, which gives the possibility of expanding erogenous zones in an alternating and growing way." From this perspective, Alizade asserts: "the woman has the privilege of not having a penis while the man is mostly limited to the genital area as an erotic zone" (2008, p. 80).

I join the many authors who, over time, have questioned the theory of the castration of women, their penis envy, and their sexual identity based on the lack of a visible external organ. I am inclined to think that what the woman has envied is not the penis, but the VOICE – the voices with which men have had a greater opportunity to express themselves. It is their voice that most women silence, because of tradition, fear of ridicule, or even fear of punishment. Is our sexuality really a dark continent, or is it simply that we need to illuminate that darkness with our own light, with our own voices?

It was Bertha Pappenhaim, the famous Anna O. in Breuer and Freud's *Studies on Hysteria* (Breuer & Freud, 1895), who introduced the idea of the need for a woman's voice when she spoke of the "talking cure" and the metaphor of "cleaning the chimney" by talking. I take this metaphor to refer not only to the psychoanalytic cure, but to the possibility of speaking in every sense, to raise our voices, to say what we think, to express our thoughts, not only to reveal the meaning of symptoms, but also to break our silence, declare our autonomy, proclaim our independence, and establish a presence in the world. Anna O. fought for women's rights and founded the League of Jewish Women, an organization that offered professional guidance to women and trained them to work and be independent. Anna O. cleaned her chimney. She spoke up and overcame her symptoms.

Freud valued her intelligence and culture, and later, he listened to Anna O. as a leader in the struggle for women's rights. Although Freud was immersed in the Victorian Vienna of the time and theorized about penis envy in women, he encouraged the presence of women in the study of psychoanalysis, valuing their intelligence and scientific contributions. In many ways, he could hear the voice of the woman much better than anyone else of his generation, despite the criticisms that are leveled against him.

Emilce Dio Bleichmar in her excellent work "*El Feminismo Espontáneo de la Histeria*" (1985). The "spontaneous feminism of hysteria" proposes that traditional conversion hysteria is an expression of the desperate scream, expressed through the body, when the woman voice cannot be heard.

Women have needed to fight throughout history to make their voices heard, and have repeatedly been ignored and relegated to only an object of man's desire.

Chasseguet Smirguel quoted Bela Grumberger who stated, in an ironic way, that

> [At] least in our civilization, women are thought to make love the essential, the central problem of their existence, while man (passes through a period of love) is obliged to deal with serious things; the amorous man easily passes for effeminate, and the "enraptured," enamored, for a more or less ridiculous figure.
>
> (Chasseguet Smirguel, 1985, p. 89 –
> [my translation from the Spanish])

I remember from my youth the lyrics of a charming song by Tito Puente, a pioneering force in Latin music. It was about how a woman should be. It is a song that I loved to hear my father sing. The song describes the idea that the most important quality defining a woman is her capacity to love a man with passion. It states that a woman *must be a dreamer and a flirt, have a fiery temperament, and must be given to love, with frenzy and ardor to be a real woman.*

This is the woman who is recognized as the object of man's desire, a woman who knows how to surrender to love.

Another aspect of the traditional woman is what I will call the "Violet Woman." She is the woman whose feminine attributes demand that she be passive, waiting to be discovered and valued, like the Violet flower. A patient told me with a mixture of nostalgia and pride, that her mother used to tell her that the woman should be discovered as a violet, and when discovered, she would offer her aroma, which would otherwise go unnoticed. It seemed that, to be a worthy and appreciated woman, one had to stay there quietly, waiting to be discovered. The violet is a flower that needs a certain humidity to live, so it prefers the shady areas, both under the trees, and next to shadowed walls, the edges of roads, or between the grasses on the lawn, a little hidden, on the edges and in the shade.

A woman, must be, a dreamer, a flirt and fiery. She must be given to love, with frenzy and ardor to be a woman. She also needs to be silent, like the violet.

Returning to paraphrase Eve, the first biblical woman, we have learned that our voice can bring us problems. Eve did not behave like the Violeta, and being carried away by her desire to know, because of her epistemological interest, she allowed herself to be seduced by the snake, and because of that desire, she was punished and expelled from paradise. From there, it seems that it was easier for women to submit and placate the desire to know, in order to avoid being expelled from the paradise we thought we had known, a space of protection and free of challenges.

Freud, in his article "*The Feminine*" (1932), takes into account that women's ideas of passivity are influence by the social environment:

> The suppression of women's aggressiveness which is prescribed for them constitutionally and imposed on them socially favors the development of powerful masochistic impulses, which succeed, as we know, in binding erotically the destructive trends which have been diverted inwards. Thus, masochism, as people say, is truly feminine.
>
> (Freud, 1932, p. 116)

Francis Tustin and Francoise Doltó agree on the primordial notion of the image of the body as the basis of sexual identity (Anzieu, 1993, p. 25).

The French author, Annie Anzieu, argues that the psyche of a woman is influenced by the representations of the interior of her body, formed by a sexual cavity. In her opinion, femininity does not imply the lack of a penis, but the notions of orifice and passage.

These days it is widely accepted that we have left behind the old notion of the woman who is made complete by man, the bearer of the phallus, which confesses to the implicit incompleteness of woman. And even Freud, while defining sexual differences based on the presence or absence of the penis, also spoke of psychic bisexuality, which leads us to identification with both parents and the appropriation of both their respective attributes. Both the boy and the girl identify with both parents, and own both the active and the passive functions, both masculine and feminine attributes.

There are many authors in the psychoanalytic world who recognize that women are as complete as men. Today we understand that the feminine is not the exclusive property of women, and that both men and women possess aspects of the feminine. The codes of behavior have changed and the limits of experience have expanded. Man is not necessarily active, strong, and powerful. And the woman is no longer required to be passive, weak, and submissive.

I dare say that a certain amount of "the feminine" in man, is one of the attributes most valued by heterosexual women today: tenderness, the ability to contain, the capacity to listen, and of course, the ability to "surrender" "to love with frenzy and ardor," which were in the past more typical of the feminine in the female. Today, the boundaries between the feminine and the masculine have blurred, far from the way in which sexual differences defined relationships and identifications a century ago. The stereotypes of what is feminine and masculine have been diluted. The distinctions of the past sound very distant and foreign to us today.

The lack conferred to women no longer seems to determine her. The lack and possession belong to everyone. The voices that were previously silenced, today are being expressed. The woman is inspired to make her voice heard in a way that shows her lights and abilities not only for love, motherhood, and restraint, but also for the expression of her desire and her aggression, to speak, to ask, to demand, suggest, and assert. Femininity has acquired a thousand and one voices in all areas: the erotic, the social, the economic, the political, in human rights, in science, in creativity, in research, in reasoning, and in leadership.

Our voices are many: the allowed and forbidden voices, the strong and weak voices, the voices of hope and the voices of lament, the happy and sad voices, the courageous and fearful voices, the voices that propose and those that respond, those that express themselves and those that are silent.

A patient used to ask me from the couch: "Who are you? In what ways are you? I only know that you are a voice."

We no longer find a clear delimitation between the feminine and the masculine. We are both male and female. Instead of asking: What does woman want? What does man want? Maybe we should ask: What does **THIS woman** want? What does **THIS man** want?

References

Alizade, M.A. (2008). *La sensualidad femenina*. Buenos Aires: Amorrortu.
Anzieu, A. (1993). *La mujer sin cualidad: Resumen psicoanalítico de la feminidad*. Madrid: Biblioteca Nueva.
Beard, M. (2014). The public voice of women. March 2014, *London Review of Books*, 36(6). Internet edition. www.lrb.co.uk/the-paper/v36/n06/mary-beard/the-public-voice-of-women
Breuer, J., Freud, S. (1895). Studies on Hysteria. Ed. J. Strachey. *The Standard Edition of the Complete Psychological Works of Sigmund Freud, Volume II*. London: Hogarth Press.
Dio Bleichmar, E. (1985). *El feminismo espontáneo de la histeria*. Madrid: ADOTRAF.

Freud, S. (1905). Three essays toward a theory of sexuality. In Ed. J. Strachey, *The Standard Edition. New Introductory Lectures on Psycho-Analysis and Other works of the Complete Psychological Works of Sigmund Freud, Volume VII.* London: Hogarth Press.

Freud, S. (1925). Algunas consecuencias psíquicas de la diferencia anatómica entre los sexos. In Ed. J Strachey, *S.E. 19*: 259–276. Buenos Aires: Amorrortu.

Freud, S. (1932). La feminidad. Conferencia 33. En Nuevas Conferencias de introducción al psicoanálisis. In Ed. J. Strachey, *S.E. 22*: 104–125. Buenos Aires: Amorrortu.

Glocer, L. (2001). *Lo femenino y el pensamiento complejo.* Buenos Aires: Lugar Editorial.

Grunberger, B. (1985). Jalones para el estudio del narcisismo en la sexualidad femenina. Ed. *Janine Chasseguet Smirguel's La sexualidad femenina,* 85–105. Barcelona: Laia/Divergencias.

Kramer-Richards, A. (2012). Freud and feminism: A critical appraisal. In Eds. Kramer, A. and Goodman N. *Psychoanalysis: Listening to Understand. Selected Papers of Arlene Kramer Richards.* New York, NY: IPBooks.

McDougall, J. (1985). *La sexualidad femenina.* Barcelona: Laia.

McDougall, J. (1998). *Las mil y una caras de eros.* Buenos Aires: Paidós.

Person, E.S. (2002). Sexo, género y el inconsciente cultural. *Trópicos, Revista de psicoanálisis.* Año X, Volumen 2, 84–94.

Torres, A. (1998). La construcción del sujeto femenino. *Trópicos, Revista de psicoanálisis.* Año VI, Volumen 1, 82–99.

Part V

Contemporary feminine scenarios

Introduction by Paula L. Ellman

I can imagine a multitude of contemporary feminine scenarios that we could be writing about and discussing in today's world, especially since the two chapters in this part were written prior to the 2020 pandemic. The most current feminine scenario could be considered as the place the woman finds herself in during this time of quarantine. Many women have been regressively pulled back to more traditional feminine positions in the household when both partners are working from home and children are educated at home. It has been considered that social crises, like the pandemic exposes the social fissures that already exist. Certainly, the painful prevalence of racism and prejudice that has been strikingly unveiled this year is one instance of a social fracture. Another instance is the gender and feminine scenario. The social fractures not only of the non-acceptance of gender diversities, but also the resumption of more rigidly defined gender roles within the family structure has become apparent and necessitates our revisiting our believes in our progressive movement.

The two chapters in this part offer an opportunity to consider two different perspectives on our contemporary feminine scenarios, and while written prior to the pandemic remain profoundly relevant to our world today in our looking forward with more hopeful medical interventions facilitated by a more functional political structure. Patricia Alkolombre's paper, "The Maternal-Feminine: Scenarios in Transition," and Paula Ellman's paper, "Self-Agency in the Feminine: What Females Need Today" consider what the feminine position is today and what women continue to "want," to desire. Alkolombre discusses in her paper the cultural changes that have emerged in contemporary times that have opened possibilities for alternative choices with regards to maternity – delayed, assisted, or no maternity, in addition to decisions to terminate pregnancies. Also, Alkolombre uses her psychoanalytic perspective in the clinical context to consider the repercussions of earlier life experiences such as abortions that are then revisited in a kind of "apres-coup" at later times of conception or maternity-related events. In a clinical vignette, Alkolombre brings our attention to those patients whose process becomes fixed, much like an obsession, on the desire for a pregnancy, and suffer again and again the disappointment each month of failed conception. Crucial for our consideration are those circumstances when the feminine need not have to depend on the choice

DOI: 10.4324/9781003180036-16

for maternity. Today's women "can want" to be women without children. These choices indicate that in a departure from the traditional feminine position, today's women can want to live differently and may make this choice with the challenge this can bring to our thinking about what constitutes the feminine.

In the second paper, I discuss the place of self-agency in today's women, as I believe that the establishment of the firm sense of self is what women want today. Through my illustration in a series of clinical vignettes, I suggest that self-agency is an area of feminine development that can prove to be at great risk. I offer some theoretical ideas on the nature of self-agency, aspects of its development and a consideration a few clinical cases, a couple in the midst of adolescent development, and others in mid-life. A consideration of the varying aspects of agency is offered. Also, I introduce my thinking on how social media interfaces with the concept of self-agency and on the manifestations of aspects of self-agency in the woman as represented in popular culture through the exploration of a television series. What had been solely relying on an explanation incorporating ideas within the realm of the development of narcissism, an alternative formulation of the formation and evolution of agency could further enrich our psychoanalytic thinking. The two chapters in this part contribute to a clarifying of the psychoanalytic lens on our current day feminine scenarios.

12 The maternal-feminine

Scenarios in transformation psychoanalysis and gender perspectives

Patricia Alkolombre

Introduction

Contemporary feminine scenarios are topics of current interest and the participation of Psychoanalysis in these debates is very important. Not less important, we must question what is changing in these fields nowadays, based on clinical observation, and explore their scopes from psychoanalytic perspectives. There are no doubts that we live in a period of deep transformations and de-constructions of the maternal-feminine, which have modified our clinical perspectives. In the midst of post-modernity, we are facing the necessity of understanding current scenarios in motherhood.

The changes in parenthood with different types of ties that bind men and women constitute a central topic. We are facing the "family in disorder," paraphrasing Roudinesco (2005), where along with the majority of traditional heterosexual families are homo-parental and single-parent families. These scenarios also include instances of assisted reproductive techniques that open new possibilities for women and men to become parents in a different way. There are so many and varied ways of being born nowadays, contemporary parenthood includes and the new scenarios of sexual and gender diversities within the LGBTIQ community (lesbian, gay, bisexual, intersex, and queer). Contemporary scenarios challenge the traditional family type as it was understood when Psychoanalysis came into being at the beginning of the last century (Alkolombre, 2017). The new ways of parenthood in this respect represent a subject that dares us, and moves us, to rethink the traditional paradigm of Psychoanalysis.

Among the transformations in parenthood, in this chapter I will discuss the current transformations of the feminine maternal from a psychoanalytical perspective and include lenses of both the historical-social and gender theories.

Initial perspectives on women's desire to have a child

If there is one feature that has without doubt characterized women in Psychoanalysis is the feminine desire, and the one true and highest desire within the Freudian framework is: the desire for children.

DOI: 10.4324/9781003180036-17

It is important to recall that the psychosexual development of girls is explained based on the primary masculinity seen in the desire for a penis, which later develops into penis-envy. Penis-envy is a central theoretical concept and alludes to the absence, the wound and the narcissistic injury of missing something essential. From this perspective, each and every woman desires to have and envies those with penis. Girls enter the oedipal stage "castrated," thus leadings to the eventual desire for a child.

A girl's masculinity is based on the non-perception of her vagina, as stated by Freud, something which was questioned by the British School[1] in the 1920s, a hundred years ago. The British School dealt with a primary femininity for both sexes and the perception of the vagina by girls.

Finally, the desire for children in the oedipal stage is defined by Freud in his 1979d paper "Some Psychological Consequences of the Anatomical Distinction between the Sexes," where he states that

> the girl's libido slips into a new position along the line – there is no other way of putting it – of the penis = child equation. She gives up her wish for a penis and puts in place of it a wish for a child. [2]

Freud's words "slips" and "equation" bring a linear and almost natural causality to his statement, especially in the idea of a prefigured symbolic equation, a pre-existing process.

The masculinization of the girl when being envisaged as a boy is linked to the androcentric and patriarchal ideals that ruled at the time, with well differentiated roles for men and women, which exist to this day. The Freudian vision of feminine sexuality was inevitably influenced by the cultural variables in which male supremacy was not questioned and there was no scientific discussion about it. Freud's contemporaries, such as Moebius and Marañón, described women as incomplete beings.[3]

The desire for a child is in Freud's work not only in the phallic stage as the resolution to the Oedipus complex, but also in other theoretical axes such as the equivalence among child = penis = feces = gift in anal erotism (Freud, 1979c); in the paper "On Narcissism, an introduction" the role of the child, described as "His majesty the baby," is associated with narcissistic parenting through the wishful dreams projected on the child to come and through transcendence. In that same paper, Freud describes a type of narcissistic object in which the child is loved as part of the mother's body (Freud, 1979b). Lastly, it is also present in the girl's pre-oedipal stage, through the identification of the girl with her mother's image: to be a mother like her mother (Freud, 1979g).

There are several theoretical assumptions underlying the Freudian developments about the desire of a woman for a child, amongst them we find phallic monism[4] in how the girl is perceived as a boy. These assumptions also rest on a binary logic in addition to an implicit hierarchy. French anthropologist Françoise Heritier (1996) points out that the difference between the sexes is one which contains a hierarchy within itself, one of them having pre-eminence over the other. She calls this "the differential valence of the sexes" within the difference between the sexes. Lastly, an essentialist perspective is present in Freud's work in the fact that he defines women's journey into femininity through motherhood, meaning that motherhood makes the feminine being, in an ahistorical and immutable way.

So if we think about how the woman's desire for a child is the theoretical core of femininity, we can see the risk of clinical interpretation privileging motherhood as intrinsic to femininity and naturalizing the maternal in an unquestionable way, a vision that is underlain by the sacralization of the maternal.

Contemporary maternities: desiring diversity

Consideration of the maternal – feminine notion today allows for scenarios that are undergoing transformation. Regarding the range of possibilities, from the desire to have a child to the desire not to have a child, motherhood raises the necessity of deconstructing the classic paradigm of the feminine in the context of Psychoanalysis. This paradigm is challenged by women's diverse experiences that do not adhere to the traditional conceptions of the feminine.

One way to explore contemporary motherhoods is revisiting Freud's questions about women, since they stem from the unknow, an unknown territory that Freud describes as a dark continent (Freud, 1979e) and the famous question he posed to Marie Bonaparte "What does a woman want?" (Freud, 1979d).

We can pose the following question: what do women want today when it comes to motherhood?

It is a question that introduces us into a plural feminine desire which moves us away from the idea that there is a unique destiny of femininity, constituted by motherhood. It is about a hegemonic wish that we inherited from the initial conceptions of women's psychosexual development. When we think of the concept of the desire for a child we can observe the hegemony of motherhood, with both the anatomical difference as biological support, and from Psychoanalysis, the theoretical support. This means that when we talk about the desire for a child, we are thinking of the Oedipus complex in women, in the symbolic penis = child equation (Freud, 1979d).

From this essentialist and binary perspective, what women want is defined in only one way – maternity – as a central part of their femininity. It holds the idea – as was previously pointed out, that there is the "nature" of femininity for all women, a conception of motherhood whose roots are found in the sediment of patriarchal culture.

In the 50's, within this cultural context, Marie Langer in her book "Motherhood and Sex" discussed women's conflicts and investigated the struggle between their professional work and their maternal instincts (Langer, 1951). She points out that self-actualization for a woman was motherhood and emphasized how culture had an influence in each woman's life. She said that a woman can develop a full life and sublimate their maternal instinct. In later years she criticized her previous ideas in a paper published in *Página 12* Newspaper (1982) about the "natural wish to procreate" and the notion of "maternal instinct" and shifted her initial essentialist perspective.

Ana María Fernández writes about this issue:

> It would seem that thinking of ourselves as being children of instinct gives us the illusion of strong anchorage, while thinking of ourselves as children of desire… desire, something so evanescent and erratic. "Children of instinct" refers us back to the illusion of being inscribed in a necessary – natural order. Children of desire confront us with the contingency in which the facts of the human order are inscribed.
>
> (Fernández, 1993, p. 171)

These ideas introduce us to a new plural feminine desire that distances us from the idea of a single desire for women. Today we can see this through a diversity of desires that unfold in new family configurations, many of which were made possible by advances in reproductive medicine.

Within all the different clinical scenarios, we find women who resort to egg donation, women who choose to be single mothers through anonymous insemination from a sperm bank – a growing practice; and others become surrogates so other women or men can become parents (this being a practice less talked about). We also find women who become mothers at a later age, other women decide to preserve their fertility through egg freezing methods, others become mothers through adoption, and we increasingly find more women who decide not to have children. There are also pregnancies pursued at any cost, stemming from a passion for a child, a concept I develop later. Lastly, there are women who, for multiple reasons, decide to terminate a pregnancy. We know from the clinical perspective the psychic consequences that the criminalization of abortion can have, the scenarios of suffering and stigmatization of women, teenagers, and girls in many Latin American countries due to legislation prohibiting abortions.

In every expression of motherhood there are fantasies and experiences associated with each woman's singular story, determined by the socio-historical context and its practices. As already pointed out, most new paths to motherhood are made possible by the advances in reproductive medicine, which were unfathomable three decades ago. We all know that the traditional ways to procreate – in the intimacy of a sexual relation – are over 2,000 years old, whereas those initiated with medical – technological intervention were inaugurated little more than 30 years ago.

Today we can say that whether it be the desire for a child or the desire not to have a child, motherhood challenges us to deconstruct the classic paradigm of maternal femininity in the light of Psychoanalysis, along with consideration of the contributions from gender theories.

Women and the desire to have a child or the desire not to

The desire for a child is unconscious and has pre-oedipal and oedipal roots in each woman's life. Contemporary maternities lead us to think that this desire is permeated by everyday contexts as well as cultural ideals and mandates transmitted throughout generations.

The maternal feminine can be expressed through a diversity of desires that move us away from the idea of a unique desire for each woman. These desires develop within the multiple feminine scenarios which we can explore and investigate within the context of gender perspectives and psychoanalytic thinking. The desire for a child is present in contemporary motherhood in hetero, homo, and single-parent families.

Today many women in their 30s and 40s who are not in an intimate relationship frequently decide to freeze their eggs. Some prefer to postpone maternity in order to advance their professional careers yet at the same time wish to preserve their fertility. Often such circumstances bring conflicts and fantasies associated with the limits of fertility and an uncertainty of whether they will become single mothers or will have a partner. In other cases, when the "biological clock" approaches, many choose to pursue maternity by means of sperm donation.

There is no doubt that the borders in this field have expanded. We see a change in the limit of age when seeking a pregnancy. Not many years ago the limit was 40 years. Nowadays, many women begin the path to motherhood from that age.

Often women seek psychoanalytic consultation in the context of their decision not to have children, previously unthinkable in psychoanalytic frameworks. It may be the woman who does not want to have children and, on the contrary, the man wants to be a father. This conflict inverts typically traditional roles where male's desire for paternity was hidden.

Women's voices

If we consider again the question about what women want today when it comes to motherhood, we find that there is much said by women about themselves. In our consulting rooms, we listen to their stories, their desires and suffering, whether or not they want to become mothers.

I would like to point out some issues that caught my interest from my experience both as a psychoanalyst in my consulting room and through my work at the public hospital. One of the most frequent stories I have heard is about induced abortions during adolescence that becomes resignified in adult life when pregnancy occurs or is desired.

Clinical vignette

Sophie (33 years old) and Alexander (41 years old) told me in their first interview that they were about to start an assisted fertilization treatment.

SOPHIE: On Wednesday we went to the doctor. I got out of there feeling badly… I had memories of the abortion. I began to have nightmares…

ALEXANDER: The doctor explained a little about the process, the egg aspiration …

SOPHIE: Aspiration … this word made me sick. Like abortion, it is the same thing but in reverse, instead of removing it they put it in.

ALEXANDER: I told her that since it's her body she should decide alone which doctor is the most reliable.

SOPHIE: I got angry when he told me that!

ANALYST: What did you think at that moment?

SOPHIE: Yes, there … (referring to abortion) my boyfriend abandoned me. I had to decide for myself. A friend recommended a doctor to me. I wanted nothing to do with the procedure. I only wanted a reliable place.

For Sophie, as in many others, the memory of a clandestine abortion powerfully emerges. In this case it is with the doctor's expressing of the word "aspiration." The earlier scene that comes back to life and returns with strength in Sophie's mind. Many women request confidentiality and secrecy when they come to the analytic consultation with a new partner, because they feel shame or fear of being rejected by them.

As we know, in Argentina when women decide to terminate an undesired pregnancy – for different reasons – they must face conditions of illegality and in many cases, precariousness and concerns about safety. In my clinical experience, the most important psychic consequences are related to the loneliness, fear, and secrecy of this situation.

When a woman is pregnant and does not want that child, she needs to be listened to. The choice made can have a subjective or de-subjective effect, whether or not they can be agents of their own desire to have a child or not to have a child. In this case, it is important to have in mind gender prejudices that may be present regarding motherhood. Especially with the prejudices suffered by women who decide not to become a mother for a variety of reasons.

The legalization of the abortion in Argentina remains a pending issue and has to do with the politicization of the female body. The promotion and the fight for reproductive rights has become much more visible through women's movements in the last few years.[5] The green handkerchief symbolizes this movement. The most meaningful change has happened in our minds, especially in new generations where there is now the possibility to identify with other perspectives and new ideals.

The passion for a child

Finally, I share a clinical vignette from a woman's analysis that led me to begin to think about a narcissistic-passionate path in the field of the desire to have a child. I have been impressed by the effort to achieve a pregnancy in women who were willing to do anything whatsoever to have a child. Many cases had a strongly sacrificial aspect, both because of the physical risk – having one assisted fertility treatment after another – as well as economic risks in finance the interventions. I compare these cases to others where adoption or life without children was considered.

Marcela was 28 years old when she came to see me. She had been married to Richard for a year, and was the middle sister of three girls, born a year after her elder sister, who was closer to their mother. The relationship with her father was always distant. Throughout her session, she spoke about her desire to have a child and also about her suffering, since she could not conceive. Each month she repeated the same nearly identical speech:

> This month I didn't get it … I'm not going to get it. Why does this have to happen to me …! Some women beg not to get it. Perhaps because of this obstacle the desire in me is greater. I don't know; I would have one after another; it's the only thing that fills me, having babies. I would like to have many.
>
> (Alkolombre, 2011[2008], p. 60)

We worked together to try to understand the roots of her complaint and the reasons for her strong fixation to the drive for pregnancy, and its relationship to her story and her femininity.

The associations and reflections are oriented initially toward the hyper-cathexis of the reproductive function, the difficulties in her bond with her mother, and the increase of castration anxiety. Also the necessity to explain the intensity of her feelings and the constant crises she suffered every month with the onset of her menses, another failed pregnancy.

After some time, I began to think that this is a problem with narcissistic-passionate roots, as in couples with a passionate functioning: *you will belong to me or to nobody*. In this case it is: *I will have a child because I have to have one*. Clinical experience has enabled me to compare this case to others with characteristics similar to that of Marcela: perseverance in cruel and non-cruel testing – patients who underwent one treatment after another – many years invested and depressive states of greater or lesser intensity. An excess of drive manifested in sacrificial and thanatic aspects associated with medical-technological treatments. And particularly two distinguishing characteristics stand out: the fixedness – or perseverance – and the affective intensity.

The passion to have a child is translated into "living for" a pregnancy; maternity becomes an ideal – as something irreplaceable – that invites pleasure and its absence generates intense suffering (Alkolombre, 1997). Consequently, I arrive at the hypothesis:

> In these women the desire to have a child is transformed into a passion to have a child: a unique object and recipient of this love. Passion is the form taken by the suffering of an ego that has submitted to the ideal of maternity.

This passion emerges in the link with the absent child, in a fixed, incessant, boundless, and demanding way. In this search for a pregnancy, women established an inner dialogue with this lack, and are constantly interrogating their body. The passion for a child is a possible destination for the desire for a child in a woman for whom the child becomes a unique, irreplaceable object, and recipient of maternal love, characterized by the fixation and affective intensity within a narcissistic-passionate dimension.

As earlier mentioned, within the scope of traditional Freudian Psychoanalysis, motherhood is described as the only destination in the resolution of the Oedipus complex in women, which entails the risk of privileging motherhood as an exclusive and hegemonic project, thus naturalizing the maternal like a condition of the feminine essence.

In these passionate searches for a child – many of them utilizing medical and technological resources – the anticathexis processes associated with the thanatic aspects existing in the "passion for a child" can be bypassed. Hence, decentering motherhood as the one true desire allows us to include other paths of desire for women in femininity and approach this "passion" as an alienating bond.

A child as the sole object (Berenstein and Puget, 2012), inasmuch as they are a primary imaginary object, is an intrapsychic bond based on the relationship between the primitive self (baby) with the external other, within a narcissistic functioning (Puget and Berenstein, 1992).

From other theoretical perspectives, Delasi de Parseval and Janaud (1983) bring forth the idea of "a child at any cost" from a critique of the implementation of assisted reproductive techniques as a voluntaristic metaphor. Tubert (1991) describes an incoercible demand in which there is no symbolic substitution, as an obsessive idea where pregnancy and motherhood are cathected as a fixed idea. Aulagnier (1992) proposes a difference between the desire for a child and the desire for pregnancy. In the first case, the child is an object separate from the mother and the desire unfolds predominantly in a symbolic dimension. On the contrary, the desire for pregnancy is dominated by the narcissistic and imaginary dimension, in a mirrored relationship.

In the proposed conceptualization, the "passion for a child" carries in itself the quality of excess in the search for a child, with a fixation and affective intensity that persists beyond the pleasure principle (Alkolombre, 2020). This is an issue rooted in narcissism, stemming from the turning back of the libido and the effort to recreate a state of fusion with the idealized object through motherhood.

In turn, we find a positive and a negative side to passion, as pointed out by Alizade (1992). The positive aspect is connected to the binding as a protective psychic bridge linked to Eros which makes the absence of a love object bearable. Libidinal intensification or hypercathexis causes a fixation to the object, making it necessary, which poses the question of how sublimation will be accomplished in the "passion for a child." The negative side to passion refers to the sacrificial and thanatic position that prevents grief work from happening.

Although passion is not a metapsychological term but a descriptive one, it is homologated to the state of being in love described by Freud as an overflow of narcissistic libido onto the object (1979b), as well as a driving force (1979a).

Anzieu (1980) argues that the passionate subject expects from the object the restitution of narcissistic fullness, and along this line, Racamier (1980) points out that the object of love in passion has a narcissistic reference value that is untouchable and unchangeable. Aulagnier (1994) in turn describes the object of passion as an irreplaceable object because it responds to a desire that has become a need. Green (1980) considers passion as a basically affective phenomenon in the love-passion, love – suffering, dyad. On the subject of "passion for a child" he points out that it can be thought of as an affective movement that stems from a desire to give life to that child (Green, 2005).

In these passionate affective constellations, sexuality is inhibited in women and a third party that could make room for desire is absent. Alienation through a passion can operate as a defense of narcissism against the suffering inherent in grief work, as pointed out by Cournut (1999). In this sense, what is characteristic of the "passion for a child" is the impossibility of carrying out a normal mourning, that would imply recovering the desire for a child whereas in the passion for a child, we are facing a sacrificial resolution.

Alongside biological and psychological foundations, motherhood and the different types of access to parenting bear a strong cultural and socio-historical imprint found in the mandates and ideals of the maternal condition. Within traditional Freudian Psychoanalysis, motherhood is described as the only path in the resolution of female sexuality. It is at this point that the question of the theoretical centrality of the desire for a child arises, inasmuch as it is the only place where the woman occupies the role of a desiring subject. The risk of privileging motherhood as a hegemonic and exclusionary destination can cause the clinical analytical interpretation to aid in these passionate searches for a child – many times through medical and technological resources – without envisaging the anticathexis processes associated with the thanatic aspects that are found in the "passion for a child." Hence, decentring motherhood as the one true desire allows other desiring paths in women to be included in femininity.

Final comments

Our social imaginary of motherhood is associated with a certain naturalization of a desire considered typically feminine. Although in analytic listening we find different theoretical lines and viewpoints, the women's desiring field is nearly totally saturated in maternity. In this regard, we can consider the different perspectives concerning the psychosexual development of women, and take into account the contemporary experiences related to motherhood. We must continue thinking about it and probe more deeply into this topic in order to de-center the maternal as the unique destiny of femininity in women, with the child as her guarantor.

These ideas are backed up in some cases by gender prejudices and leave out other aspects of the maternal-feminine in women who, for different circumstances, cannot or do not want to become mothers.

We argue that today the maternal constitutes a heterogeneous territory that develops alongside the changes in the cultural ideal, the different family structures and gender identities. It is a theoretical conception that harbors in itself different experiences of women ranging from the desire for a child to the non-desire, within a desiring diversity. It is deeply immersed in a perspective that contemplates the criticism of the patriarchy and gender perspective, and takes into account the decline of traditional paradigms.

There is still much to ponder about women, desires and today's motherhoods, around a decentralized interpretation of binarism and essentialism, within a desiring diversity.

Notes

1 The so-called "British school" was formed by Melanie Klein, Ernest Jones, and Karen Horney.
2 Freud (1979d).
3 Cited by Langer (1951, p. 31).
4 Freud points out the preeminence of a single sex under the phallic primacy, in the phallic-castrated dichotomy (Freud, 1923), A.E., T. XIX.
5 While I was editing the paper, the law on legal, safe, and free abortion in Argentina was approved by the government. It is a great achievement of reproductive women's rights after years of struggles. Women now can decide about their bodies and their lives.

References

Alizade, A. M. (1992). *La sensualidad femenina*, Buenos Aires: Paidós.

Alkolombre, P. (1997). "Female Sterility: her baby, her passion," *International Psychoanalytical Studies Organization, IPSO Journal,* July 1997, pp. 99–104. *Barcelona.*

Alkolombre, P. (2011). [2008]. *Deseo de hijo. Pasión de hijo. Esterilidad y técnicas reproductivas a la luz del psicoanálisis,* Buenos Aires: LetraViva Editorial.

Alkolombre, P. (2017). "Vicissitudes of the desire to have a child in contemporary parenthoods: reproductive techniques and the new origins", *Changing Sexualities and Parental Functions in the Twenty-First Century,* comp. Sé Holovko C., Thomson-Salo, F., pp. 87–101. London: Karnac.

Alkolombre, P. (2020). "Pasión de hijo", *Diccionario de Psicoanálisis Argentino,* Nuevos Términos A-Z, pp. 355–358, Buenos Aires: Asociación Psicoanalítica Argentina.

Anzieu, D. (1980). "Une passion pour rire: L' esprit", en *La passion, Nouvelle Revue de Psychanalyse,* n° 21, Paris: Gallimard.

Aulagnier, P. (1992). "Qué deseo, de qué hijo", *Revista de Psicoanálisis con niños y adolescentes,* n°3.

Aulagnier, P. (1994). *Los destinos del placer: alienación, amor, passion,* Barcelona: Petrel.

Berenstein, I., Puget, J. (2012). "Objeto único," en *Diccionario Argentino de Psicoanálisis, Revista de Psicoanálisis* 69(04): 1015–1017.

Cournut, J. (1999). "L' énergie de la passion," *De la passion,* Paris: Puf.

Delaisi de Parseval, G., Janaud, A. (1983). *L' enfant à tout prix*, Paris: Du Seuil.

Fernández, A.M. (1993). "Madres en más, mujeres en menos: los mitos sociales de la maternidad", en La mujer de la ilusión. Capitulo 7, pp. 159–184, Buenos Aires: Paidós.

Freud, S. (1979a). "Un recuerdo infantil de Leonardo da Vinci," *Obras completas*, T. XI, Buenos Aires: Amorrortu.

Freud, S. (1979b). "Introducción del narcisismo", *Obras completas*, T. XIV, Buenos Aires: Amorrortu.

Freud, S. (1979c). "Sobre las trasposiciones de la pulsión, en particular el erotismo anal," *Obras completas*, T. XVII, Buenos Aires: Amorrortu.

Freud, S. (1979d). "Algunas consecuencias psíquicas de la diferencia anatómica entre los sexos," *Obras completas*, T. XIX, Buenos Aires: Amorrortu.

Freud, S. (1979e). "Sobre el análisis ejercido por legos," *Obras Completas*, T. XX, Buenos Aires: Amorrortu.

Freud, S. (1979f). "Sobre la sexualidad femenina," *Obras Completas*, T. XXI, Buenos Aires: Amorrortu.

Freud, S. (1979g). "La feminidad," *Obras completas*, T. XXII, Buenos Aires: Amorrortu.

Freud, S. (1979h). "Esquema del psicoanálisis," *Obras completas*, T. XXIII, Buenos Aires: Amorrortu.

Green, A. (1980). "Passions et destins des passions," *Nouvelle Revue de Psychanalyse*, n° 21, Paris: Gallimard.

Green, A. (2005). Comunicación personal.

Heritier, F. (1996). *Masculin / Féminin. La pensée de la différence*, Paris: Editions Odile Jacob.

Langer, M. (1951). *Maternidad y sexo*, Buenos Aires: Paidós.

Langer, M. (1992). Oh, madre! Libérame de eso que llaman instinto maternal, Buenos Aires, *Página 12*, *Newspaper*. www.pagina12.com.ar/diario/psicologia/9-13777-2002-12-05.html.

Puget, J., Berenstein, I. (1992). *Psicoanálisis de la pareja matrimonial*, Buenos Aires: Paidós.

Racamier, P.C. (1980). "De l'objet- non- objet. Entre folie, psychose et passion," en *La passion Nouvelle Revue de Psychanalyse*, n° 21, Paris: Gallimard.

Roudinesco, E. (2005). *La familia en desorden*, Buenos Aires: Fondo de Cultura Económica.

Tubert, S. (1991). *Mujeres sin sombra. Maternidad y tecnología*, Madrid: Siglo XXI.

13 Self-agency in the feminine

What females need today

Paula L. Ellman

Introduction: self-agency

What Do Women Want Today is a compilation of chapters that considers the current situations for women from perspectives of analysts from North and Latin America. The thrust of the chapters offers contemporary challenges to what calls on more traditional patriarchal thinking in the question "what do women want?" Women's desires in current times allows for challenges to classical analytic theories, and from these challenges new ideas, new conceptualizations are born. In this chapter I consider the specific question of agency in women, theoretically, developmentally, and clinically. I also examine aspects of our current world with regard to social media and popular culture in terms of their contributions to and reflections of self-agency in the feminine.

I am writing about self-agency in the female. In Ungar's chapter (in this volume) she references the *enigmatic* question Freud outlined to Marie Bonaparte: "What does woman want?" or "*Was will das Weib*?" where she writes that Kristeva explains that the question does not refer to *desire* (*Wunsch*), but to *want/will* (*Wollen*). Ungar writes,

> The question here **is not** what woman wants. We are not talking here about *desire*, but about *want/will* (*Wollen*). In the past, this was simply not possible. Nowadays, a woman can ask many things, and first if she wants to be a woman. And also, if she wants to be a wife, if she wants to be a mother. In Freud's times, there was absolutely no space available for these questions.
> p. 2 (Ungar – this book)

The idea of "will" has an immediate connection to agency, the sense of self-agency, one's will. Based on recent clinical experiences, I want to consider what is agency (will) for the woman and how do we understand it. I bring into my discussion aspects of psychoanalytic theory about self-agency and also describe what stands out in my clinical work with vignettes of my work with two female adolescents and a middle-aged woman, and in greater clinical depth with the mother of two young children. I also wonder about how social media may enter into a discussion on agency. Is it agency when young women post

DOI: 10.4324/9781003180036-18

Instagram selfies with 500 plus followers – capturing the mirrored reflections of their bodies in their new clothes or bathing suits, or putting on display their fun social times with friends? How might the use of social media contribute to the development of agency? Is it a mechanism by which young women are internally working on their sense of agency? I will consider how current usage of social media relates to self-agency. Lastly, I will address how current popular culture, such as television series, speaks to this topic of self-agency in women. I intend this chapter to clarify the place of self-agency in females, and also address times when problematic conflicts and experiences serve to compromise the fluid development of agency in the woman.

Recently a male patient described an experience with his wife; she consistently finds fault with him and he is troubled by her ongoing complaints of people that are closest to her. Then I hear from him that she asks for his direction in simple decisions that could not be more obvious – for instance, should she loan her ski socks to her son's girlfriend on their family ski trip. I wonder: Might her highly critical self and her profound self-doubt both be related to a problem with her stable sense of self-agency?

In our journals recent contributions focus on efforts to understand the nature of self-agency. Sugarman (2018) writes about self-agency in terms of self-responsibility and discusses a case where he emphasizes an entitlement that includes an effort to avert a too-severe superego. He presents a case of a young woman who disavows self-responsibility; she shows no awareness of the self as an agent in her creation and perpetuation of her difficulties. The patient had a procrastination difficulty, and was laissez-faire about this problem, often resorting to using manipulation to make her way through her life. Sugarman theorizes that narcissistic traits and superego difficulties account for this particular version of self-agency difficulties. He references Tyson (1996) and Loewald (1979b) as offering perspectives on this topic where their emphases are on the absence or presence of a neurotic structure. Loewald (1979a) emphasizes self-responsibility as an essential structural attainment that helps to define neurosis. "This sense of mastery only occurs if an individual has a superego capable of self-responsibility" (Sugarman, 2018, p. 4).

> Responsibility to oneself, within the context of authoritative norms, consciously and unconsciously accepted or assimilated from parental and societal sources, is the essence of the superego as internal agency. ... [Self-responsibility]... involves appropriating or owning up to one's needs and impulses as one's own. ... Such appropriation ... means to experience ourselves as agents.
>
> (Sugarman, 2018, p. 392)

Coen (1989) also notes the relationship between the superego and a sense of self as agent, or its lack thereof. He finds that patients with an excess of entitlement avoid responsibility and self-agency to ward off the self-criticisms of their harsh superego. It is impossible to experience agency if one does not experience one's internal world. With the capacity for choice comes greater ownership of responsibility.

I want to broaden this discussion of agency beyond the concept of the sense of self-responsibility related to the importance of nature of the superego function, with its focus on the neurotic v. narcissistic question. I want to consider agency in terms of something more primary, more related to psychic structure, more a way of grounding in self-hood, direction, purpose, identity. Agency accompanies aspects of sexual and gender identity – agency today is not just accepting the assignment of gender identity, but choosing it. Psychoanalysis grants the awareness of unconscious fantasy (Ellman & Goodman, 2017) affecting facets of the mind's structures, thereby freeing up the motivation and the capacity to make choices, and strengthening the establishment of agency. The nature of the unconscious fantasy may contribute to the state of agency and experiences of the self.

A recent column in the New Yorker (8/19/19) "A year without a name" by Cyrus Grace Dunham captures this in his poignant personal history narrative:

> Twenty years later, my girlhood was dissolving, with no clear alternative in place. I felt less embodied than ever… . My unease was far-reaching. I felt like vapor trapped in a container. A windowless room with no doors, a single dangling light that never turned off. I was dysphoric, I'd have to decide whether to do something about it… .
>
> (pp. 24–25)

And later: "… . I am him now. I need to be him now. I choose to move towards something like manhood" (p. 27). This piece impressed me as one in which the author demonstrates his process of claiming agency, the agency to desire and to choose.

Establishing agency in the female was discussed in a panel entitled "Issues of Power and Aggression in Women" (Garfield, 2003) where Ethel Person argues that issues of self-agency, assertiveness, self-determination, and regulation of interpersonal relationships arise from what she termed a "power motive."

> This is inborn, though distinct from the drives of classical theory. She traces the development of the power motive from its biological roots to its shaping by interpersonal and cultural contexts. Power was viewed not as primarily destructive but as an essential and universal aspect of human nature.
>
> (p. 643)

Although the infant is helpless at birth, Person notes, there are early signs, within the first days of life, of self-assertion. Through interactions with parents and caretakers, the child continues to develop methods of personal and interpersonal power. If this development goes awry, destructive aggression may result either from the frustration of the power motive or from an experience of narcissistic injury. Person continues stating that a sense of personal power is no less important than a sense of interpersonal power. In fact, personal power is "generally a prerequisite to stable interpersonal relationships." By personal power she is referring to the capacity to "define ourselves and our needs in a world that seems bent on defining us and shaping us to respond to its demands…" (p. 644). Gradually the child develops an awareness of the intention to assert oneself: "To wield personal power, we must possess some ability to write our own life stories, to choose the direction our lives take, to control our time and the uses to which we put our minds and bodies" (p. 644).

Person describes the impact of cultural values on the acquisition of power and the frequency of the woman's inhibition of self-assertion, self-determination, and capacity for regulating interpersonal relationships. Chodorow (1996) links the elements of establishing gender identity with creating the internal space relevant to agency: "Each woman creates her own psychological gender through emotionally and conflictually charged unconscious fantasies that help construct her inner world, that projectively imbue cultural conceptions, and that interpret her sexual anatomy" (p. 215). Chodorow addresses that for most people, unconscious fantasies seem an important primary ingredient in personal gender, where each woman creates her own "prevalent animation of gender" by attributing varying importance to factors of self, object and body. Through psychoanalysis, with its work on unconscious fantasy (Ellman and Goodman, 2017) gender and self becomes organized around dominant or subordinate fantasies, and by freeing up the capacity for choice, strengthens the establishment of agency.

Clinical material

I now move to the clinical material hoping to bring more life to these concepts. I am working with two adolescent females, one 14 years old and one 18 years old, in the midst of their development. The 14-year-old has a brother who excels at everything in his life: academics, friendship, and athletics. My patient opts out of engagement with school and friendships. She struggles with suicidal ideation. She and her father have a tremendously conflict-filled way of relating and she professes to me her hatred for him. She presents with a masculine way of moving and is strongly identified with her athleticism – she is a star team player, yet remains remote from her team peers. Her athletic excellence brings her pleasure and a sense of power. She reports her distress with the horrible hateful exchanges she has with her father and wishes him dead. My 18-year-old patient had previously been ridden with panic attacks – fear of disease, fear of flying, fear of disaster, earthquakes, destruction, all had been horribly disabling for her. She too has a tumultuous relationship with her remote academic father. Developing herself as a writer is her life passion and she is pursuing writing in college; she takes pleasure and comfort in finding her voice through writing creatively. These young females both are in the midst of an internal battle to establish their sense of self-agency. Both have especially close relationships with their mothers, at times enmeshed, and conflict-embroiled relationships with their fathers. Both fathers are isolative and emotionally labile, often rageful, and who cannot seem to engage their daughters in nurturing relationships, nor provide the possibility for a triadic world.

Here let us think about the function of the "father." I find quite helpful Birksted-Breen's concept of the "penis-as-link," a function which I think may be foundational to the smooth establishment of agency for the woman. The penis-as-link is about the triadic and oedipal in object relations, and in intercourse within one's mind and between two, between analyst and analysand.

> As opposed to the binary aspect of the phallic vision along the lines of presence and absence, the structuring and linking function of the penis of the tripartite world of the mother, linked with but different from the father, and child in relation to the parents, makes for a more complex world ... In this position, good and bad, powerful and powerless, masculine and feminine are encompassed rather than being mutually exclusive.
>
> (2016, p. 130)

The "penis-as-link" functions just as the oedipal couple functions to connect and create. The resolution of the oedipal complex, the movement into the depressive position, the possibility of the creation of the triangular space, the third, creates a place of equivalency where the other is seen in like-terms, where perspective shifts.

The use of the word "link" is crucial in recognizing the bond that becomes possible when the constellations of fantasies about penis include relationships and love. While there may be fantasies about the phallus and distinctively about penis-as-link, their content in relation to sexual excitement and to the other are quite different in their aim.

> While the phallus belongs to the mental configuration that allows only for the "all-or-nothing" distinction, hence to the domain of omnipotence, and is an attempt away from triangulation, the penis – as-link – which links mother and father, underpins Oedipal and bisexual mental functioning and hence has a structuring role which underpins the process of thinking.
>
> (Birksted-Breen, 2016, p. 137)

This new modality is the symbolic world of the mind, or the formation of a "triangular space" as Ron Britton describes (Britton, 1989). Britton addresses the importance of the oedipal space in the establishment of the sense of what I think of as self-agency:

> The acknowledgement by the child of the parents' relationship with each other unites his psychic world, limiting it to one world shared with his two parents in which different object relationships can exist. The closure of the oedipal triangle by the recognition of the link joining the parents provides a limiting boundary for the internal world. It creates what I call a "triangular

space"—i.e., a space bounded by the three persons of the oedipal situation and all their potential relationships. It includes, therefore, the possibility of being a participant in a relationship and observed by a third person as well as being an observer of a relationship between two people.

(Britton, 1989, p. 86)

Britton continues: "to clarify this point it is helpful to remember that observed and imagined events take place in a world conceived of as continuous in space and time" he references Rey (1979) here,

> ... and given structure by the oedipal configuration. The capacity to envisage a benign parental relationship influences the development of a space outside the self, capable of being observed and thought about, which provides the basis for a belief in a secure and stable world.
>
> (p. 86)

While the limits of the "maternal container" challenge the oedipal, the father function not functioning as the third interferes with the development of the capacity to integrate observing and experiencing. It is only with the possibility for integrating observing and experiencing, and the development of mentalization that creative thought becomes possible.

In the context of treatment, the "penis-as-link," the triangular space, the capacity to integrate experience with observation brings contact between analyst and analysand and serves to facilitate observing and thinking in the analytic session, as the knowledge of the oedipal couple brings structure and containment to powerful affects including desire, envy, and acceptance of reality. The "penis-as-link," the triangular, creates space and depth and the possibility of meaning that resides in the multiple layers of the unconscious. "Mental space and the capacity to think are created by the structure that allows for separateness and link between internal objects, and the self and other, instead of fusion and fragmentation" (Birksted-Breen, 2017, p. 136).

These concepts shed light on ways that the structuring of the mind leads to the capacity to think and to the development of self-agency. How this unfolds developmentally is captured most poignantly at the time of adolescence. Silber (2012), references feminist scholar Gilligan (Gilligan et al. 1990), in writing about how girls lose their voice at adolescence, and how "they must gain the ability to resist cultural norms to stay connected to and further develop an authentic sense of self" (Silber, p. 122).

> It is a huge challenge for the female adolescent to assert herself and take charge of her self-definition: to own her desire, to construct and reconstruct her boundaries, and to speak in her own voice. What culture do you know that supports this developmental challenge for the female adolescent? I can't think of one.
>
> (Silber, p. 122)

Winnicott's work (1971) on object usage is critical to understanding the adolescent developmental challenge. Essentially, he is pointing to the subject's need for the object to survive the felt aggression to be "used" (that is, if you can survive my anger you can see me and I can be seen) and to arrive at the experience of real self-agency (p. 130). The cultural sanctions against the direct expression of aggression and becoming a subject of desire interfere in the teenage girl's negotiating the passage of adolescence and arriving at both connection and separation. By managing the tension of both as she works through her passage – by being aggressively self-directed and simultaneously interested in taking care of others, she solidifies the use of thirdness within the intersubjective space (Winnicott, 1971, p. 130).

I now turn to considering my work with two adult female patients, both who passed through a similar adolescence in relation to their mothers and fathers.

A woman in her late 50s (a married mother of three) recently came for her first psychotherapy and within the first ten minutes told me that she has never told anyone this and broke into sobbing. When she was in her last year of college she was engaged to a young man, quite handsome and desirable. He would come to visit her regularly where she worked at the front desk of a college facility that was infrequently used. At each visit they would both go into a nearby closet, shut the door, and have "sex." My patient expressed that she knew she did not want to have sex, but believing she had no choice, she would close her eyes and collapse to the floor and "play dead" until her fiancé stopped. They never spoke. This went on for some time and eventually and fortunately she ended the engagement. She struggles to permit herself a once a week psychotherapy since even that feels like a shameful indulgence. She speaks of her professional and personal relationships where she cannot help but put the "other" first, believing herself selfish to do otherwise. She is profoundly unhappy, bedraggled, and burdened. While the dictates of a religiously observant early life are present in her mind, I am inclined to think about how her developing a sense of agency was somehow hijacked in the course of her development, perhaps the hijacking contributed to by the family's strict religious dictates.

Barbara, a woman in her 40s came to consult with me because she was painfully convinced that her husband was having an affair with another woman, or that he is homosexual and having a homosexual affair. She told him about her worries and he insisted that he is faithful to her. The couple does not engage in sexual intimacy; husband is passive and my patient disinterested. The absence of her husband's interest fueled my patient's painful mistrust, and she could not help but to speak to her husband regularly about her jealous worries.

Early on in her treatment Barbara described her husband as not being enough, feeling that something was wrong with him. Over the course of the past few years Barbara's concerns have evolved to be more about herself, not feeling like she is enough, and that something is missing in her. With searing distress, this becomes her felt experience as she meets up with the challenges of parenting her two young children and the developmental difficulties that have arisen for them. The oldest in kindergarten shows some learning challenges with reading, and mild behavioral problems, and her toddler has some difficulties with language development. Barbara easily construes her children's difficulties as being due to her faulty mothering, that she lacks something essential that they need from a mother.

Barbara describes that her children's needs and demands are too much for her. She wants to be alone. She feels guilty relying on her babysitter, but insists she needs time away. She describes feeling bored whenever she is with her children. Recently she described her distressing worry that her 5-year-old is a narcissist as evidenced by his repetitive drawings of himself as a king positioned at the top of the fort, with his friends beneath him fighting off the enemies and protecting him. She reflected on her own early life fantasy of being a princess while playing alone in her family's backyard. Then she reluctantly and with embarrassment admitted that she had imagined herself not a princess but a goddess, her own longings for a sense of power, suggesting her struggle with her experience of powerlessness.

Barbara was an only child. Her parents divorced when she was 6 years old. Her contact with her seeming ineffectual father was limited to weekends; she dreaded her visits to him – her father had a new young wife and they both hit her to keep her out of their bedroom when she came to their closed door with frightening night terrors. Her father died of a heart attack in her adolescence. Her mother dated many men over the years – with little stability in any of her romantic relationships. Her mother's current boyfriend is a man who was Barbara's elementary school teacher – a sign to me of the mother's enmeshment with her daughter.

Barbara's mother tells Barbara that she was "such a good baby," allowing mother to do whatever she pleased, Barbara's needs never getting in her way. Barbara shares her childhood memories of sitting on the floor outside the bathroom each morning "for hours" while her mother engaged in her time-consuming application of her makeup and styling her hair.

Barbara repeatedly expresses to me her eagerness for and anticipation of her mother's visits to her and her family, yet with each visit relates what has become her predictable rage at her mother for her mother's frequent undermining of her parenting and competition for her grandchildren's attention and love. Her mother never expresses any curiosity in Barbara's mind, her thoughts, her work. Barbara describes her mother's demands of her. Her demands appear to be her way of her entering Barbara's family as a kind of occupying force, often usurping her daughter's place. The space between the two collapses and Barbara's mental space also collapses. While initially thrilled with her anticipation of her mother's visits, she quickly turns resentful and furious, angrily lashing out, and feeling torn between her rage and her guilt.

Barbara has few friends. Friendship often carries oppressive comparisons; while at times her comparisons will bring her a sense of triumph where she can feel superior, more often the comparisons lead to self-condemnations of inadequacy and worthlessness. So fluctuating is Barbara's sense of self; so quickly she can be thrown into states of uncertainty, anxiety, a belief in her lacking, and her missing something internal that she thinks is essential. What is missing for Barbara is her firm sense of agency. We may be accustomed to thinking of this as a narcissistic problem. Might we consider this as a problem of self-agency.

I suggest that the establishment of agency in the young female is centered in aspects of the relationship to the internalized maternal and paternal objects. Lachman finds that as the infant's recurrent affect states are responded to by caregivers, the infant's sense of self develops (Lachmann, 2008). "Sense of self" here refers to the way the infant begins to know his affect states, differentiates between those that are distressing, and eventually comes to experience himself as a separate but connected being in relation to others. Affect is the primary organizer of self-experience.

Stolorow and Brandchaft (1987) suggest the idea of the way affect organizes experience in their conceptualization and study of transformation as it occurs in adult treatment. They state that "as the analyst's affective responsivity furthers the patient's affect integration, the patient's sense of self develops" (p. 249). If the early object is excessively narcissistic, unable to hold and affirm the inner world of the child, and/or the function of the third is compromised, rendered ineffectual at creating space in the maternal dyad to facilitate the developing experience of the child's inner world (penis as link), the inner world becomes limited, at times collapsed, and the establishment of self-agency is compromised.

> … [T]he possibility that the capacity to experience ourselves as conscious intentional agents in a coherent world of objects is not merely a modality of perception but rather a maturational and development achievement that is … vulnerable to neglect and maltreatment …
>
> (Fonagy and Allison, 2016, p. 5)

We can witness the ways that developmental experience nurtures or compromises the establishment of self-agency, and the vicissitudes of self-agency in the course of the development and the establishment of the sense of self in the female adolescent and in the adult woman's worlds. "Self-agency" provides a useful concept in articulating aspects of the founding of the sense of self.

Social media

Nowadays adolescence often brings an early crescendo to interest and participation in social media. Might the presence of social media in our culture offer a possible avenue for the development of self-definition, self-agency? Or might the engagement in social media touch only the surface of the mind and internal engagement within the psyche is minimal leaving the sense of self in a continued state of vulnerability. Further from Silber (2012),

For authentic selfhood, the adolescent female must find strength to defy cultural messages by organizing the feedback from her primary attachment system. She struggles to stay connected, … to simultaneously strengthen the paradoxical need for attachment and autonomy to which she is attempting to give resonant voice.

(p. 123)

Here are the complementary processes in development of differentiation and connection/attachment. While social media can allow for the experience of connection, the adolescent mind may be challenged with sustaining and growing the autonomous sense of self.

An outstanding question for consideration is the relationship between engagement in the external world of social media to the internal state of agency. Certainly, central to the establishment of self-agency is the experience of "being seen." Lemma (2013) speaks to the "being seen" visually and mentally in her work with transsexuals. In these instances, there is an incongruity between the given body and the "true" body. I think the essence here is relevant to understanding the establishment of self-agency: that an internal congruity must be established, and the sense of embodied self is established with the experience of the "being seen." Social media is one platform where the central purpose is to be seen.

Winnicott's and Bion's theories both call attention to the place of mirroring and transformation of the child's experience as mediated by the primary object's capacity to accurately reflect the child's internal experience while indicating clearly that s/he has a different experience (i.e., the mirroring is "marked"). This process facilitates the "mentalization" of experience (Fonagy and Target, 2000). Lemma notes that this line of thinking represents a point of convergence between psychoanalysis and contemporary elaborations of attachment theory and mentalization, notwithstanding their different epistemic assumptions (Fonagy, 1999). The coherent sense of self is rooted in the experience of the body, and social media is currently where the body is put forward to the public eye.

At an American Psychoanalytic Association (APsaA) panel, in 2014, Freeman, Hartman, Gabbard, and Camden discussed phenomena considered as virtual reality, the technological advances creating the new world of cyberspace, and its significant impact on human experience (Stevens, 2014). In 2015 Lemma presented at the Boston International Psychoanalytical Association (IPA) Congress on social media and psychoanalysis. Her early ideas began the discussion of the social network and its impact on internal psychic economies. She suggests that contact can be made virtually, virtual is not necessarily less real, and virtual does not necessarily mean disembodied. When connecting virtually, we can see that there is an interest in the reconstruction of bodies online. Relevant to consider is how these online activities inform, or not, one's offline experience of embodiment and hence the sense of identity. Lemma notes that cyberspace can be considered a transitional space where identity can be played with. Cyberspace may be used as a refuge by some young people, while for others the real body can be denied, and relationship between external and internal reality is altered. Lemma asks the question, does the online self become a creation of an idealized self that is different from the offline self, or is there a virtual realization of a possible self and social validation that allows this self to become more authentic, thereby impacting the development of the offline self. An important question related to the effect of social media and cyberspace on the development of agency is whether the self engaging with technology elicits authentic or inauthentic self-expression. Alternatively, might it be a space of experimentation and that the sense of the individual transcends the on and offline.

Muchnick and Buirski (2016) note that as social media shares characteristics as a selfobject experience, it may be used as a reparative space for painful past relation experiences.

> While social media sites are communities of people and are designed to facilitate interpersonal engagement, interacting with the sites themselves is not necessarily a relational process. For example, one common usage of social media sites is voyeuristically browsing or monitoring for enlivening experiences without actually engaging with another. In doing so, a person may stumble upon portrayals of others' experiences that feel personally familiar but the user's passive stance makes it a one-person activity and not a relational one. Because such a virtual experience, however, engaging in the moment, is fleeting and transitory, the experience may offer the promise of … . selfobject experience but does not deliver it.
>
> (pp. 142–143)

The presence of an attuned other allows for experiences of a relationship as well as a new understanding of oneself or the forming of new organizations of experience. Social media can mimic the longed-for self-other experience. It may offer the potential for connection where the risks of the painful past are less present:

> Facebook… (has the)…ability to connect them to others while simultaneously protecting them from the emotional risks inherent in real-time, face-to-face interactions… . (T)he experience may provide a feeling of oneness with another and decrease the harrowing feeling of being alone in the world.
>
> (Muchnick and Buiski, 2016 pp. 147–148)

However, there may be a half of the dyad that remains unaware of the other and the need may go unfilled. "(W)hen this attempt to be seen occurs online and in a forum without the richness that face-to-face affective experience provides, one can experience only the illusion of feeling known and understood …" (p. 148).

In other words, the online social media experience is not truly in an internal realm, but it lies somewhere between external reality and our internal world. When we sit at the computer, we are both real and not real.

> There is a fundamental paradox in cybercommunication: it presents a radical challenge to our traditional notions of privacy but also offers us a place to hide. It allows for the possibility of a playful expansion of the self. This screen persona is both me and not-me … . Moreover, to an alarming extent, the assortment of electronic instruments that hold us hostage – Twitter, social networking, blogging, email, texts, etc. – may conspire to turn us away from the internal realm and demand us to attend to the external signals that surround us and command our attention… turning us away from the self-reflective process of analytic inquiry (Gabbard, 2015, p. 529).

Another contributor speaks to an alternative view of virtual reality, with its potential for being transformative of the development of the sense of self. Mann (2019) writes of

> … how virtual reality may promote reclaiming unlived potentialities, unconscious or disavowed … that virtual aspects of the self, its potential capability, are unconscious (or unknown) until met by someone or something that promotes their transformation into a conscious state of mind and supports their realization. In this sense, the virtual experiences of the self are drawn from the preconscious.

Mann offers clinical vignettes that show the potential for transformation that are given rise to by virtual experiences that respond to the self's needs when they are perceived as recognizing and responsive to the Self's needs. "Cyber reality converses with conventional reality and, thus, is appreciated as a mode of psychic advance toward a new kind of self-consciousness" (2019, p. 282). While Mann (2019) and Muchnick and Buirski (2016) both speak to aspects of self-psychology when describing the transformative nature of connecting on social media, Mann offers a more hopeful perspective on the potential for social media to be transformative to the sense of self.[1]

There is the place of the "Selfie" for us to consider in this discussion for self-agency. Suler (2015) states:

> As a longstanding tradition ever since the invention of photography, the self-portrait represents what makes humans unique: our highly developed self-awareness that motivates us to capture and preserve ourselves in some material way, so we can re-experience, re-examine, and perhaps better understand not just ourselves, but also the very process of capturing our own self-awareness.
>
> (p. 175)

Suler reviews the impact of the invention of digital photography and the internet where opportunities for self-portraits became abundant, no cost for unlimited photos and endless possibilities for editing and sharing online. Suler, both as a lifelong photographer and a psychoanalyst interested in studying online behavior, took interest in the impact of self-portraits and online communities.

> Because our mind intrinsically rivets to the characteristics of the human face, seeing someone's self-portrait in social media makes them feel more real, more so than simply typing text. Self-portraits are a highly effective method of revealing oneself in cyberspace while attempting to control that projected self-awareness.
>
> (p. 175)

He points out that the more recent uses of the "selfie stick" creates the illusion that someone else might have taken the photograph – someone at a distance. Even more so, if looking away from the camera and avoiding a self-conscious facial expression, the self-portrait suggests someone else is the photographer. Suler explores "the selfie" as a narration of one's life, a kind of storytelling, or at times a wish-fulfillment of being a star in a show of their own making. Here there is a post-idealized version of oneself on social media…. "… a kaleidoscope of images that reveal a more complete, multifaceted representation of the photographer … which can serve to enhance the sense of self-continuity and cohesion" (p. 179) and I add "self-agency" here, the opportunity to witness what is it about the self that changes and what remains the same. So, like with participation with Facebook and other online communities, "the selfie," too, can serve the purpose of superficial engagement or can allow for the self-reflective process over time, an opportunity to develop a more stable sense of self-agency.

Popular culture

Issues of women's self-agency have a central presence in our popular culture. With the fairly recent outbreak of Covid-19, many television series have been popular and recently suggested to me was a four episode television series entitled "Unorthodox" that poignantly captures these principles of equality of opportunity and of self-agency. The series (based on the autobiographical memoire of its producer) depicts a young woman, Esty (for Esther) raised in a sect of Hasidic Jews in New York, and her flight from her community as she poignantly discovers her voice once outside the restrictive confines of her prior highly ritualized life. Esty lived according to the strictures of her religious community, and was raised by a loving religiously observant grandmother as her mother had left the community when Esty was three years old; Esty was falsely told that her mother had abandoned her and was "dead" even though her mother fought as best she could to keep Esty, failing in the end in the midst of family threats of legal proceedings within the religious community. Esty and her grandmother had a secret – Esty's exquisite singing voice. Because of Hasidic prohibitions against women performing in any way, Esty's voice was not permitted to be heard. Esty made the decision to leave her newly matched husband and community, seemingly because of the loveless marriage of which the only aim was to procreate in the most dispassionate mechanistic (and painful) way. Not only was sexual intercourse terribly unpleasant for Esty, but also her husband proclaimed to her that he wanted a divorce because "something was wrong with her," and her mother-in-law made frequent unannounced visits to lecture her on the need to make her son feel like a "king" in the bedroom. Upon discovering her pregnancy (her husband did not yet know) Esty took flight to Berlin using the German citizenship her German mother had left her with (offering her a way out of the imprisonment of the community). It was with her departure from her religious community, and from the tight hold of her grandmother (her grandmother died of a heart attack on the same day Esty auditioned at a music conservatory in Berlin, symbolically freeing her from her past) that Esty could seek her own life path. Esty found her "voice," found her agency, found what she longed for, thereby enabling her to pursue the equal opportunity to set her own direction in her life. This series is a moving narrative of a woman finding her self-agency, her freedom to choose. In keeping with concerns of feminine agency, also new to television is a series entitled "Mrs. America," an excellent depiction of the early 1970's second wave feminist movement at the time of the ratification of the Equal Rights Amendment which includes portrayals of Gloria Steinem, Shirley Chrisholm, Betty Friedan, Bella Abzug, and Phyllis Schlafly. In my mind, there is no coincidence that the "Mrs. America" series, speaking to the critical importance of the woman having charge of her body, is of popular interest now when Roe v. Wade is under attack and the essence of women's self-agency is being challenged.

Women have come far from the time of the ratification of the Equal Rights Amendment. Nonetheless, with our legal and even technological developments, we continue to see frequent instances when women's self-agency is all too fragile and life is then lived in a greatly compromised way, with much pain and uncertainty. Our analytic work will be enriched and fortified if we hold in mind the concept of agency and its place in the evolution of the female psyche.

Conclusion

This paper considers theoretically the concept of self-agency. I offer a clinical discussion of two female adolescents and two middle-aged mothers, one with young children, one with grown children, where the place of the self-agency is clarifying to both the conceptualizing of their minds and of the therapeutic intervention. In these instances, clinical work becomes crucial in the building of the experience of an inner life, of an internal space – that has the potential to move forward a more fluid development of agency – of an internal grounding in self-hood. Also in this discussion is the consideration of the place that social media has in the development of one's sense of self-agency, both those that see cyberspace as being potentially transformative and those that bring more skepticism to its possibility for affecting the development of agency. Lastly, I discuss recent narratives in our popular culture depicting the current relevance of concerns for the self-agency in the woman. We continue to hone our theories stemming from varied psychoanalytic perspectives in an area that deserves our continued thought – *Self-agency in the feminine: What females need today.*

Note

1 This paper was written before the 2020 Covid-19 Pandemic. The world has turned to virtual ways of connecting in all realms. In our work, in our professional development, in our education systems, in our social exchanges, we have all turned to using virtual spaces to engage. Psychoanalysis has continued in virtual spaces. Our conceptualizations of connecting using virtual space are in the process of being formulated and further developed. I believe that before the Pandemic we never could have imagined that in so many areas of human living we could use virtual space to proceed. While working virtually cannot substitute for embodied encounters, a virtual connection has been a viable temporary alternative. Time will tell us to what extent our worlds will continue to function in virtual spaces.

References

Birksted-Breen, D. (2016). Phallus, penis and mental space. In Birksted-Breen, D. *The Work of Psychoanalysis: Sexuality, Time and the Psychoanalytic Mind.* London: Routledge.

Britton, R. (1989). The missing link: Parental sexuality and the Oedipus complex. In Steiner, J. (ed.) *The Oedipus Complex Today: Clinical Implications.* London: Karnac.

Chodorow, N.J. (1996). Theoretical gender and clinical gender: Epistemological reflections on the psychology of women. *Journal of the American Psychoanalytic Association,* 44S (Supplement): 215–238.

Coen, S. (1989). Intolerance of responsibility for internal conflict. *Journal of the American Psychoanalytic Association,* 89: 37–943-964.

Ellman, P. & Goodman, N. (2017). *Finding Unconscious Fantasy in Narrative Trauma and Body Pain: A Clinical Guide.* London: Routledge.

Fonagy, P. & Allison, E. (2016). Psychic reality and the nature of consciousness. *International Journal of Psycho-Analysis,* 97(1): 5–24.

Fonagy, P. & Target, (2000). Playing with Reality:III. The persistence of dual psychic reality in borderline patients1. *International Journal of Psycho-Analysis,* 81: 835–873.

Gabbard, G. (2015). Privacy, the self and psychoanalytic practice in the era of the internet. *Rivista di Psicoanalisi,* 61(2): 529–542.

Garfield, R. (2003). Aggression and women. *Journal of the American Psychoanalytic Association,* 51(2): 6377–6649.

Gilligan, C., Lyons, N. Hanmer, T. (1990). *Making Connections: The Relational Worlds of Adolescent Girls and Emma Willard School.* Boston, MA: Harvard University Press.

Lachmann, F.M. (2008). The process of transforming. *International Journal of Psychoanalytic Self Psychology.* 3(1): 1–15.

Lemma, A. (2013). The body one has and the body one is: Understanding the transsexual's need to be seen. *International Journal of Psycho-Analysis.* 94(2): 277–292.

Lemma, A. (2015). Psychoanalysis in times of technoculture: Some reflections on the fate of the body in virtual space. *International Journal of Psycho-Analysis*, 96(3): 569–582.

Loewald, H. (1979a). The waning of the Oedipus complex. *Journal of the American Psychoanalytic Association*, 27: 751–776.

Loewald, H. (1979b). Reflections on the psychoanalytic process and its therapeutic potential. *Psychoanalytic Study of the Child*, 35:155–167.

Mann, G. (2019). Virtual reality as a self-object function: Towards reclaiming unlived potentialities. *Psychoanalytic Inquiry*, 39(3–4): 282–291.

Muchnick, R. and Buirski, P. (2016). Social media as organizing but not transforming self-experience. *International Journal of Psychoanalytic Self Psychology*, 11(2):142–151.

Rey, J.H. (1979). Schizoid phenomena in the borderline. In J. LeBoit & A. Capponi (Eds.), *Advances in the Psychotherapy of the Borderline Patient* (pp. 449–484). New York, NY: Jason Aronson.

Silber, L. (2012). Adolescent girls and the transgenerational relational catch. *Journal of Infant, Child & Adolescent Psychotherapy*, 11(2):121–132.

Stevens, D. (2014). Online and on-the-couch virtuality: the real, the imagined, and the perverse. Panel Report. *Journal of the American Psychoanalytic Association*, 62(6): 1105–1116.

Storolow, R.D. and Brandchaft, B. (1987). Developmental failure and psychic conflict. *Psychoanalytic Psychology*, 4(3): 241–253.

Sugarman, A. (2018). The importance of promoting a sense of self-agency in child psychoanalysis. *Psychoanalytic Study of the Child*, 71: 108–122.

Suler, J. (2015). From self-portraits to selfies. *International Journal of Applied Psychoanalytic Studies*, 12(2): 175–180.

Tyson, P. (1996). Neurosis in childhood and in psychoanalysis: a developmental reformulation. *Journal of the American Psychoanalytic Association*, 44:143–165.

Ungar, V. (2022). *Femininity, Desire and Agency in Psychoanalysis: What Do Women Want Today*. London: Routledge. Current volume.

Winnicott, D.W. (1971). *Playing and Reality*. London: Tavistock Publications.

Concluding remarks

What do women want today?

Margarita Cereijido

This book examines and supports women's growing perception of themselves as subjects with their own desires and projects. As part of that, women are exploring new gender identities, dynamics, and family configurations. That is captured by the book's cover picture showing Rosy the Riveter, with her arm up, urging women to go to work and unionize.

Our starting point was a revisiting of Freud's classic question, "What do women want?" Freud's response to his own question was that women want to be loved.

Yes, women want to be loved. And women also want to be free of violence against them. However, instead of talking about women wanting to be objects of love and an end to discrimination and abuse against them, the book focusses on contemporary women as desiring subjects who pursue their own ideals. These ideals are changing thanks, to a great extent, to the new identificatory models provided by feminist movements.

This focus on ideals is in line with Julia Kristeva's interpretation of Freud's classic question. In her view, Freud was also referring "… to the relationship of the feminine to the ideals of life, and to life itself, inseparable from cultural ideals" (Kristeva, 2019). His response that women want to be loved was the response that fit the time.

The Covid pandemic has offered an x-ray on the complexity of current gender dynamics. Many more women than men have lost their jobs, domestic violence against women has increased, and in spite of having their own jobs, women have been the primary parent in charge of young children and domestic chores. On the other hand, some gender dynamics have become less binary as men have become more involved with child care and house chores. This x-ray reminds us that while they pursue their own ideals and projects, most women also still want and are fighting for their basic human rights. The book aims to stimulate ongoing discussion on the multiple desires of women.

DOI: 10.4324/9781003180036-19

Concluding remarks

Paula L. Ellman

Since the contributors wrote the chapters in this collection, the nature of "Today" has shifted dramatically. We have endured 15 months of a global pandemic, a time when women's career have suffered immeasurably more than men, and misogyny and violence against women has exacerbated. A recent NY Times column, "'The Choice Was Made for Me': What Losing Work in the Pandemic Cost 15 Mothers" captures the current plight of many young women. A recent conference co-sponsored by The Committee on Women and Psychoanalysis (COWAP) featured two papers written by contributors to this book relevant to this topic, "The Impact of the Pandemic Crisis on Gender Dynamics: From Othering to Openings for Change" by Margarita Cereijido and "Women in Freefall: The Pandemic's Unveiling" by Janice Lieberman

> discussed the tragic loss of two and a half million (U.S.) jobs during the pandemic, most of them held by women. This reverses the many gains made by women over the past 60 years. In many cases, married women with children left their jobs in order to care for their children, homeschool them, and do most of the domestic chores in the home, while their husbands worked.

The reductionistic aspects of gender stereotypes addressed in the chapters of this book have been especially prevalent in this pandemic time. The complications of women having both traditional and contemporary gender ideals abound. Many women have retreated to traditional gendered roles in the household. In a time of such uncertainty women struggle with their desires and identities, and have made sacrifices to what they want. While desires inside and outside the home have developed for women over the past decades, the in-home demands of the pandemic have dramatically curtailed the choices available to women. The fissures in our social fabric unveiled by the pandemic have ignited desires in many women related to gender conceptualizations, racialization, and cultural oppressions. "What do Women Want Today," addressed here by many voices of current psychoanalytic thinkers, continues to be a crucially pertinent question.

Concluding remarks

Nancy R. Goodman

From the beginning of planning the COWAP 2019 conference in Washington, D.C. on "What Do Women Want, Today" with Margarita Cereijido, I wanted a gathering of the most insightful and knowledgeable psychoanalysts we could think of. Here in this book, we have the chapters addressing this question from contemporary international psychoanalysts who had previously written the creative innovative papers about femininity and female development. The chapters in this book take up the question about "What Women Want, Today?" with focus on the body, desire, gender stereotypes, societal restrictions, and opportunities for women.

Some of the issues of the day are similar to those present when Marie Bonapart first brought this question to Sigmund Freud. Even with the new knowledge about the unconscious underpinnings of hysterical symptoms of women and recollections of traumas including sexual seductions in childhood, women were still depicted as needing to be at home, raising children, supporting husbands, and relinquishing desires related to envy of the penis and envy of men and their freedoms. There was a double bind concerning being able to speak up about subjugation – doing so meant femininity was not accepted. It was unfeminine to complain and want more.

There is voice in this book and whichever chapters one begins to read will immediately bring resonance to the tones of liberation women have gained and continue to want for enhancement in their individual life and for oppressed women in societies around the world. Psychoanalytic theory and organizations have been woven through with threads of misogyny which is openly addressed here. The first woman president, Virginia Unger, of the International Psychoanalytic Association writes of the achievements and continued need to incorporate room for women and to break glass ceilings in our own organizations. Paula Ellman as overall Chair of COWAP, depicts the vitality of conferences all around the globe and the topics covering motherhood, sexuality, needs for safety, and traumas. These themes are echoed in the chapters of the book.

My own topic addresses the question about what women want with the answer that women want the freedom to dream and need active bystander witnesses to bring this about. Misogyny produces trauma and trauma shuts down the mind and vitality. This book provides the witnessing necessary to open the mind and to allow all women to feel known and to be understood deeply in whatever wishes they have for their lives today.

Index

deconstructing "what do women want today?" question 4–7, 104–105
Delasi de Parseval, G. 168
Deleuze, G. 56
depression: gender relations 73, 74; hatred, origins of 72; queerness 90; wives 134
Derrida, J. 50
desires: and difference 57–58; plurality of 45–58; poiesis 56–57
Deutsch, F. 36
Deutsch, H. 11, 36–39, 42
difference: and desire 57–58; recognition and valuing of 61; understandings of 95; *see also* otherness
Dio Bleichmar, E. 154
discrimination: equality, failure to assert right to 71; as illegal and socially condemned 72; in the workplace 120
divorce settlements 134
Doltó, F. 155
domination, desire for 72
Doolittle, H. 61, 62
dreams 141, 142, 148–150
dress 17
Dunham, C.G. 174

economic context 8
education: authority 19; black and white women, relations between 108; and defining oneself by appearance 117; Karve family 97–98; limitations 72; misogyny 141; power and authority 22; thwarted ambition 93
Ehrenberg, D. 143
Eizirik, C. 14
elder care 61, 135
election campaigns 17
Elise, D. 39, 42, 124
Ellman, P. 6, 9, 145, 190
emotions: control over one's 123; "ugly" 118
employment *see* labor market
envy: birth of a sibling 39; Freud's female patients 76; penis *see* penis envy; power 3, 10
Epstein, J. 120
equal pay 72–73, 103, 130
equal status/power 9, 15, 16, 17, 61, 64–65; failure to assert right to 71–72; marital relationship 74; stereotypes 120
erogenous zones 54, 153
eroticism 36, 37, 38, 43n2

ethical issues: power and authority 23; will 6, 15
Ever After (film) 119

fairy tales 114, 115–116, 118, 119, 121, 122
family: cultural changes 8; disorder 161; feminine ideals 8; Freud's "what do women want?" question 16; parents and gender identity 6; siblings 39; *see also* father–daughter relationship; marital relationship; mother–daughter relationship; motherhood
Fanon, F. 88, 103
fantasies 54, 55
father–daughter relationship: Deutsch 37, 39; gender individuality 40, 41; self-agency 175, 176, 179
female, liberating from "femininity" 29–42
female genital mutilation 63, 71, 141
femaleness 29; Elise 39, 42; "sense of" 40–41
femicide: active bystander witness 141, 149; statistics 71; trends 15, 48; women's movements 7
feminine, the 27–28; conceptions of 5, 6, 53; defined in terms of a negative 78; "eternal" feminine 30–35; gender relations 81; leadership 9; motherhood 9; plurality of desires 45–58; psychoanalytic explorations 10–11; stereotypes 156; traditional and new ideals, co-existence of 8; transformation 6, 25; voice 156; what men want of women 63–65; what women want 61–63
feminine conundrum 46
feminine enigma 45, 46, 48
femininity: aggression, affirmation, and ambition 77; clinical resonances 41–42; conceptions of 46, 53; liberating "female" from 29–42; as masquerade 88; primary 149, 162
feminist movement: ambition 88; black and white women, relations between 108; carceral feminism 107, 111n15; contraceptive pill 149; cultural changes 7–8; cultural feminism 92; Deutsch 36; equality/inequality 15, 64; gender norms 76–77, 78; identificatory models 188; individual variations 81; intersectionality 106–107, 110; "Mrs. America" (TV series) 185; patriarchy 75, 107, 110; queer theory 94; suffrage 85; *see also* women's movements
Ferenczi, S. 72

For Product Safety Concerns and Information please contact our EU
representative GPSR@taylorandfrancis.com
Taylor & Francis Verlag GmbH, Kaufingerstraße 24, 80331 München, Germany

www.ingramcontent.com/pod-product-compliance
Lightning Source LLC
Chambersburg PA
CBHW070329270326
41926CB00017B/3822

9 7 8 1 0 3 2 0 1 7 8 1 5